Routledge Revivals

World War Debt Settlements

World War I left in its wake an unparalleled amount of international debt. Within a period of 5 years a larger sum of international obligations existed than had been built up by ordinary processes during the whole of the preceding century. These debts were, moreover, inter-governmental in character and resulted almost wholly from the destructive processes of war. At the end of the war there was surprisingly little realization in the world of the all-pervasive and far-reaching political and economic implications of the war debts. Originally published in 1927, this book discusses the amount and origin of each of the debts; the nature of the various negotiated settlements; the changes in national policies which occurred and the issues which remained unresolved at the time of publication.

World War Debt Settlements

Harold G. Moulton and Leo Pasvolsky

Routledge
Taylor & Francis Group

First published in 1927 by George Allen & Unwin Ltd

This edition first published in 2024 by Routledge
4 Park Square, Milton Park, Abingdon, Oxon, OX14 4RN

and by Routledge
605 Third Avenue, New York, NY 10158.

Routledge is an imprint of the Taylor & Francis Group, an informa business

© 1927 Harold G. Moulton and Leo Pasvolsky

ISBN 13: 978-1-032-94885-0 (hbk)
ISBN 13: 978-1-003-58219-9 (ebk)
ISBN 13: 978-1-032-94889-8 (pbk)
Book DOI 10.4324/9781003582199

WORLD WAR
DEBT SETTLEMENTS

BY

HAROLD G. MOULTON

AND

LEO PASVOLSKY

With the Aid of the Council and Staff
of the Institute of Economics

LONDON: GEORGE ALLEN & UNWIN, LTD.

Ruskin House, 40 Museum Street, W. C. 1

1927

First Published in Great Britain in 1927
Printed in the United States of America

DIRECTOR'S PREFACE

THE WORLD WAR left in its wake a volume of international indebtedness of unparalleled extent. Taking both inter-allied and reparation debts into account, there came into existence in the space of about five years a much larger total of international obligations that had been built up by ordinary processes in the course of the preceding century. These debts were, moreover, inter-governmental in character and resulted almost wholly from the destructive processes of war rather than from constructive commercial enterprise.

At the close of the war there was surprisingly little realization in the world at large of the economic difficulties that might be involved in the liquidation of this indebtedness. Since they were obligations between governments, it was popularly assumed that all these debts would be readily settled merely by the transfer of money between government treasuries. Only gradually has the world come to realize the all-pervasive and far-reaching political and economic implications of the war debts. The existence of these debts, indeed, has proved to be the greatest single obstacle to world reconstruction. Not only has it been productive of currency disorders and trade demoralization, but the whole reparation and

vii

debt problem has become a network of controversies that has at times threatened the very peace of the world.

A cycle of discussion and negotiation has practically been completed during the present year. Between 1921 and 1926 a whole series of debt and reparation settlements has been negotiated, and practically all of the important outstanding obligations have now been funded and regularized with definite annuity payments provided. Aside from the Russian debt, only a few minor obligations remain unfunded, although the French debt agreements with both the United States and Great Britain have not as yet been ratified.

The purposes of this volume are: first, to present the salient facts as to the amount and origin of each of the debts; second, to describe the nature of the various settlements that have been negotiated; third, to indicate the changes in national policies that have occurred; and fourth, to outline the issues that are still in suspense. We enter into no discussion of the future capacity of the various debtor countries to meet the terms of the settlements; nor do we attempt to analyze the effects of debt and reparation payments upon the creditor countries. The pertinent documents and the texts of the agreements are given in the appendices.

HAROLD G. MOULTON, Director.

Institute of Economics,
    July, 1926.

CONTENTS

ix

CHAPTER IV

CHAPTER V

CHAPTER VI

CHAPTER VII

CHAPTER VIII

CHAPTER IX

CHAPTER X

APPENDICES

APPENDIX A

WORLD WAR
DEBT SETTLEMENTS

WORLD WAR DEBT SETTLEMENTS

CHAPTER I

THE PROCESS OF PAYING AN INTERNATIONAL DEBT

WHILE the liquidation of international indebtedness involves many technical questions, the problem of such liquidation is not so involved that it cannot readily be understood by the layman. In all discussions regarding the debt problem there is one primary fact that must be constantly borne in mind, namely, that all debts, whether between individuals or governments, whether domestic or foreign, represent, at bottom, an exchange of goods or services. Debts are created when goods or services pass from the lender to the borrower. When debts are repaid, the direction is reversed, and goods or services pass from the borrower to the lender. They may be different kinds of goods and different types of services; but a transfer of goods or services there must always be in the process of creating or liquidating a debt. That is the crux of the whole problem.

Debts are usually expressed and contracted in

terms of money and they are repaid in money. A debt is created when one man buys something from another on credit, the payment being deferred to a later date. Such a purchase may involve any of a great variety of goods and services. Whether it is a loaf of bread, or a suit of clothes, or a house, or the attendance of a physician, or the right to witness a theatrical performance, the purchaser receives something which he wants, and gives his promise to pay for it later.

In order to obtain the necessary means of repaying his debt, the man who has bought on credit or has borrowed money with which to buy the things he wants, must be able to produce goods or render services which can be exchanged for money, and he must also be able to find some one willing to purchase his goods or services. When he fulfills these two conditions, he comes into possession of a certain number of monetary units, which he then turns over to his creditor, the latter thus receiving the means of acquiring a certain amount of goods or services which he may want to purchase. The debt is now liquidated, and what has happened in the process is that goods or services have changed possession several times.

Exactly the same thing happens when in the creation or repayment of debts national frontiers intervene between creditors and debtors. The only difference is that the payment of a debt in a foreign country requires the use of foreign money, which can be procured only through international trade and service operations.

The necessity of paying in goods and services may, however, sometimes be obscured by the resort to new credit operations. A debtor may borrow the means with which to meet a maturing obligation. For example, when a European government has to meet a debt payment to the United States it may borrow the necessary funds—from private sources in the United States, or from private or public sources in other countries.[1] In this manner the original debt payment would be liquidàted, but a new debt would be created in its place, leaving the total indebtedness unchanged. Such liquidations of indebtedness by means of borrowing operations may be repeated more or less indefinitely. But, in the end, a net indebtedness cannot be wiped out except by making payments in goods and services to the final creditor.

HOW WAR DEBTS WERE CONTRACTED

With all their energies engaged in war efforts, the Allied powers found themselves in need of large amounts of goods which they could not themselves produce and the purchase of which in other coun-

---

[1] For a discussion of the extent to which international debts can be adjusted by means of borrowing operations, the transfer of securities, and other temporary expedients, see Moulton, Harold G., and McGuire, Constantine E., *Germany's Capacity to Pay* (Investigations in International Economic Reconstruction, Institute of Economics, Washington), 1923, Chapter I.

tries exceeded their immediate paying capacity. They bought on credit, promising to pay later.

European countries bought in the United States flour and meat and lard to feed their armies and their civilian population. They purchased cotton to manufacture into military clothes and bedding, or to use in making explosives. They bought guns and shells and explosives, to hold their war-scarred trenches or blast their way through the enemies' lines. They acquired ships, locomotives, and tractors. They procured tobacco, and supplies of every kind and description. And for nearly everything they gave only their promises of future payment.

Before the United States entered the war, the Allied governments borrowed heavily from private citizens in this country, either in the form of money loans from those who had savings, or in the form of credit from those who had for sale the commodities which the Allied countries needed. Some of the Allied powers, notably Great Britain, were in a stronger credit position than others. So France, Russia, Belgium, and Italy borrowed from Great Britain, while Great Britain in turn contracted debts in the United States.

After the United States became a participant in the struggle, the financing of all the Allied purchases here was undertaken by our government. Bills for these purchases, as well as for such services as the transportation of the goods that were exported, were paid by the United States Treasury. The Treasury in turn accepted from the foreign governments their promises to repay these amounts at some future date. After the war the same arrangement was continued for a time in the form of relief credits, in order to afford the hardest pressed countries a breathing spell in which to begin the process of readjustment to peace-time conditions.

It was in this manner that war debts came into existence. At the end of the war, the United States found herself with outstanding accounts against practically all the Allied nations. Great Britain, while owing a substantial amount to the United States, found herself the creditor of a large number of nations; France, while owing large amounts to both the United States and Great Britain, was also a creditor of some of her Allies. All the other Allies (with the exception of Italy, which had small outstanding credit accounts) found themselves in a position of debtors to one or more of the three great creditors.

GOVERNMENT BUDGETS AND FOREIGN TRADE INVOLVED IN REPAYMENTS

The process of paying off these obligations is similar to the process whereby they were created. When our Treasury paid for Allied purchases in this country it had first to collect from the people of the United States the money thus to be used. This money was in fact obtained partly through taxation and partly from the flotation of Liberty Loans. The goods which were then purchased were furnished directly to the European governments, and thus the trade side of the problem was simplified. In the repayment process the budget part of the problem is similar, but since the United States government does not necessarily wish to receive whatever sorts of goods and services the debtor may chance to offer in payment the commercial side of the question involves different considerations.

When the government of Great Britain, for example, has to make a repayment to the United States it must first collect from its citizens the sums required for the given payment. For a short time these revenues may be raised by means of internal borrowing operations, but in the long run they can only be provided out of taxation receipts. Such revenues are in pounds sterling while our Treasury wishes to be paid in dollars, which are the only legal tender currency in the United States.[2] The problem before the British government is to convert the pounds sterling into dollars. This is where the international trade and service operations enter into the picture.

If Great Britain is to pay in dollars British citizens must somehow be able to earn dollars, and this can be accomplished only through the sale of goods

[2] The Treasury is, however, willing to accept a certain portion of the payments in the form of our own Liberty bonds. This merely means that the debtor governments have to purchase these bonds, chiefly in American markets.

or the rendering of services, directly or indirectly, to Americans. It is necessary to say indirectly, as well as directly, for the reason that Great Britain might earn dollars from roundabout as well as from direct trading operations. For example, Americans might purchase goods in Brazil or Japan and pay dollars for their purchases. Then the Brazilians or the Japanese might purchase goods from the British, paying for them with the dollars obtained from American purchasers. But no matter through how many hands these dollars may pass, their acquisition by Great Britain indicates two things: first, that somebody in the United States has bought something outside his country; and, second, that somebody in Great Britain has sold something outside his country.

Not all of the dollars received by Great Britain through selling goods or rendering services to the United States, however, can be used in paying debts. A large part of the proceeds must go to pay for Britain's necessary imports of foodstuffs and raw materials. Only the surplus of exports over necessary imports is available for payments on debt account.

To summarize, a debtor country, in order to meet its annual payments on a foreign debt, must have, year in and year out, two things: a state budget in which there is an excess of revenues over expenditures equal to the amount of the annual payment; and a foreign trade surplus of exports over imports, corresponding in magnitude to the amount of the payment.

If we take again the illustration of Great Britain and the United States, whenever Great Britain meets the above two conditions and thus has in her possession an amount of dollars equal to the payment which she makes, two things have already taken place: Great Britain has already sold somewhere in the world an amount of goods or services exceeding the amount which she had bought by at least the equivalent of this payment, while the United States has already purchased from somewhere in the world an amount of goods and services exceeding the amount which she has sold by at least the same sum. It is in this manner alone that the war debts can be paid.

NATURE OF REPARATION OBLIGATIONS

Besides these debts bequeathed to us by the war, there is another set of international obligations which differ in their origin from the war debts. These are the reparation obligations which are a penalty imposed upon Germany and the other Central Powers for the damages suffered by the Allied nations during the war. By the terms of the treaties of peace these damages are assessed against the Central Powers.

While the reparation debts have originated in a different manner from the other international debts, the process of their liquidation is identical with the process involved in the repayment of any sort of international debts. Germany is the principal reparation debtor, and in order to discharge her obligations, she has to make large payments to her various reparation creditors. This involves fiscal and trade problems similar to those involved in paying the war debts.

CHAPTER II

GERMANY'S REPARATION OBLIGATIONS

THE treaty of Versailles required Germany to make reparation for all damage "done to the civilian population of the Allied and associated powers and their property by the aggression of Germany by land, by sea, and from the air." The treaty did not, however, fix the total amount for which Germany was thus made liable. It merely set forth the character of the damages for which Germany was to make reparation, and left the assessment of the total sum to a Reparation Commission, which was to be established for the purpose of collecting reparation payments and distributing them among the Allied powers.

THE CHARACTER AND EXTENT OF GERMANY'S LIABILITY

During the peace negotiations there was some question as to the specific damages for which Germany was actually liable. It was readily admitted that the physical devastations resulting from the German occupation, especially of Belgium and northeastern France, had to be repaired. The Germans had destroyed houses and public buildings, roads and railways. They had dismantled factories and either destroyed or removed into Germany machinery and other equipment. They had flooded coal mines and blown up mine shafts. They had cut down forests and had slaughtered or carried away live stock. For all these damages Germany was obviously liable. But if this were all, Great Britain's share of the reparation payments would have been negligible. Political conditions in England which made it imperative for the British negotiators to bring home a substantial claim against Germany, and the natural desire on the part of the Continental allies to receive as large a recompense as possible for the losses sustained during the war, led to an insistence upon the inclusion of pensions in the bill of claims.

President Wilson was opposed to the inclusion of pensions, and the Germans protested vigorously. The American objections, however, were finally overcome, and the German protests overruled. Pensions and allowances went into the reparation bill, and the total amount subsequently assessed against Germany was thus made more than double what it would otherwise have been. A large number of other items, such as the Belgian war debt, the expenses of the Allied armies of occupation in Germany, and so on, were also to be included in the final bill.

The treaty of Versailles was signed on June 28, 1919. Under its provisions the Reparation Commission was given almost two years in which to fix the total amount of the reparation debt, the arrangements to be completed by May 1, 1921. It was on April 27, 1921, that the Reparation Commission was finally ready to announce the amount of Germany's liability. It fixed the total amount of damage for which reparation was due at 132 billion gold marks, or 33 billion dollars. During the two years that had elapsed since the signing of the Versailles treaty, Germany had, however, already made certain payments to the Allies. A part of these payments had been made in cash; another part consisted of German property handed over to the Allies; still another part represented deliveries in kind. The value of all these payments was to be credited to Germany against the total amount, which was finally fixed at 136 billion gold marks, 4 billions being added to the Reparation Commission figure to cover the war debt of Belgium.

During this interval, too, the Allies had agreed upon the manner in which the reparation payments were to be divided among them. At a series of conferences held in the summer of 1920, the most important of which was at Spa, it was decided that the costs of military occupation were to have first claim on German payments, while all that remained was to be divided in the following manner: France was to receive 52 per cent; Great Britain, 22 per cent; Italy, 10 per cent; Belgium, 8 per cent; Japan and Portugal, three-fourths of 1 per cent each; the remaining 6.5 per cent were reserved for Greece, Roumania, Yugoslavia, and other countries not represented at the conferences.[1]

LONDON SCHEDULE OF REPARATION PAYMENTS

Almost immediately after the Reparation Commission had announced the amount of Germany's liability an Allied Conference met in London. On May 5, 1921, an ultimatum was sent to Germany, informing her of the amount of the reparation bill and of the conditions under which payments on it were to be made. The schedule of annual payments worked out at this London conference imposed upon Germany the obligation to pay to the Allies every year the sum of two billion gold marks in cash (about $500,000,000). In addition the Allies were to receive 26 per cent of the proceeds of German exports, and certain fixed amounts of coal and other materials, known as "reparations in kind." Notice was served upon Germany that in case of her refusal to accept these terms, the Allies would occupy the Ruhr valley and seize German customs and certain other revenues. Germany accepted the ultimatum, though under protest that she could not possibly carry out its provisions.[2]

By September, 1921, Germany actually paid one billion gold marks in accordance with the London

[1] For the full text of the Spa Protocol see Appendix A.
[2] For the text of the London Schedule of Payments see Appendix A.

schedule of payments. But by the beginning of
1922 the Reparation Commission found it necessary to lighten the burden of payments by granting
Germany short-term, partial delays or moratoriums.
All through the year 1922 there were numerous negotiations between the Reparation Commission and
the German Government, which finally resulted, on
August 31 of that year, in a temporary suspension
of all cash payments. Deliveries in kind were continued, though with some deviations from the prescribed program.

HOW REPARATION PAYMENTS WERE MADE

It was pointed out in the preceding chapter that
in order to pay foreign debts a nation must ,in the
long run have both an excess of budget revenues
over expenditures and a surplus from interna-.
tional trade and service operations. During the
years that Germany had been making these payments, however, she did not possess either a budget
surplus or a foreign trade surplus. The payments
had been made in the following ways: First, Germany had parted with a considerable part of her
reserves of gold and silver which constituted the
basis of her monetary system. Second, she had sold
large quantities of paper marks to foreign purchasers. Third, she had liquidated some remnants
of foreign investments which she still owned at the
end of the war. Fourth, she had turned over to the

Allies considerable amounts of property situated in other countries. Fifth, she had utilized to some extent the proceeds from the sale of German securities and real estate to foreigners. And finally, she had made some direct deliveries in kind, consisting chiefly of coal and chemical products. Up to the end of 1922, she had been credited by the Reparation Commission on account of these various operations with payments of a little more than 8 billion gold marks.[3]

One important means of making restitution for the damages done might have been but was not to any great extent utilized. It would have been possible for Germany to provide the materials and the labor for the actual reconstruction of the devastated areas. She did indeed offer on numerous occasions to restore in this manner the devastated regions of France. In this connection, France was confronted with the choice between providing work for her own laborers or permitting German labor to do the work of reconstruction. In the matter of materials there was a similar dilemma, for, with the exception of coal and a few other commodities, French producers were desirous of supplying the materials required. It is not surprising, therefore, that France refused to permit any German labor to enter her territory for the purpose of reconstruction and that she al-

[3] For a full discussion of these payments and the conflicting estimates as between the German government and the Reparation Commission of the value of the payments made, see Moulton and McGuire, *Germany's Capacity to Pay*, Chapter III.

lowed the importation of only small quantities of reparation materials.

A real effort was however made to facilitate both the work of reconstruction and the making of German reparation payments by the signing on October 6, 1921, of the so-called Wiesbaden Agreement, whereby France agreed to receive from Germany for a period of 14 years reconstruction materials to the amount of not more than one billion marks a year. The actual deliveries requested and accepted by France under this agreement were, however, almost negligible. France preferred to carry on the work of reconstruction with her own labor and materials and to charge the costs up to Germany for future reimbursement in cash.

The payments that Germany had been making during these years by the surrender of capital assets could be continued only for a short time— that is, until such assets had been exhausted. Regular payments over a long period of years can, as we have seen, be made only out of current international income derived from the sale of goods and services, and the availability of such income depends upon whether or not Germany can sell to the rest of the world more goods and services than she buys from the rest of the world.

FRANCO-BELGIAN OCCUPATION OF THE RUHR

The temporary expedients described above by means of which Germany had been making payments were practically exhausted in 1922, and the German financial and economic organization was rapidly deteriorating. There was a huge deficit in the German budget, and in the international accounts there was a substantial excess of imports over exports. While Germany was thus drifting toward a complete breakdown of her economic organization there was developing a difference of view between the two principal reparation creditors, France and Great Britain. France insisted on a rigid application of the London schedule of payments and upon the enforcement against Germany of the various penalties for non-fulfillment of the payment terms provided for in the treaty of Versailles and the London schedule, while Great Britain leaned toward a greater degree of moderation.

The whole situation finally came to a head on January 9, 1923, when the Reparation Commission, by a majority vote of three to one (the French, Belgian, and Italian delegates as opposed to the British), declared Germany in wilful default on coal deliveries. The French Government immediately decided to take drastic measures, and two days later French and Belgian troops marched into the Ruhr.[4]

From that time on all prescribed reparation payments ceased and were not resumed until the sec-

---

[4] For a discussion of the political setting of the occupation of the Ruhr and the economic factors involved, see Greer, Guy, *The Ruhr-Lorraine Industrial Problem* (Investigations in International Economic Reconstruction, The Institute of Economics, Washington), 1925, Chapter VII and Appendix B.

ond half of 1924. During that period the only receipts on account of reparation consisted of the proceeds of the Franco-Belgian exploitation of the mining and industrial resources of the Ruhr district, the customs and other revenues collected in the occupied territory, and the 26 per cent tax on German exports to Great Britain collected by the British Treasury.

The Franco-Belgian occupation of the Ruhr completed the post-war economic and financial disorganization of Germany. But it also resulted in a thorough reconsideration of the whole reparation problem.

THE DAWES PLAN—A RESTATEMENT OF THE PROBLEM

During 1923 the reparation question definitely entered a new phase. France finally agreed to the appointment of international committees of experts to consider the question of Germany's capacity to pay. Two such committees were appointed on November 30, 1923, by the Reparation Commission—the first, under the chairmanship of General Charles G. Dawes, to determine how much Germany could pay and in what manner, and the second, headed by Mr. Reginald McKenna, of Great Britain, to find out how much money had left Germany during the period of inflation and was on deposit in foreign banks.

The Dawes committee drew up the reparation

plan under which the whole problem of payments is now handled. This plan was presented to the Reparation Commission on April 9, 1924, and was officially adopted by the prime ministers of the countries concerned at the London Conference, held on July 16, 1924.

The reparation plan introduced a number of new elements into the situation. First of all, the annual payments fixed in the 1921 schedule of payments were found to be impossibly high. The plan fixed the maximum annuity at two and one-half billion gold marks, which was not, however, to be reached for several years.

But even more important, the plan finally and definitely did away with the idea that the manner in which these payments are made is solely Germany's concern. On the contrary, the plan which made an economic restoration of Germany the first prerequisite to any payments, provided a mechanism for the purpose of regulating payments in such a way that the creditors' receipts would be the maximum compatible with the maintenance of economic stability in Germany.

The plan emphasized over and over again the fundamental principle that a country can pay its international debts only if it has in its state budget an adequate excess of receipts over expenditures and in its foreign trade a corresponding excess of exports over imports. It also made it perfectly plain that when a country does not actually meet these basic requirements, a continued pressure for foreign payments disorganizes its whole economic life.[5]

THE DAWES PLAN IN OPERATION

The plan was put in operation on August 30, 1924. The German budget was reorganized and some of the revenues were specifically assigned to reparation payments; the German railways were pooled into a huge corporation, and, together with some of the larger industries, were made partly responsible for providing the means of payment. Under the plan the German government collects, in German marks, the amounts necessary for meeting the annual instalments, and these sums are paid into a special reparation account under the control of the Agent General for Reparation Payments. The responsibility of Germany ends with these internal payments. It devolves upon the Agent General to transfer the proceeds to the Allied governments. This is to be done in part by the purchase of such German goods as the Allies may wish to have delivered and in part by the purchase of foreign bills of exchange resulting from German exports.

During the first year under the new reparation plan (August 30, 1924 to August 31, 1925), the Agent General received into his account the one billion marks which he was supposed to receive,—

[5] For the full text and a discussion of the Dawes Plan see Moulton, Harold G., *The Reparation Plan* (Investigations in International Economic Reconstruction, Institute of Economics, Washington), 1924.

COMPOSITION OF GERMAN ANNUITY UNDER THE EXPERTS' PLAN *
(In millions of gold marks)

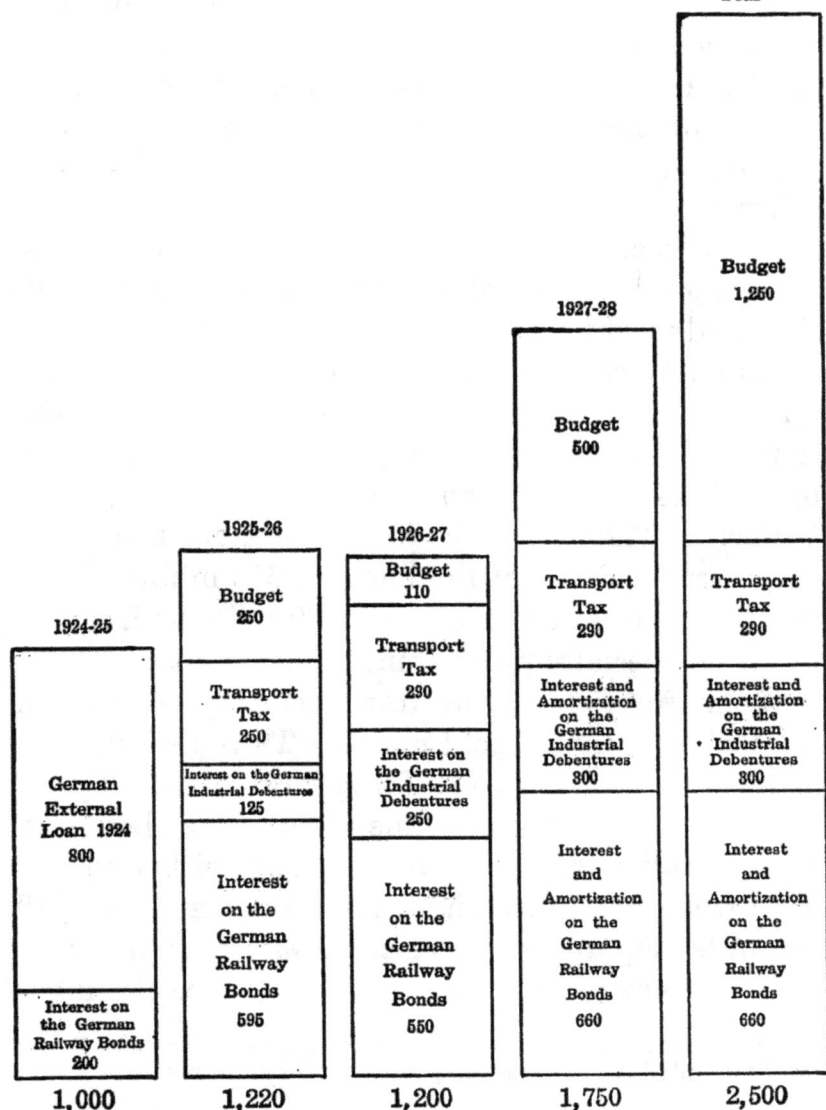

1928-29
and thereafter
"Standard
Year"

1927-28

1925-26

1926-27

1924-25

1924-25
German
External
Loan 1924
800

Interest on
the German
Railway Bonds
200

1,000

1925-26
Budget
250

Transport
Tax
250

Interest on the German
Industrial Debentures
125

Interest
on the
German
Railway
Bonds
595

1,220

1926-27
Budget
110

Transport
Tax
290

Interest on
the German
Industrial
Debentures
250

Interest
on the
German
Railway
Bonds
550

1,200

1927-28
Budget
500

Transport
Tax
290

Interest and
Amortization
on the
German
Industrial
Debentures
300

Interest
and
Amortization
on the
German
Railway
Bonds
660

1,750

1928-29
Budget
1,250

Transport
Tax
290

Interest and
Amortization
on the
German
Industrial
Debentures
300

Interest
and
Amortization
on the
German
Railway
Bonds
660

2,500

* From the Reports of the Agent General for Reparation Payments.

800 millions of which were provided by the reconstruction loan which was floated in other countries, principally in the United States. The remainder came not from a budget surplus but from the sale of railroad securities. The Agent General used a part of these funds to defray the costs of armies of occupation, control commissions, and so on, and the rest in financing deliveries of coal and other commodities.[6]

In the second year—September 1, 1925 to August 31, 1926—the total collections amount to 1,220 million gold marks, and again none of it comes from the budget proper. The bulk of it is derived from interest on railroad bonds and from the sale of railroad securities. The full payments do not begin until the so-called "standard year," beginning September 1, 1928, when 1,250 million gold marks are to be provided out of the budget; 660 millions from interest on railroad securities; 300 millions from interest on specially pledged industrial bonds; and 290 millions from a special transport tax,—making a total of 2.5 billions gold marks. Thus the full test of the plan will not come for several years.

Up to the present time there has been no demonstration of Germany's capacity either to collect from her own internal resources the full amounts required or to make possible their transfer by means of an export surplus. Since the inau-

[6] The Agent General for Reparation Payments publishes annually detailed reports regarding the operations of his office.

guration of the Dawes Plan the German government and German citizens have borrowed very heavily from abroad, the sums equalling several times the amount of the payments that have been made. In accordance with the spirit of the plan the Allied nations have been engaged in resuscitating Germany, partly with a view to rehabilitating the shattered economic fabric of Europe and partly, of course, in the hope that in due course a restored Germany would be able not only to meet the foreign obligations resulting from these new loans, but also to make substantial payments on reparation account.

CHAPTER III

GREAT BRITAIN'S DEBT POLICY

DURING the period of the Great War the British government was both a great lender and a great borrower. Great Britain was a lender to her Continental allies; and she was a borrower chiefly from the United States. Thus Great Britain emerged from the war a debtor as well as a creditor, although, as we shall see, the sums owed to Great Britain greatly exceeded the amount of her own foreign indebtedness.

GREAT BRITAIN AS DEBTOR AND CREDITOR

Great Britain's wartime requirements of materials and supplies were so great that it was necessary for her to borrow heavily in the United States. Moreover, because of her stronger credit position here, Great Britain acted in reality as banker for the other Allies, who also had to purchase materials in this country. At the same time Great Britain made very large direct loans to her Continental allies. The results of these transactions, together with certain minor credit operations following the war, are indicated in the following paragraphs.

On April 1, 1925, the total external debt of the British Government was 1,122 million pounds sterling, or a little less than 5.5 billion dollars. Eighty per cent of this amount represents the British debt to the United States, and more than nine-tenths of this American debt is owed directly by the British government to the United States Treasury.

On the other hand, Great Britain is the creditor of a large number of nations. The nominal amount of Britain's advances to her allies during the war, together with the accumulation of interest was (on April 1, 1925) 2,062 million pounds sterling, or about 10 billion dollars. Her largest war debtor is Russia, whose obligations constitute over one-third of the total British war claims. Then comes France with about 30 per cent of the total, followed by Italy with about 25 per cent. The remainder—about 10 per cent of the total—is distributed among the smaller Allies. The Belgian war debt is not included in these figures, as it is an integral part of the German reparation debt.

Next to France, Great Britain is the largest creditor of Germany on the reparation account. Under inter-allied agreement she is entitled to 22 per cent of the reparation receipts under the Dawes Plan.

Finally Great Britain is creditor of a large number of small countries, particularly in Central Europe, on account of post-war relief and reconstruction loans. The total amount of these loans, however, is not very large.

It is clear from the above figures that Great Britain has come out of her international financial operations connected with the war as a net creditor. Taken at their nominal value, and including reparations claims, she has coming to her at least three times as much as she owes.

BRITISH DEBT SETTLEMENT POLICY

Great Britain's first official declaration of policy with regard to the handling of the inter-allied debts created by the war was made in the summer of 1922. Prior to that time there had been developing in Great Britain no little sentiment in favor of the cancellation of all war debts. Such a policy could not, however, be carried out without the consent of the United States as the largest international creditor. Although there had been a number of semi-official conversations between the British representatives in Washington and our government with regard to an adjustment of the debts, the British government felt that, as a debtor, it could not take the initiative in the matter. It was not until the American policy was publicly defined that the British government had an opportunity to state its position.

The creation by Act of Congress of the World War Foreign Debt Commission, in February, 1922, followed by the official request of the United States government that all its debtors take the necessary steps toward the funding of their debts, clearly defined American policy. As a consequence of this, Mr. Arthur J. Balfour, the British Secretary of State for Foreign Affairs, addressed on August 1, 1922, a note to the debtors of Great Britain asking them to take the necessary steps toward funding their war debts to Great Britain. Mr. Balfour stated, however, that this policy had been adopted with reluctance, for Great Britain had been in favor of a general cancellation of both war debts and reparation claims. He pointed out that it was the American policy that was responsible for the change in the British policy. The Balfour Note announced, however, that the British Government was still prepared to go as far as it could in the direction of a reduction of war claims. It laid down what has come to be known as the Balfour principle, which is that the British Government will seek to collect from its debtors only such amounts as would in their aggregate equal the sums paid by Great Britain to the United States.[1]

THE ANGLO-AMERICAN DEBT SETTLEMENT

Great Britain was the first debtor country to send a debt-funding mission to Washington. This mission, consisting of Mr. Stanley Baldwin, then Chancellor of the Exchequer, and Mr. Montagu C. Nor-

[1] For further discussion of British policy as laid down in the Balfour Note, see Chapter IX; and for the full text of the Balfour Note, see Appendix C.

man, Governor of the Bank of England, arrived in the United States at the beginning of January, 1923. In the course of the negotiations the British representatives protested that it was impossible for their country to arrange for the payment of the whole indebtedness within the 25-year period specified in the act of Congress creating the Foreign Debt Commission. They also argued that it was hardly fair to charge interest at 4.25 per cent in view of the fact that the market rate had fallen to about 3.5 per cent and was likely to continue permanently at approximately that level. The American Debt Commission recognized the fairness of the British position, and the final agreement, which was signed on June 19, 1923, carried terms considerably different from those laid down in the Act of 1922. The terms were, however, approved by Congress in an amendment to the original act which laid down the terms of settlement.[2]

By the terms of the agreement the total indebtedness of Great Britain—the principal of the debt and unpaid interest as of December 15, 1922—was fixed at $4,604,128,085.74. The British government turned over to our Treasury long-termed bonds of the amount of $4,600,000,000 and paid the remainder in cash. The amount of these bonds is to be paid off in 62 annual installments. Interest is fixed at the rate of 3 per cent for the first 10 years and 3.5 per cent for the remaining 52

[2] For the full text of the amendment see Appendix B.

years,[3] making the total annual payments, principal and interest, about \$160,000,000 a year during the first ten years, and about \$180,000,000 during the remaining years.

GREAT BRITAIN'S NEGOTIATIONS WITH HER DEBTORS

Since the spring of 1924 Great Britain has had debt negotiations with all three of her principal war debtors. In the negotiations with Russia the question of the war debts was left in abeyance, the only problem taken up being concerned with the pre-war debts; these negotiations will be discussed in Chapter VI. With France and Italy complete settlements were in due course negotiated.

A tentative agreement with France was reached in the summer of 1925, when M. Caillaux, the French Minister of Finance, negotiated with Mr. Churchill, the British Chancellor of the Exchequer, a settlement involving payment by France of 12.5 million pounds sterling annually. The French Minister had not the authority to sign the agreement definitely, but he took it with him to France and laid it before his colleagues. Soon after that the French government accepted the settlement in principle, but made this acceptance subject to subsequent discussion. The overthrow of M. Caillaux and the setting in of a severe political and financial crisis in France pre-

[3] For a discussion of the cancellation involved in this settlement, see Chapter VIII; for the full text of the Anglo-American debt settlement and the complete schedule of annual payments, see Appendix B.

vented the immediate resumption of the Anglo-French debt negotiations.

New negotiations were begun on May 19, 1926, by the Minister of Finance Péret, but these again failed to result in a final settlement. On July 12, 1926, however, M. Caillaux, who in the meantime had again become the French Minister of Finance, went to London once more and concluded a debt funding agreement.

The total of French payments to Great Britain under this agreement is fixed at 855,000,000 pounds sterling, of which, however, 53,500,000 pounds are made subject to future agreement. The French debt to Great Britain stood at the time of the settlement at 653 million pounds including accrued interest to that date. The agreement, therefore, provides for the repayment of the principal and accrued interest to the date of settlement, and for current interest at the rate of less than 1 per cent, although no distinction is made in the annual payments between interest and principal, the two being lumped into one sum.

The 12,500,000-pound annual payment rate, adopted during the first Caillaux negotiations, was used as the basis for determining the total of the French payments. The payments during the first four years, however, were made lower than this rate, the difference being funded over the last 31 years of the 62-year period, making these latter payments higher than the basic rate and increasing the whole total because of the accumulation of interest on the deferred payments. In accordance with this arrangement, France is to pay Great Britain 4,000,000 pounds in 1926-27 (plus 2,000,000 pounds required as a payment for 1925); 6,000,000 pounds in 1927-28; 8,000,000 pounds in 1928-29; and 10,000,000 in 1929-30. Then for 27 years, from 1930-31 to 1956-57 inclusive, the annual payments are 12,500,000 pounds, and for the remaining 31 years, 14,000,000 pounds.

These payments account for 801,500,000 pounds, leaving 53,500,000 pounds of the total agreed upon subject to special agreement, embodied in article 7 of the settlement. This sum is the equivalent of the amount of gold shipped by France to Great Britain puring the war as security for the loans extended to France, to be returned to France upon the liquidation of the French war debt to Great Britain. Under the British-French debt agreement, this gold remains in British possession as a non-interest-bearing loan, while an equivalent amount of French debt to Great Britain remains outstanding, also as a non-interest-bearing loan. The final liquidation of these two balancing accounts is left to future negotiation.[4]

The terms of the French settlement were much less lenient than those extended to Italy in the settlement signed with that country on January 27, 1926. The total amount of the Italian payments, including interest charges over a period of 62 years,

[4] For the full text of the British-French settlement see Appendix C.

is fixed at 276,750,000 pounds sterling (about $1,350,000,000). The principal of the Italian debt, including accrued interest to December 15, 1925, was at the time of the settlement 610,840,000 pounds sterling. In making its agreement with Italy the British government thus wrote off all of the interest and even a part of the original principal.

The annual payments are, as in the French settlements, inclusive, no distinction being made between principal and interest. During the first year Italy is to pay 2,000,000 pounds; during the next two years, 4,000,000 pounds a year; during the next four years, 4,250,000 pounds a year; then for 55 years her annual payments are to be 4,500,000 pounds; and finally, for the last year, 2,250,000 pounds. The payments thus run for 63 calendar years.

There will be deductions, however, from these fixed amounts. During the war Italy shipped to Great Britain gold to the amount of 22,200,000 pounds, on the same terms as the French shipments described above. Under the Anglo-Italian debt settlement the amount represented by this gold deposit will be released in annual instalments spread over the whole period of Italian payments, starting with 1928. These instalments will be deducted from the fixed annuities in such a way that the net Italian payments from 1928 to 1986 will be about 4,000,000 pounds sterling a year.[5]

[5] For the full text of the Anglo-Italian settlement see Appendix C.

THE BALFOUR PRINCIPLE IN OPERATION

The Anglo-Italian and the Anglo-French settlements contain a proviso which embodies the principle set forth in the Balfour Note of August 1, 1922. Section 6 of the Italian agreement and Section 5 of the French provide that if at any time Great Britain's total receipts from her allies on account of the war debts and from Germany on account of reparation payments should exceed the total payments made by Great Britain to the United States, then Italy and France would be credited with a share of this excess proportionate to their respective total payments. On the other hand, in case Great Britain's receipts should thereafter fall short of the British payments to the United States, Italy's and France's payments will be similarly increased, within the limits, however, of the credits previously allowed them.

It is the intention of the British government to write a similar proviso into all of its debt settlements. In this manner Great Britain is carrying out the pledge contained in the Balfour Note of not collecting from her own war debtors a penny more than she has to pay the United States. Under this principle it will be seen that Great Britain becomes merely a transmitting agent.

Great Britain's payments to the United States during the financial year 1926-27 will be 33,500,000 pounds sterling. Against this she expects to receive

4,000,000 pounds from Italy and about 10,000,000 pounds as her share of the Dawes annuity. The terms of her settlement with France provide for a partial moratorium in the French payments for the first four years. The aggregate amount owed Great Britain by her other war debtors is very small, and is not likely to make much difference in the situation, while the Russian war debt may, almost with certainty, be considered as lost. Thus at best during the current year the British receipts will be less than half of the British payments. Even when the French payments reach the sum of 12,500,000 pounds a year—and assuming that her other debtors will be paying her by that time one or two millions a year—Britain's aggregate annual receipts from her allies will scarcely constitute one-half of her annual payments to the United States, which by that time will be substantially larger than at present. The difference would have to be made up out of the British share of the German reparation payments.

When the Dawes annuity reaches its full amount, the British share of it will be about 23,000,000 pounds sterling. This sum would be quite sufficient to cover the difference between Britain's receipts from her allies and her payments to the United States, provided the full amount of this annuity is really forthcoming.

The application of the Balfour principle to the British debt settlements thus links together almost indissolubly the German reparation payments, the payments on the Allied debts to Great Britain, and the British debt payments to the United States.

HOW GREAT BRITAIN HAS BEEN PAYING

Under the terms of the British debt settlement with the United States, Great Britain made her first payment in June, 1923, and she has since regularly met her annual instalments. Thus, in a period during which Great Britain was receiving nothing from her debtors, except small sums on reparation account, she has demonstrated her capacity to meet her own obligations out of her own resources.

In the first chapter it was pointed out that to meet a foreign debt year after year a nation must possess a surplus of budget revenues and also a foreign trade surplus. Fortunately, Great Britain has during the years in question possessed these requisites. During the past few years British government revenues have shown a surplus over expenditures, and although the tax burden has been an onerous one Great Britain has been able regularly to collect within the country the necessary sums required for meeting the instalments on account of the foreign debt.

Great Britain has also been able to convert British pounds sterling into dollars, thanks to a net income from international trade and service operations. In the matter of trade, Great Britain has a large excess of imports over exports, but her income from foreign investments, from shipping, from the tourist trade, and from banking and other commissions more than offsets the trade deficit. So long as this situation obtains Great Britain can continue to meet her debt payments irrespective of collections from her own debtors.

To the degree that Great Britain is able to obtain payments from her debtors, in accordance with the policy enunciated in the Balfour Note, she will be able to mitigate her own burdens in meeting her obligations to the United States. In fact, since Great Britain is meeting her obligations almost entirely from her own resources, she will be able to reduce her domestic taxation to the precise extent that she receives additional payments from her debtors.

CHAPTER IV

THE FRENCH DEBT SITUATION

At the outbreak of the Great War the French government was entirely free from foreign indebtedness. During the course of the conflict a huge debt was created as a result of foreign borrowing both from public and private sources, and this indebtedness has been somewhat increased by additional borrowings since the Armistice. On the other hand, as a result of the peace treaty, France has become a large creditor on the reparation account. The war has thus resulted in making France both a debtor and a creditor country.

FRANCE AS DEBTOR AND CREDITOR

Including accrued interest on the war debt, the French government on January 1, 1925, owed abroad—principally to Great Britain and the United States—about 40 billion gold francs. About 85 per cent of this amount comprises the so-called "political" debt, that is, the sums borrowed by the French government from the Treasuries of Great Britain and the United States "for strictly war purposes." The other 15 per cent represents the so-called "commercial" debt, that is, all the other foreign borrowing of the French government, the largest item being the sum owed to our Treasury on account of the purchase by France of surplus war materials.

As an offset to these foreign obligations of the French government may be put the loans of France to her allies during and after the war, amounting to approximately 3 billion gold francs. Leaving reparation claims out of account, the French government is thus a net debtor to the extent of approximately 37 billion gold francs, or a little more than 7 billion dollars.

France is, however, the principal creditor of Germany on the reparation account, being entitled under allied agreement to 52 per cent of the total payments. She is also a creditor for small amounts on account of the Austrian, Hungarian, and Bulgarian reparation obligations.[1] If Germany should pay the full sums prescribed by the London settlement of 1921, France would receive between 16 and 17 billion dollars.

If, on the other hand, Germany should pay only the capitalized value of the standard Dawes annuities, or about 42 billion marks, France would receive as her share only about 5 billion dollars. In such an event France would be a net debtor even though she should be repaid for her war loans to Russia and other countries, and receive her share of the Austrian, Hungarian, and Bulgarian reparation claims.

[1] For details see Chapter VII.

Up to the present time (July, 1926) France has been meeting no interest obligations on account of her political debt. Provision has, however, been regularly made in the French budget for meeting the interest on the commercial debt amounting to about 30 million dollars annually, of which 20 million dollars a year goes to the United States Treasury.

NEGOTIATIONS WITH CREDITORS AND DEBTORS

France made her first serious attempt to negotiate a settlement of her war debts when the French Minister of Finance, M. Caillaux, visited London and Washington in the summer and autumn of 1925. In London, M. Caillaux negotiated with the British government a tentative agreement for the repayment of the French debt to Great Britain. In the course of these negotiations, the British proposed a settlement on the basis of annual payments by France amounting to 12.5 million pounds sterling (a little over 60 million dollars) over a period of 62 years, which was tentatively accepted by France, subject, however, to subsequent discussion of such points as the initial annuities and the return of the gold shipped by France to England during the war.

M. Caillaux then proceeded to Washington, where he laid before our World War Foreign Debt Commission a proposal involving the payment by France of 25 million dollars a year during the first five years; 30 million dollars a year during the next five years; 60 million dollars a year during the following 10 years; and 90 million dollars during the following 42 years. These payments, which were to include the 20 millions of annual payments on account of the commercial debt, were to be considered as extinguishing the total indebtedness—principal and interest.

The French offer was rejected by our Debt Commission on the ground that the payments offered were too small. The French then made a new tentative offer, involving payments spread over a 68-year period, with 40 million dollars paid annually during the first five years; 60 millions annually during the following seven years; and 100 millions annually during the remaining 56 years. This offer was also rejected by our Commission on the ground that the total payments would merely equal the principal of the debt with interest at the rate of less than 1 per cent *per annum.* Throughout the negotiations the French insisted upon a so-called "safeguard clause," the principal provision of which was that the amount of French payments might be reduced in the event that reparation payments did not come up to expectations. This provision was also a reason for rejecting the French offers.

Finally, the American delegation submitted a counter proposal which provided that the whole question be left in abeyance for five years, at the end of which time it would be taken up again. In the meantime France should pay a total of 40 million dollars a year on account of current interest. As in his negotiations with Great Britain, M. Caillaux took this proposal to Paris to lay it before his colleagues. But almost immediately after his return to France, he was defeated in the Chamber of Deputies and resigned his post. With his downfall, the question of the debt settlement entered upon a period of new delays.

The negotiations with the United States were resumed in the spring of 1926, with Senator Bérenger, the French Ambassador in Washington, acting as a special plenipotentiary for the French government. An agreement was signed on April 29, the details of which will be found below. The settlement had, however, not been ratified either by the French Chamber of Deputies or the American Senate up to July, 1926.

Negotiations were also resumed with Great Britain by the French Minister of Finance, M. Péret, in May, 1926, but disagreement arose over the amount of the initial payments. The figure arrived at during the Caillaux negotiations the year before, namely, 12.5 million pounds sterling a year, was used as the basis for the Péret negotiations, but the French Minister was not prepared to agree to the British demand that the payments during the first five years should average no less than 9 million pounds. Two months later, however, on July 12, 1926, an agreement was signed between Great Britain and France,[2] the instalments during the first few years being materially reduced.

As far as her debtors are concerned, France has not succeeded as yet in making any definite arrangements for repayment. She has, however, accepted the Dawes plan for the regulation of reparation payments and the decisions of the Reparation Commission with regard to the Austrian and Hungarian reparation payments. She has also opened negotiations with Russia, her principal debtor.

THE AMERICAN-FRENCH DEBT AGREEMENT

The American debt settlement with France, which was signed on April 29, 1926, differs somewhat from the terms discussed at the time of the Caillaux negotiations in October, 1925. The total amount of principal and interest over the whole 62-year period of payments is larger by $627,000,000, but the payments during the first ten years aggregate about $40,000,000 less than those offered by M. Caillaux. The "safeguard clause" was definitely eliminated in this final agreement; but the actual schedule of payments by France was worked out with implied reference to her expected reparation receipts, as well as to other factors in the French economic situation.

The explanation of the reduction in the amount of payments in the earlier years, as explained to the Ways and Means Committee of the House of Repre-

[2] See also discussion in Chapter III, pp. 30-1.

sentatives by Secretary Mellon, is as follows: "The slightly smaller payments for the first five years were made necessary because the present fiscal condition of France is less strong than it was at the time of the negotiation last autumn." [3]

During the first two years, 1926 and 1927, France is to pay on account of principal, $30,000,000 a year; during the next two years, $32,500,000 a year; and in the fifth year, $35,000,000. The payment for the sixth year is only $1,350,000; for the seventh, $11,363,500; for the eighth, $21,477,135; for the ninth, a little over $36,000,000; and for the tenth, slightly over $42,000,000. During the next 35 years, the annual payments fluctuate between $51,000,000 and $80,000,000. Then they rise gradually, and are over $100,000,000 a year during the last six years of the paying period. The principal of the French debt is fixed at $4,025,000,000.

The fluctuations in the payments on account of principal are due to the effort to graduate the total amount of the annual payments, the distribution as between interest and principal being merely arbitrary. No interest at all is charged during the first five years (1926-1930); hence the annual instalments for the period are all attributable to principal. For the next 10 years, from 1931 to 1940 inclusive, interest is charged at the rate of 1 per cent. This absorbs the greater portion of the annual payments required in the first part of this period, leaving only

[3] For the full text of the Secretary's statement see Appendix B.

the small sums attributable to principal in those years.

The interest schedule for the complete period is as follows: No interest at all is charged until 1931; for the next 10 years interest is computed at the rate of 1 per cent; for the following 10 years at 2 per cent; and for the next eight years at 2.5 per cent. Then from 1959 until 1965, the interest rate is 3 per cent; and from 1966 until the end of the 62-year period, in 1987, it is at 3.5 per cent.[4]

THE BRITISH-FRENCH DEBT AGREEMENT

The British debt settlement with France is along the same lines as the American. The period of payments is 62 years. The annuities provide for the repayment of the whole amount originally borrowed, accrued interest to the date of settlement, and current interest during the period of payments. There are, however, the following differences between the two settlements: (1) the amount of interest charged by Great Britain is smaller than that charged by the United States, and (2) the initial period of graduated payments is shorter in the British settlement than in the American.

The table given on p. 45 shows the actual amounts originally borrowed by France from the United States and from Great Britain, the amount of inter-

[4] For a discussion of the cancellation involved in this settlement see Chapter VIII; for the full text of the agreement and the schedule of annual payments see Appendix B.

est France has agreed to pay to each of her creditors, and the totals of the annual payments stipulated in the respective agreements (figures in millions of dollars):

Countries	Amount Actually Borrowed	Accrued Interest	Current Interest	Total Payments in 62 Years
United States.....	3,340	735	2,773	6,848
Great Britain.....	2,725	453	983	4,161

The amount actually borrowed by France from
the United States was about one-fifth larger than
the amount borrowed by her from Great Britain.
But the total of the 62 annual payments to the
United States is larger than the aggregate payments
to Great Britain by more than one-half. This is due
to the fact that the rate of current interest charged
by the United States is considerably higher than
the rate fixed for the British annuities.

The initial period of small payments in the case
of the British settlement is only four years. In the
American settlement, the initial period of graduated payments extends over 16 years, the payments
rising, however, rather rapidly after the fifth year.
The effect of this on the size of the payments to be
made to the two countries is shown below (figures
in millions of dollars):

Countries	Payments During 1st Five Years	Payments During 2nd Five Years	Payments During 3rd Five Years	Payments During 4th Five Years
United States	160	305	520	620
Great Britain	207	304	304	304

Thus during the first five years, Great Britain will receive much larger sums from France than will the United States. During the next five years, the receipts of the two countries will be the same. Starting with the third five-year period, however, the payments to the United States will greatly exceed those to Great Britain.[5]

HOW FRANCE HAS MET "COMMERCIAL" DEBT PAYMENTS

We have seen that since 1920 France has been paying annually about 30 million dollars on account of her so-called "commercial" indebtedness, and it is necessary to point out in conclusion how these payments have been made. France has not had a balanced budget; on the contrary, the deficit has ranged from about 38 billion francs in 1920 to approximately 15 billions in 1925, the revenues in the latter year equalling approximately two-thirds of the total expenditures. So far as international income is concerned, up until 1924 the value of French imports was greater than the value of exports and services, so that France in the earlier years had neither a domestic budget surplus nor a net international income with which to meet foreign obligations. And yet France was paying interest on the commercial debt. The explanation of this phenomenon is somewhat similar to that which we

[5] For the text of the British-French agreement see Appendix C.

have given for German reparation payments during the years prior to the establishment of the Dawes Plan.

By the flotation of securities in the domestic market and by currency inflation France has been able, even up to the present time, to raise internally the sums required to meet this portion of her foreign indebtedness. Until 1924, in order to convert these funds into dollars and pounds it was necessary to resort to foreign borrowing and to the sale abroad of French currency and property. Since 1924, France has, however, had an excess of international income over outgo, and thus has experienced no difficulty in connection with the transfer problem.

But meeting indebtedness by means of borrowing operations cannot continue indefinitely. The effects of France's unbalanced budget and of the huge credit transactions that have been entailed in consequence, have already been manifested in the persistent, and recently catastrophic, decline of the franc.[6]

Whether France will be able to meet the increased payments which debt settlements with the United States and Great Britain will entail, will depend upon her ability to procure and maintain both an excess of budget revenues and a net international income. If, following the ratification of debt set-

[6] For a full discussion of the French fiscal and debt situation the reader is referred to Moulton, Harold G., and Lewis, Cleona, *The French Debt Problem* (Investigations in International Economic Reconstruction, Institute of Economics, Washington), 1925.

tlements, large foreign loans are granted to France she might of course for a time be able to meet debt payments out of the proceeds of the loans, just as Germany has been doing under the Dawes Plan. But such a procedure would not in reality mean a reduction in the total of the French debt; it might, on the contrary, mean an actual increase. In the long run, France's capacity to pay depends upon her ability to meet the fundamental budget and trade requirements to which we have alluded.

CHAPTER V

ITALY'S DEBT PROBLEM

ITALY, like France, came out of the war heavily indebted to both Great Britain and the United States. She was also a creditor on reparation account, but unlike France and Great Britain, Italy is not a creditor on any significant scale as a result of loans to war-time allies. Hence her capacity to meet the payments on her war debts to Great Britain and the United States will depend wholly upon her own resources, plus possible reparation receipts.

HOW ITALY CONTRACTED HER DEBTS

Italy did not enter the war until May 20, 1915. When she cast her lot with the Allies, it was with the guarantee that she would have the financial assistance of Great Britain in the handling of her foreign purchases. In July, 1915, Great Britain granted Italy her first credit, amounting to 60 million pounds sterling. Other credits followed in an ever-increasing volume up to the first part of 1917, when the United States entered the war, and the task of rendering financial assistance to Italy was assumed largely by our Treasury.

Altogether Italy borrowed from Great Britain 377 million pounds sterling. Following its usual custom, the British Treasury provided for capitalization of interest from the very start on all loans made to Italy. This interest was compounded monthly on a basis governed by the current cost of money to the Bank of England, and averaged during the war about 5 per cent *per annum*. As a result of this compounding of interest, the total amount owed by Italy to Great Britain at the end of 1925 was 611 million pounds sterling, the accrued interest thus amounting to 234 million pounds.

In connection with the first credit granted to Italy, the British Treasury arranged for the transfer to Great Britain of a considerable amount of gold taken from Italy's metal reserves. Altogether a little over 22 million pounds sterling worth of gold was thus shipped to Great Britain under an arrangement similar to that concluded with France and Russia. This gold was to be retained by Great Britain up to the time of a complete liquidation of the war debt, when it would be subject to a return to Italy.

The first American credit to Italy was granted by our Treasury on May 2, 1917, or less than a month after we entered the war; the last credit was extended on April 30, 1919. During these two years Italy borrowed from our Treasury 1,648 million dollars.

Accrued interest at the time of the debt settlement

was calculated from the termination of the war, and was charged from that date until December 15, 1922, at the rate of 4¼ per cent per annum; from December 16, 1922, to June 15, 1925, interest was charged at the rate of 3 per cent. In this manner, the accrued interest at the time of the settlement was 394 million dollars, which became a part of the total funded debt.

AMERICAN-ITALIAN DEBT SETTLEMENT

The negotiations between the Italian Debt Funding Mission, headed by Count Volpi, and the United States World War Debt Funding Commission took place during the first half of November, 1925. They lasted 10 days (November 2-12), and the final agreement was signed on November 14.

The principle of "paying capacity" was conceded at the very outset. The discussion centered around the question as to precisely what factors are involved in determining this capacity, and the fixing of payments accordingly. A "safeguard clause," making Italian payments definitely contingent upon reparation receipts, was not insisted upon by Italy, but as in the case of the French settlement the annual instalments as worked out had implied reference to expected Italian reparation receipts, as well as to other factors in Italy's economic situation.

The Italian Mission attempted to obtain a longer period of payment than had been applied to the previous debt settlements made by our Debt Funding Commission. The principal Italian proposal provided for a 77-year period, with no payments during the first few years. This proposal was rejected by our Commission, and it was finally agreed that payments should begin immediately, that these payments should be spread over 62 years, and that the interest rate at the beginning should be very low. In accordance with this agreement, our Commission submitted to the Italian Mission a schedule of payments, which was promptly accepted by the latter.

The sum which Italy undertook to pay was fixed at 2,042 million dollars. This sum, which became the principal of the funded debt, was made up of 1,648 million dollars which Italy actually borrowed during the war, and of accrued interest amounting to 394 million dollars, calculated in the manner described above. The sixty-two payments into which the total sum is divided, range from $5,000,000 during each of the first five years to $79,400,000 in 1987. The only substantial jump in the annual payments is during the sixth year, when the amount increases from $5,000,000 to $12,100,000, plus interest at the rate of $\frac{1}{8}$ of 1 per cent. From that time on the rise is gradual.

No interest at all is paid during the first five years. From 1930 until 1940 the interest rate is $\frac{1}{8}$ of 1 per cent; from 1940 until 1950, it is $\frac{1}{4}$ of 1 per cent; from 1950 until 1960, it is $\frac{1}{2}$ of 1 per cent; from 1960 until 1970, it is ¾ of 1 per cent; from 1970 to 1980, it is 1 per cent; and from 1980 until 1987, it is 2 per cent. Altogether, when Italy shall have completed the payments, the total amount collected by our Treasury will be $2,407,000,000.[1]

BRITISH-ITALIAN DEBT SETTLEMENT

Italy's debt settlement with Great Britain was made in January, 1926. The nature of this settlement differed from the settlement with the United States in three important respects: (1) the payments are uniform through practically the whole of the 62-year period of the payment schedule; (2) the lump payments from the beginning include both principal and interest, with no differentiation made between the two, and (3) the reduction of the total debt is greater in the case of Great Britain than of the United States.

Italy undertook to pay to Great Britain a total sum of 276,750,000 pounds sterling. The payment for the first year is fixed at 2 million pounds, and during the last year at 2.25 millions. During the second and third years, the payments are 4 million pounds annually; and during the remainder of the period 4.5 millions annually. However, the return of the gold held by the Treasury for Italy's account

[1] For a discussion of the cancellation involved in this settlement see Chapter VIII; for the full text of the agreement and the schedule of payments see Appendix B.

is also spread over the same period of years and is so arranged that the annual payments between the second and sixty-first years will be practically uniform at the rate of 4 million pounds a year.

No attempt was made in the settlement to fix the rate of interest as no distinction is made between principal and interest. When Italy shall have concluded her annual payments set forth in the schedule, her total indebtedness to Great Britain will be considered liquidated.[2]

The reduction of Italy's debt to Great Britain involved in the settlement is very substantial. The figures below (in millions of dollars) show at a glance the difference between the two settlements:

Countries	Amount actually borrowed	Total payments in 62 years	Payments during first 5 years	Payments during second 5 years
Great Britain........	1,830	1,346	87	97
United States........	1,648	2,407	25	75

It is clear from the above table that when the British-Italian war debt account shall have been entirely liquidated, Italy will have in effect paid Great Britain no interest whatever and only 73 per cent of the amount actually borrowed. In the case of the United States, Italy will have paid at the end of the 62-year period of payments all of the money borrowed during the war and, in addition, 759 million dollars in interest. So far the United States seems to have fared better than Great Britain in

[2] For the full text of the settlement see Appendix C.

the debt settlement with Italy, since, if all the payments are really made, the American Treasury will receive twice as much as the British, although originally the United States loaned Italy less than did Great Britain.

But, on the other hand, the British settlement has the advantage of larger payments during the earlier years of the paying period. This is especially true of the first five years, when Great Britain's receipts are three and one-half times as large as those of the United States. During the second five-year period, American receipts are three-quarters of the British. It is not until after the first 15 years that Italy's payments to the United States will exceed her payments to Great Britain.

HOW ITALY MAKES HER PAYMENTS

Almost immediately after the signing of the American-Italian debt agreement, Italy paid to the United States Treasury not only the minor sum of $199,466.34 required to round out the principal as funded, but also the first annual instalment of 5 million dollars which was not due until June 15, 1926. The check for this payment was drawn against the proceeds of a 50 million dollar credit extended some months previously to the Bank of Italy by the firm of J. P. Morgan & Company of New York. Several days later, the Italian Mission concluded an arrangement with a group of New

York bankers for the floating of a 100 million dollar Italian government loan, which yielded Italy about $90,000,000.

Thus for the first annual payment, at any rate, the Italian government did not have to rely upon the two requisites of international debt payments which we discussed in Chapter I, namely, a surplus in the government budget and a net international income from trade and service operations. Indeed, as a result of this and other borrowing transactions, the proceeds of which can be mobilized for government purposes, Italy ought not to have any difficulty, for the next few years, in providing for foreign debt payments. At the end of the first five years, however, Italy's net indebtedness abroad will almost certainly be larger than at the end of 1925. It nevertheless remains true that in the long run—that is, over the whole period of debt payments—the sums necessary for the discharging of the Italian government's obligations to the American and the British Treasuries must come out of Italy's own resources, that is, the budget and the foreign trade.

As matters stand at the present time, Italy has the necessary budget resources with which to meet her payments both to Great Britain and the United States. During the fiscal year, 1924-25, the Italian budget showed a surplus of 417 million paper lire, and for the year 1925-26 the surplus stood at 1,489 millions. In addition, Italy has, since the inauguration of the Dawes Plan, been receiving reparation deliveries of a value of 400 to 500 million paper lire a year. Since Italy's payments in 1926 to Great Britain and the United States aggregate a little less than $15,000,000 or, at the rate of exchange prevailing in June, 1926, about 450 million paper lire, it will be seen that so far as the budget problem is concerned Italy did not need to rely upon borrowed revenues.

On the transfer side of the problem Italy's situation is less satisfactory. Italian foreign trade shows a large excess of imports. This excess is scarcely covered by the international revenues derived from service operations, principally from the emigrant remittances, the tourist trade, and shipping. In 1924, there appears to have been a small net income on international account, but in 1925 there was apparently a deficit approaching 500 million paper lire. The situation in 1926 may turn out to be approximately the same. These figures, however, again do not include reparation receipts, which yielded, in 1925, about 400 million paper lire and are expected to yield in 1926 about 500 million paper lire.

Thus, since 1924, there has been—even including reparation receipts—merely an approximate equilibrium in the international accounts, with no net income available for the purpose of meeting debt instalments. It is this situation, together with the instability of the Italian currency and the scarcity

of working capital, which has necessitated the re
cent new borrowing operations.[3]

[3] For a detailed discussion of Italian problems see McGuire,
Constantine E., *Italy's International Economic Position* (Investi-
gations in International Economic Reconstruction, Institute of
Economics, Washington), 1926.

CHAPTER VI

RUSSIA AND HER DEBTS

In the case of the four international debtors which we have thus far been considering—Germany, Great Britain, France, and Italy—there has not been any question as to the acceptance by these countries of liability for their debts. These obligations have always been officially recognized. Russia is unique among the present-day international debtors in that her government refuses to acknowledge its liability for the debts contracted prior to 1918. In this chapter we shall trace the origin and the extent of Russia's foreign indebtedness, the position taken with regard to it by the Soviet government, and the basic factors involved in the solution of the Russian debt problem.

EXTENT AND ORIGIN OF RUSSIA'S FOREIGN DEBTS

Unlike the other great governments of Europe, the Russian government was a large and continuous borrower for many years before the Great War. Foreign loans were floated for the purpose of financing wars, for covering ordinary budget deficits, and for the financing of railroad and other public enterprises.   The Great War necessitated even larger credit operations, which continued until the Bolshevist *coup d'état* in 1917.

At the outbreak of the Great War the Russian government owed abroad about 4.2 billion roubles (or approximately 2.1 billion dollars). It was also responsible, through its guarantee, for about 870 million roubles of loans contracted in other countries by the privately owned railroad lines. In addition to these obligations of the Imperial government, Russian municipalities owed 420 million roubles in other countries, and Russian industries, banking, and commercial establishments, insurance companies, and so on, had borrowed foreign capital to the extent of over two billion roubles.

Thus Russia's pre-war foreign indebtedness—public and private—aggregated 7.5 billion roubles, or about $3,750,000,000.   The greater part of this money, it will be seen, was borrowed for purposes of economic development.   Half of the debt owed directly by the government was contracted for railroad construction.   Railways and factories were built with foreign money, mines were opened and cities improved with money borrowed abroad.   Out of the 7.5 billion roubles borrowed altogether, only about 2 billions were spent by the government for political purposes.

France was Russia's most important creditor, her share in the pre-war Russian debt being no less than two-thirds of the total.   Next in importance was Great Britain, followed by Germany (whose claims, however, were wiped out by the war), Belgium, and the United States.

Through the war period Russia borrowed 7,681 million roubles, thus doubling her foreign indebtedness. The larger part of this war borrowing—5,375 billion roubles—was from Great Britain. Next in importance came France, with 1,492 millions, and the United States, with 553 millions.

The above figures do not, however, represent Russia's net foreign indebtedness today. A part of the railroad mileage constructed with foreign money is located in Poland and the Baltic States, which are no longer a part of Russia. At least 350 million roubles of the railroad debt would have to be assumed by these countries, reducing Russia's debt proportionately. Moreover, Russia shipped to Great Britain during the war 640 million roubles' worth of gold, which was to have been held by the British government until the liquidation of Russia's war debts, in the same manner as similar deposits of gold made by France and Italy. Finally, at the time of the Bolshevist *coup-d'état,* the Russian State Bank had on deposit in various foreign banks large amounts of gold, which were taken over by the Allied governments. Altogether, about a billion roubles have to be deducted from Russia's war debt on account of these gold deposits.

Making all these deductions, we find that Russia's net foreign indebtedness today, not counting any accumulations of interest since 1917, when all interest payments ceased, is about 13.8 billion roubles, or in the neighborhood of 6.9 billion dollars.[1]

SOVIET POLICY OF DEBT REPUDIATION

One of the earliest official acts of the Soviet government following its establishment in November, 1917, was the promulgation of a decree, repudiating all foreign debts. Issued on January 21, 1918, this decree stated that, as of December 1, 1917, "all foreign debts are annulled, unconditionally and without exception."

In issuing this decree, the Soviet government took the position that it was not responsible for the debts, contracted in the name of Russia, by its two predecessors, the Imperial and the Provisional governments. Proclaiming itself as the first direct and true spokesman for the Russian people, it laid down the proposition that the governments preceding it borrowed money abroad without the consent of the people, and that the Russian people, and consequently the Soviet government, were not liable for these debts.

The position thus assumed by the Soviet government with regard to the foreign debts of Russia became a vitally important factor in the relations

[1] For a detailed discussion of the Russian debts see Pasvolsky and Moulton, *Russian Debts and Russian Reconstruction* (Investigations in International Economic Reconstruction, Institute of Economics, Washington), 1924, Chapters II and III.

between Russia and the rest of the world. The great world powers, which are at the same time Russia's creditors, refused to extend official recognition to the Soviet government, principally because of the latter's position on the debt question.

For four years following the establishment of the Soviet régime the debt problem remained entirely in abeyance. It was only at the conferences held at Cannes and Genoa, in 1922, that the first attempt was made to find some common ground with reference to the debt problem as between Great Britain and France—Russia's principal creditors— and the Soviet government. The work begun at Genoa was continued at another conference, held at The Hague later in the same year for the special purpose of taking up the Russian question.

The Hague conference failed completely to find any basis for an understanding on the debt question. The Russian representatives refused unconditionally to consent to an abrogation of the annulment decree. They expressed their willingness, however, to discuss a possible arrangement for the repayment of some of the debts, but they made this discussion entirely conditional upon a promise, given in advance, by the Allied powers, that large credits would be extended to Russia. The Allied representatives rejected these proposals, and The Hague conference broke up.

The Russian debt question again hung fire for a year and a half, until at the beginning of 1924 the MacDonald government in Great Britain extended to the Soviet government an official recognition, without any commitments on the part of the latter with regard to the Russian debts. With that event the Russian debt question entered upon a new phase.

BRITISH-RUSSIAN DEBT NEGOTIATIONS

Soon after the official recognition was extended to the Soviet government by Great Britain, an Anglo-Russian conference met in London to discuss the question of the debts and other matters pending between the two countries. The conference lasted from April 14 to August 5, 1924, and two treaties were finally concluded and signed by the British and the Russian delegations, subject to the ratification of the British Parliament and the Soviet government.

Just as in the negotiations at Genoa and at The Hague, all categories of Russian foreign debt were treated by the British representatives as obligations of the Soviet government, since, by virtue of nationalization, all the private enterprises in which British capital had been invested had been confiscated by the Soviets. And just as at Genoa and at The Hague, the Russian representatives were adamant in their refusal to accept liability for all these obligations, although they were willing to discuss repayment on condition that they receive assurances of new credits.

In the London negotiations the Soviet point of view prevailed almost completely. The treaties which were finally signed contained no assumption by the Soviet government of any responsibility for Russia's foreign debts. The war debts were described as held in abeyance pending some general international arrangement regarding all the inter-allied debts. As for the pre-war debts, the Soviet government agreed to satisfy "the claims of British holders of loans issued or taken over or guaranteed by the former Imperial Russian government, or by the municipalities of towns in the territory now included in the Union, payable in foreign (non-Russian) currency." This represented only a small part of the total debt. It also undertook to enter into negotiations "with British nationals in respect of industrial businesses or concessions which have been nationalized or cancelled by it, in order to arrange for just compensation of such claims." In exchange for these vague and indefinite commitments, the British government undertook to obtain from Parliament the necessary approval for granting credits to Russia. And the Soviet undertakings were made conditional upon the success of the British government in carrying out its undertaking.[2]

Thus under this Anglo-Russian arrangement, the Soviet government retained in its entirety the principle of debt repudiation and of the confiscation of

[2] For the full text of the Anglo-Russian agreement, see Appendix C.

private property. Its concession with regard to the satisfaction of some of the claims was specifically made the price to be paid for new credits. The arrangement failed, however, of going into effect. The MacDonald government was overthrown before the Anglo-Russian debt arrangements could be ratified by Parliament. The elections which followed placed in office the Baldwin government, which was definitely hostile to the ratification of the arrangement. The MacDonald treaties with Russia were never presented to Parliament for ratification, and consequently lapsed.

Since then there have been no further official negotiations between Russia and Great Britain regarding the question of the debt. Nevertheless that question crops up every little while, especially in connection with the Russian credit position in Great Britain.

OLD DEBTS AND NEW BORROWINGS

The British government has a system of export credits granted under the so-called Trade Facilities Act. Under this system, the British Department of Overseas Trade undertakes to stimulate British export trade by guaranteeing the credit of certain foreign purchasers whose position appears to it entirely sound, but to which the British exporters cannot sell on credit because their bankers, for some reason or other, do not care to undertake the risk. Efforts have been made repeatedly to extend the facilities of this scheme to Russian trade, but so far the government has not acquiesced in such a policy. The government policy in this regard was stated officially in the House of Commons, on May 12, 1925, by Mr. Guinness, the Financial Secretary of the British Treasury, to be as follows:

To refuse credit facilities to the Soviet government, or its agencies, until the Soviet government itself establishes such conditions in the treatment of debts or compensation for confiscated property as will restore confidence and credit.

The matter came up again in parliamentary debate in February and March, 1926. In the course of this debate, Mr. Samuel, the Secretary of the Department of Overseas Trade, after pointing out that "if it (the Soviet government) has defaulted once, it may do it again," declared:

If a case were to come to me from the Credit Export Advisory Committee asking me to authorize the use of public money for the purpose of giving credit facilities to Russia under the scheme, I should decline to accede to it.

Thus the net result of Great Britain's experience with Russia during the past two years has been to dissociate, so far as Russia's European creditors are concerned, the question of debt repudiation from that of the official recognition of the Soviet government, and to accentuate still more the connection between the old debts and the new foreign borrowing of Soviet Russia.

France, under the Herriot government, which came into power soon after MacDonald became Prime Minister of Great Britain, followed the British example in the question of the recognition of the Soviet government. Just as in the case of Great Britain, diplomatic relations were established between France and Russia without any reference to the debt question. And again as in the case of Great Britain, the debts were taken up at a Franco-Russian conference, which, however, failed to achieve any results.

The debt negotiations were resumed at a second Franco-Russian conference which opened in Paris at the end of February, 1926, and is still in progress (July, 1926). Just as in the case of Great Britain, the Soviet debt negotiations with France are tied up with discussions of new credits, and the same difficulties stand in the way.

LEGAL LIABILITY AND PAYING CAPACITY

In all the negotiations conducted so far on the subject of the Russian debts, the question at issue has always been whether or not the Soviet government is legally liable for the pre-war and war debts of Russia. The Soviet government has maintained, and still maintains, that it bears no responsibility whatever for this huge mass of indebtedness, which it holds was contracted without the consent of the Russian people. Russia's creditors, on the other hand, maintain that the principle of government succession applies to the Soviet government, irrespective of the circumstances under which it came into existence, and that consequently the Soviet régime inherited from its two predecessors all of Russia's foreign obligations, as well as her national resources.

This difference of views on a question as formal and technical as the principle of legal liability is more important than it might appear to be. It acquires special significance in connection with the question of Russia's capacity for paying her debts.

It is readily admitted by both sides that Russia has at the present time no paying capacity whatever. More than that, the tragic events of the past decade in her history have wrought so much havoc in her national life that she is in sore need of foreign credits for the rehabilitation of her economic system. Until the process of Russia's economic restoration, at least to the pre-war level of operation is somewhere near completed there can be no question of any debt-paying capacity.[3]

Russia is today pretty much where she was during the last decade of the nineteenth century, when she was just beginning her economic development on a large scale. She then needed a stable monetary system based on gold, a network of railways, and industrial equipment. She succeeded in acquiring

[3] For a discussion of the Russian paying capacity see Pasvolsky and Moulton, *Russian Debts and Russian Reconstruction*, Chapters VI-X.

all these, such as they were, through foreign loans. Today she again needs a sound monetary system; her railways require enormous expenditures for their rehabilitation; her industrial equipment needs repair and renewal. She cannot accomplish any of these things without new borrowing abroad.

She can borrow only in the countries which are. already her creditors on account of her pre-war and war debts. And the task which now confronts the Soviet government is either to give up its policy of debt repudiation by accepting legal liability for the existing debts and thus lay a foundation for a credit position, or else to obtain from Russia's present creditors an acceptance of its repudiation policy and to convince them that they ought in any case to make new loans to Russia.

The principle of legal liability for the existing debts is thus the crucial factor in Russia's present-day credit position. In this way it is a vital element in the determination of Russia's future paying capacity, since that depends upon the availability at the present time of new foreign loans, which, in turn, depends upon Russia's international credit position.

CHAPTER VII

DEBT PROBLEMS OF THE SMALLER EUROPEAN COUNTRIES

FROM the point of view of the amounts involved, the obligations of Germany, Great Britain, France, Italy, and Russia represent the bulk of international indebtedness. Nearly all of the remaining countries of Europe have, however, emerged from the war burdened with foreign obligations of greater or lesser amount, and in this chapter we shall examine some of the outstanding features of the foreign debt position of these smaller European countries.

REPARATION ARRANGEMENTS WITH AUSTRIA, HUNGARY, AND BULGARIA

The treaties of peace which terminated the World War were five in number, namely, that of Versailles with Germany, that of St. Germain with Austria, that of Trianon with Hungary, that of Neuilly with Bulgaria, and that of Sèvres with Turkey. With the treaty of Sèvres, which was superseded in 1923 by the treaty of Lausanne, we are not here concerned. But the other four treaties are of direct interest to us because each one of them contains a provision for reparation payments by the respective country with which it was signed. In Chapter II we examined the reparation provisions of the Versailles treaty and traced the vicissitudes of the German reparation problem since the signing of that treaty. We shall now make a similar examination of the reparation problem as relating to the remaining three countries upon which reparation liability was imposed by the peace treaties.

Neither the St. Germain nor the Trianon treaties fixed the amount of reparation payments for which Austria and Hungary were made liable. In this respect the two treaties conformed to the precedent established in the Versailles treaty. The determination of the precise amounts, the manner of payment, and the distribution of receipts was left to the Reparation Commission, which was given, in the case of Austria and Hungary, just as in the case of Germany, a sort of "blanket" mortgage on all the national resources of these countries as security for the carrying out of the reparation programs.

The conference at Spa, held in 1920, fixed not only the percentages of the total reparation payments from Germany to which each of the recipients was entitled, but also similar ratios for the distribution of the reparation receipts from Austria and Hungary. The total amounts due were not, however, fixed at that conference and were again left to a determination by the Reparation Commission.

These amounts have not been fixed to the present

day. On the contrary, because of the events which led, in 1922 and 1923, to international action, under the auspices of the League of Nations, for the financial salvaging of Austria and Hungary, the determination of these amounts has been definitely postponed for a period of 20 years.

By virtue of the protocols of Geneva, signed in October, 1922, which placed the finances of Austria under the control of the League of Nations, Austria was freed from any reparation payments until 1942. Moreover, the Reparation Commission, prior to the signing of the protocols, agreed to waive its mortgage rights to certain specified resources of the country. This was done in order to enable Austria to float a foreign loan, secured by a part of the revenues of the government.

In the case of Hungary, the Reparation Commission was not quite so lenient. Under the League reconstruction scheme, which went into effect early in 1924, a schedule of reparation payments was prescribed for Hungary for a period of 20 years. However, these payments were made very small, averaging over the whole period about 10 million gold crowns (about $2,000,000) a year.[1]

Bulgaria was treated differently from Austria and Hungary in that the total amount of her reparation liability was fixed by the treaty of Neuilly. Under

[1] For the decisions of the Reparation Commission with regard to Hungarian reparation payments and the schedule of payments, see Appendix A.

the terms of this treaty Bulgaria undertook to pay the Allies the sum of 2,250,000,000 gold francs, in half-yearly payments spread over a period of 37 years from January 1, 1921. The distribution of these payments among the recipients was fixed by the Spa conference.

The scheme for the distribution of all these reparation payments is very intricate. The receipts from Austria and Hungary are divided into two equal parts. Of the first half, the great powers, that is, France, Great Britain, and Italy, receive practically the whole amount; of the second half, Rumania and Serbia are the principal recipients. Of the Bulgarian payments, the three great powers receive about 70 per cent. Taking all these payments into account, we find that the distribution is approximately as follows:

France	26	per cent
Italy	25	" "
Rumania	15	" "
Great Britain	11	" "
Serbia	10	" "
Belgium	4	" "

The remaining 9 per cent are divided among the smaller Allies, principally Greece and Portugal.

LIBERATION PAYMENTS OF THE SUCCESSION STATES

In connection with the reparation obligations imposed by the peace treaties on Austria and Hungary, there is a rather curious arrangement affecting the five other so-called Succession States, those countries which contain territories formerly included within the boundaries of the Austro-Hungarian Monarchy—namely, Poland, Czechoslovakia, Rumania, Yugoslavia, and Italy. By virtue of special agreements, the governments of these countries undertook to make certain contributions "towards the expenses of liberating" the territories ceded to them.

These liberation payments originated in the feeling, which was rather prevalent at the time of the peace negotiations, that the territories in question should not be wholly freed from the reparation liability attaching to the countries from which they were separated. The total sum of the payments has never been fixed, though it was specifically provided in the original agreement that it should not exceed 1,500,000,000 gold francs and should be divided among the various territories "on the basis of the ratio between the average for the three financial years, 1911, 1912, and 1913, of the revenues acquired by them from the former Austro-Hungarian Monarchy."

However, four of the countries liable for these liberation payments are also entitled to the receipt of certain amounts of reparation payments. Czechoslovakia alone has no reparation claims, since her territory was comprised in its entirety within the frontiers of the former enemy powers. Her liberation debt, therefore, if its total should ever be fixed, would be an actual debt. Under the terms of the original agreements, the portion chargeable to Czechoslovakia cannot, however, exceed one-half of the total. Poland has potential reparation claims, since she comprises a part of the former Russian territory, and under Article 116 of the treaty of Versailles and Article 187 of the treaty of St. Germain there is reserved for Russia, and consequently Poland, a possible future claim on account of reparations. This claim might be used to offset the liberation payments. As for Italy, Rumania, and Yugoslavia, their reparation claims are far in excess of any share of liberation payments that might be assigned to them.

AUSTRO-HUNGARIAN PRE-WAR DEBTS

Besides imposing reparation and liberation payments on the countries carved wholly or in part from the territory of the former Austro-Hungarian Monarchy, the peace treaties with Austria and Hungary also provided for the general manner of handling the Austro-Hungarian debts, both those created before the war and those arising out of the war. These are to be partitioned among the various new states, in accordance with percentages fixed by the Reparation Commission. In the last three years certain definite arrangements have been made with regard to some of these debts.

Very considerable sums are involved. The territories which had formerly constituted the Austro-

Hungarian Monarchy are nominally liable for no less than 18 billion crowns, or over 3.5 billion dollars at the pre-war rate of exchange. However, most of these debts are expressed in paper crowns and have become practically worthless because of the depreciation of the crown. But something like one-quarter of the total indebtedness is expressed in gold or in stable foreign currencies, and these debts, which are all pre-war, are subject to payment.

The Reparation Commission apportioned these debts in the following manner: The bulk of the debts contracted by the former Austrian Empire has been assigned to Czechoslovakia (42 per cent), present Austria (37 per cent), and Poland (14 per cent). The bulk of the debts contracted by the former Kingdom of Hungary has been assigned to present Hungary (46 per cent), Rumania (22 per cent), Czechoslovakia (16 per cent), and Yugoslavia (14 per cent). This division was made mainly on the basis of the share of each of the countries in the economic resources of the former Monarchy.

In June, 1923, the Reparation Commission called a conference of the representatives of the British, French, Swiss, Dutch, Belgian, Italian, and German associations of foreign bondholders, as well as of the representatives of the seven Succession States, to discuss the question of the pre-war Austro-Hungarian debts. The conference met at Innsbruck, and drew up a protocol embodying an agreement on some of the questions under consideration.

It was agreed that payments should begin in 1925 on practically all the railroad loans, and on two categories of Austrian and three categories of Hungarian public loans. There was no cancellation made in the amounts of these debts, but it was stipulated that during the initial period the interest and amortization charges on the loans involved would be reduced by 68 per cent, and in some cases even by 73 per cent. A *Caisse Commune,* or Joint Office of foreign holders of pre-war Austrian and Hungarian bonds, was created by the Innsbruck protocol. All the payments allotted under the protocol are to be paid into this Joint Office and are to be distributed by it.

The Innsbruck protocol failed of immediate ratification by some of the countries concerned, notably Rumania, and in November, 1925, the Reparation Commission called another conference, held in Prague to consider certain questions which had arisen out of the discussion of the protocol. The result of the Prague conference was the putting into operation of the Innsbruck protocol, and the scheme set up under it is now in effect.

This scheme is to continue in its present form until October, 1937, although the rates of payment may be changed within the first six years of the scheme's operation, provided the economic condition of the paying countries warrants such a modification.

EXTENT OF WAR AND RELIEF LOANS

During the war the smaller Allied countries found it necessary to borrow money from their more powerful allies, notably from the United States and Great Britain. After the war, all of the new or reorganized countries in Central Europe, running from the Baltic to the Ægean seas, had to borrow money for relief purposes in order to be able to pay their way during the initial period of their post-war existence. These two sets of borrowing are responsible for the foreign debts of these countries which are subject to funding and repayment under the arrangements made by the World War Debt Funding Commission of the United States and under similar arrangements in Great Britain.

As far as the United States is concerned almost all of these debts have now been funded. The sums actually borrowed by the smaller countries with which debt-funding agreements have been signed were as follows:

Belgium	377.0	million dollars
Czechoslovakia	91.8	" "
Esthonia	14.0	" "
Finland	8.3	" "
Hungary	1.7	" "
Latvia	5.1	" "
Lithuania	5.0	" "
Poland	159.7	" "
Rumania	36.1	" "
Yugoslavia	51.0	" "

With the exception of Russia, whose policy of debt repudiation applies to the 192 million dollars borrowed from the United States Treasury during the war, there remain two unfunded accounts. Greece borrowed 15 million dollars and expects soon to negotiate a settlement. Then there is the Austrian debt of 24 million dollars, the funding of which has been postponed until 1942 by a Congressional Joint Resolution, approved by President Harding on April 6, 1922.

Altogether, the war and relief loans of the United States Treasury to the smaller European countries amounted to 789 million dollars, of which 750 millions have been funded.

Great Britain extended war credits to four of the smaller Allies; namely, Serbia, Rumania, Portugal, and Greece. The total amount of these loans outstanding in 1925, together with accrued interest, was about 500 million dollars, almost equally divided among the four countries. The relief loans extended by Great Britain were made to eight countries, and aggregated about 100 million dollars. Finally, Great Britain loaned Belgium about 60 million dollars for reconstruction purposes, and extended small credits, aggregating about 7 million dollars, to Czechoslovakia, Poland, Yugoslavia, Rumania, and Latvia for the purpose of repatriating their prisoners of war. Practically all of these British accounts, totalling, in 1925, 667 million dollars, still remain unfunded.

French loans to the smaller Allies during the war were small in amount.

CHARACTER OF AMERICAN DEBT SETTLEMENTS WITH SMALLER NATIONS

Outside of Great Britain, France, and Italy, 10 European debtors have now funded their war debts to the United States. Of these debt-funding agreements, one was concluded in 1923; three in 1924; five in 1925; and one in 1926.

The debt settlement with Finland was signed on May 1, 1923. This was the first debt-funding agreement actually consummated, since the British agreement was not signed until June 19, 1923, although the British negotiations began earlier than the Finnish. The total principal and accrued interest for which Finland assumed responsibility under this agreement is $9,000,000. It is payable in 62 annual instalments, starting with $45,000 in 1923 and rising gradually to $345,000 in 1984. Interest is charged at the rate of 3 per cent during the first 10 years, and 3.5 per cent during the remainder of the period.

In 1924 debt-funding agreements were signed with Hungary (April 25), Lithuania (September 22), and Poland (November 14). Hungary assumed responsibility for a total sum of $1,939,000, which is to be paid in 62 annual instalments, rising from $9,600 in 1924 to $75,000 in 1985. Lithuania became responsible for $6,030,000; her instalments range from $30,000 in 1925 to $227,000 in 1986. The total of Poland's debt was fixed at $178,560,000;

her instalments range from $560,000 in 1923 to $9,000,000 in 1984. All these payments are on account of the principal of the debt. Interest in all three cases is fixed at the rate of 3 per cent during the first 10 years and 3.5 per cent during the remaining 52 years.

The four agreements described above conform to the model set up in connection with the British debt settlement. In each case the amount actually borrowed is to be repaid in full, plus accrued interest at the rate of 4.25 per cent. The sum of these two amounts constitutes the new principal, interest on which is to be charged at the rate of 3 per cent during the first 10 years and 3.5 per cent during the remaining 52 years.

In 1925 debt-funding agreements were signed with Belgium (August 18), Latvia (September 24), Czechoslovakia (October 13), Esthonia (October 28), and Rumania (December 4).

The Belgian settlement represented the first important departure from the model set up by the British settlement. The whole Belgian debt was divided into two parts—that contracted before and that contracted after the Armistice. The pre-Armistice debt was fixed at $171,780,000, which was the amount agreed upon in Paris during the Peace Conference and approved by President Wilson for inclusion in the Belgian war debt, which, under the treaty of Versailles, was to be assumed in full by Germany. On this portion of the debt Belgium is to pay no interest whatever. The total sum is to be discharged in 62 instalments, starting with $1,000,000 in 1926 and rising gradually to $2,900,000 in 1932; then continuing at that rate until 1987, when the last instalment equals $2,280,000.

The post-Armistice debt of Belgium, amounting, with accrued interest, to $246,000,000, is treated in the same manner as the debts funded prior to the Belgian agreement. The principal is to be repaid in 62 annual instalments, rising from $1,100,000 in 1925 to $9,600,000 in 1932. Interest on the post-Armistice debt is fixed not on a percentage basis, but in lump sums for each year, representing much less than the 3 per cent rate used in the other settlements. Starting with the eleventh year, interest will be charged at the rate of 3.5 per cent.

It is interesting to note that, in the language of the American debt commission, "the adjustment of early payments on the (Belgian) debts have been made to meet the present difficulties of Belgium in obtaining foreign exchange because of the unfavorable balance of her commodity trade and the deficiencies in her income from foreign investments, tourist travel, and other forms of 'invisible' exchange." [2]

The Czechoslovak settlement also represented a departure from the British model, but only in the manner of handling the interest payments. After

[2] Statement given to the press by the World War Foreign Debt Commission, August 19, 1925.

some controversy between the Debt Commission and the Czechoslovak delegation, the principal of the debt was finally fixed at $115,000,000, and Czechoslovakia agreed to repay it in 62 annual instalments, with the rate of interest fixed at 3 per cent for the first 10 years and 3.5 per cent during the remaining 52 years. She asked, however, for the privilege of deferring a part of the interest due during the first 18 years to the later period. In this manner, the first 18 annuities were fixed at $3,000,-000 each, while the deferred portion of the interest during the period was added to the remaining 44 annuities, making the total funded debt $131,-000,000.

The Latvian and the Esthonian settlements, one of which preceded and the other followed the settlement with Czechoslovakia, conformed to the model of the settlement with Great Britain.

The settlement with Rumania followed the Czechoslovak model, rather than the British. The period during which Rumania is to defer interest payments is, however, 14 years, rather than 18 as in the case of Czechoslovakia.

On the other hand, the settlement with Yugoslavia, signed on May 3, 1926, followed the model of the Italian settlement, which represented a much greater departure from the original British model than any of the other settlements. Yugoslavia is to pay no interest at all during the first 12 years; from 1927 until 1940, she is to pay ⅛ of 1 per cent;

from 1940 until 1954, ½ of 1 per cent; from 1954 to 1957, 1 per cent; from 1957 until 1960, 2 per cent; from 1960 on, 3.5 per cent.[3]

Of the 10 smaller settlements made by the Debt Commission, only three conform entirely to the British model. These are the settlements with Finland, Hungary, and Lithuania. Five others carry the same rates of interest as the British settlement, but differ from it in the options provided for the initial period. Poland, Latvia, and Esthonia are given the option of deferring three-quarters of the payments due for principal and interest during the first five years to the remaining 57 years, the deferred payments being funded at 3 per cent. Czechoslovakia has the right to defer a quarter of her payments during the first 18 years, while Rumania has a similar right for the first 11 years. The only real departures from the straight application of the British model are in the case of Belgium and Yugoslavia.

POST-WAR BORROWING

France was the only one of the creditor nations that continued to extend government credits after the war and the initial period of reconstruction.

---

[3] It should be noted that the amount of the total funded debt given in the case of each of the countries discussed here is put in round figures; in each case a small cash payment was made at the time of the settlement for the purpose of rounding out the exact amount. For a discussion of the cancellation involved in each of these settlements see Chapter VIII; for the full text of the agreements and the schedules of payments see Appendix B.

Altogether her war, relief, and post-war loans to the smaller countries of Europe aggregated up to 1925 about 8 billion paper francs, or approximately 400 million dollars at the 1925 value of the franc. Her principal creditors on these accounts are Belgium, Yugoslavia, Rumania, Poland, and Czechoslovakia.

The American and the British Treasury loans ceased after the relief credits had been completed. All the borrowing done by the smaller European countries since that time has been from private investors.

The most important of the post-war loans for the smaller European countries has been the reconstruction loan to Austria, floated in 1923. It was for 625 million gold crowns (about 125 million dollars), and was allocated among several countries, the largest shares being taken over by Great Britain and the United States. It was a loan extended to the Austrian government, but it was guaranteed, as to principal and interest, by Great Britain, France, Italy, Czechoslovakia, and several smaller countries.

A similar loan was extended to Hungary in 1924. It was for only 250 million gold crowns, and did not carry any international guarantee. Smaller loans have been arranged in the United States by the governments of Czechoslovakia, Poland, and Yugoslavia. These loans were handled through ordinary banking channels.

On the whole, the post-war borrowings by the

governments of the smaller European countries have been, so far, smaller than their accumulated war and relief debts, and represent for these countries a much smaller burden of foreign debt than their obligations incurred during the war or those imposed upon them in consequence of the peace treaties.

FACTORS INVOLVED IN DEBT PAYMENTS

The factors which are involved for each of these smaller countries in the meeting of their debt payments are precisely those which we set forth in Chapter I and discussed in connection with each of the five great international debtors of Europe. Every one of them, in order to be able to make the necessary payments, must in the long run have an adequate surplus in its government budget and a corresponding excess of exports over imports in its foreign trade.

Even apart from the debt payments, the budgetary problem for all of the countries here under discussion has been exceedingly difficult to adjust. With the exception of Belgium and Greece all of these countries are either new or have been re-constructed by the peace treaties; and both Belgium and Greece suffered great disorganization as a result of the war. After the Armistice these countries accordingly found themselves forced either to create or readjust their governmental systems, and the process has involved serious fiscal difficulties.

Much progress has, however, been made in recent years. Indeed, the Baltic countries—Finland, Latvia, Esthonia, and Lithuania—have for some time possessed balanced budgets. Moreover, Austria and Hungary, Czechoslovakia and Yugoslavia, have during the past year achieved budgetary equilibrium. Yugoslavia's budgetary position, however, is still precarious, owing principally to the fact that her currency has not been stabilized. Belgium, Poland, and Rumania are, on the other hand, still experiencing great difficulties in making non-borrowed revenues equal expenditures.

The financial condition of the last three countries is greatly complicated by the fact that their currencies have not been put on a stable basis. Poland attempted stabilization in 1924 but the stability was of short duration, and critical conditions have since prevailed. The currency depreciation is in part a reflection of budgetary deficits but it is also in part attributable to unfavorable balances of trade.

While all of these countries have thus attained budgetary equilibrium or made great progress in that direction, nearly all of them have still to demonstrate their ability to develop an excess of revenues over expenditures equal to the debt payments required from them.

As for the transfer problem, practically all of the countries under discussion here have to depend mainly upon an excess of exports over imports in their merchandise trade for the means with which to make their payments abroad. With the exception of Belgium, Austria, and Czechoslovakia, none of these countries has any great amount of international income from service operations. Some of them, however—notably the Baltic states—have developed an export surplus. Czechoslovakia has also had a fairly satisfactory foreign trade situation for several years, although the size of her favorable trade balance has fluctuated considerably.

Some of the countries of Eastern and Southeastern Europe periodically have a foreign trade surplus; but since they are primarily agricultural countries the fluctuation in the yield of crops produces very considerable variations in the volume of their exports. For example, it was the virtual failure of the harvest that brought Poland to the verge of economic disaster in 1925 and destroyed the stability of her currency.

Faced with budget and trade difficulties, a number of these countries have, like Germany and Italy, resorted to borrowing operations in order to make possible the initial payments on their foreign obligations. Poland floated a loan of 100 million dollars in the United States soon after her debt was funded, and Czechoslovakia one for 25 million dollars. Belgium, Rumania, and Yugoslavia have likewise been negotiating for loans since the funding of their obligations. Hungary's payments, both on account of reparations and debts, have thus far been made primarily from the proceeds of her international reconstruction loan; and in the summer of 1926 she was negotiating a new loan in Great Britain.

Thus in the case of most of the countries under discussion in this chapter the occasion has not yet arisen for actually putting to the test the two primary requisites involved in international debt payments.

CHAPTER VIII

THE EXTENT OF AMERICAN CANCELLATIONS

At the conclusion of this survey of the debt problems of the several countries under consideration, it will be of interest to recapitulate the results from the point of view of the United States—the principal creditor nation. What is the actual creditor position of the United States Treasury with respect to these obligations since they have been funded? And to what extent have the agreements that have been negotiated altered the original creditor position of the United States government?

THE CREDITOR POSITION OF THE UNITED STATES TREASURY

The total amount of cash advances made by the Treasury under the Liberty Bond Acts aggregated $9,598,236,575.45. In addition foreign governments were indebted to the Treasury for obligations contracted in the following ways: (1) through the purchase of surplus war supplies; (2) through the receipt of relief credits; (3) through the purchase of flour held by the United States Grain Corporation;

and (4) for credits extended by the United States Shipping Board. The combined total of the cash advances and the other obligations amounted to the sum of $10,338,058,352.20, exclusive of accrued interest.

This money was loaned to 20 different countries, of which 16 were in Europe. Of the non-European borrowers, Armenia, which has no government at the present time, received $11,959,917.49. Liberia received $26,000, and this sum has not as yet been refunded. Cuba borrowed $10,000,000 and has already repaid it. Nicaragua purchased on credit $166,604.14 worth of war supplies and has so far repaid about one-half of this sum.

Of the European debtors, Austria has obtained a postponement of any considerations of her debt, amounting to $24,055,708.92, until the year 1942.[1] Greece with a total debt of $15,000,000 and Russia with obligations amounting to $192,601,297.37 have as yet taken no steps towards the funding of their indebtedness. The other 13 European debtors have concluded debt-funding agreements, but as previously noted the agreements with France and Yugoslavia have not as yet received final ratification.

The interest on these obligations prior to the dates at which they were definitely funded has been added to the principal. Although at the time the original loans were granted the interest rate was nominally

[1] For the text of the Congressional Resolution authorizing this postponement see Appendix B.

5 per cent,[2] at the time of the British debt-funding negotiations the rate of accrued interest was definitely fixed at 4.25 per cent, the rate at which the United States government floated its later Liberty Loans. In adjusting the principal of the British debt, accrued interest up to December 15, 1922, was added to the amount actually borrowed and this figure was rounded off to an even number by a small cash payment.

In the case of all the other settlements the rule was adopted that the rate of accrued interest should not exceed that laid down in the settlement with Great Britain. Arrears of interest were therefore generally calculated at the rate of 4.25 per cent up to December 15, 1922, and at the rate of 3 per cent from then until the date of the various settlements. This latter rate was in accord with the rate Great Britain had been paying on her debt, since December 15, 1922. The original principal plus the accrued interest became, with minor adjustments, the principal of the funded debt.

The table on page 94 shows the total amounts to be received by the United States Treasury on account of principal and interest in accordance with the settlements that have been effected.

As the table indicates, the rate of interest is practically identical in nine of the thirteen adjustments,

---

[2] With the exception of the small amount of obligations transferred to the Treasury from the United States Grain Corporation, which were on the basis of a 6 per cent rate.

TOTAL PRINCIPAL AND INTEREST TO BE PAID TO THE UNITED STATES BY 13 WAR DEBTORS

Country	Principal	Interest	Total	Average Interest Rate (approximate) over the Whole Period of Payments, Per Cent
Great Britain	$ 4,600,000,000	$ 6,505,965,000.00	$11,105,965,000.00	3.3
Finland	9,000,000	12,695,055.00	21,695,055.00	3.3
Hungary	1,939,000	2,754,240.00	4,693,240.00	3.3
Poland	178,560,000	257,127,550.00	435,687,550.00	3.3
Esthonia	13,830,000	19,501,140.00	33,331,140.00	3.3
Latvia	5,775,000	8,183,635.00	13,958,635.00	3.3
Lithuania	6,030,000	8,501,940.00	14,531,940.00	3.3
Czechoslovakia	115,000,000	* 197,811,433.88	312,811,433.88	3.3
Rumania	44,590,000	* 77,916,260.05	122,506,260.05	3.3
Belgium	417,780,000	310,050,500.00	727,830,500.00	1.8
France	4,025,000,000	2,822,674,104.17	6,847,674,104.17	1.6
Yugoslavia	62,850,000	32,327,635.00	95,177,635.00	1.0
Italy	2,042,000,000	365,677,500.00	2,407,677,500.00	0.4
Total	$11,522,354,000	$10,621,185,993.10	$22,143,539,993.10	

*Includes deferred payments which will be funded into principal. See p. 84.

namely 3.3 per cent.[3]   This rate is slightly less than
the standard rate of 3.5 per cent merely because
during the first 10 years interest is charged at the
rate of 3 per cent.   At the end of 62 years these nine
debtors will, therefore, have repaid the actual
amounts borrowed, accrued interest to the date of
settlement, and in addition interest on the principal
of the funded debt at an average rate of 3.3 per
cent.   The other four debtors will also have repaid
in full the amount borrowed and the accrued interest, but the average rate of current interest varies
widely.   It is 1.8 per cent for Belgium, 1.6 per cent
for France, 1.0 per cent for Yugoslavia, and 0.4 per
cent for Italy.

THE PERCENTAGES OF CANCELLATION

The original obligations of foreign governments
held by the United States Treasury called, as we
have seen, for a 5 per cent rate of interest, and prior
to the funding of the debts, accrued interest on all
these obligations was entered on the books of the
Treasury at this rate.   Thus at the time of each
settlement there was outstanding against the negotiating country a total indebtedness consisting of
the amount originally borrowed, plus accrued interest calculated at the rate of 5 per cent.   For con-

---

[3] The rate for Czechoslovakia and Rumania is slightly larger
than 3.3 per cent; there are also other slight variations, appearing
in the second and third decimal places.

venience, we may call this outstanding indebtedness "the debt prior to funding."

As noted above, the accrued interest was recalculated at the time of the settlements on a 4.25 per cent basis (3 per cent for part of the time in the case of the later settlements). The actual funded principal was thus made somewhat smaller than the debt prior to funding. This obviously represented a certain amount of reduction, or cancellation, of the outstanding indebtedness as recorded on the books of the United States Treasury.

It will also be recalled that the rates of current interest charged in the settlements are considerably below not only the original 5 per cent rate, but also the 4.25 per cent rate fixed as the minimum in the Act creating the World War Foreign Debt Commission. This reduction of current interest represents a further, and much more considerable, cancellation of indebtedness.

To estimate the amount of the cancellation that has occurred it is necessary to compare the amount of the debt prior to funding with the present value of the actual settlements. The present value of the settlements is the sum which in 62 years, at a given rate of interest, would yield a total equal to the principal and interest payments called for by the various agreements. The amount of the present value will, however, obviously vary, depending upon whether interest is computed at 5 or 4.25 per cent. In the table on page 97 the present value is computed on a 5 per cent basis, the rate which the obligations originally bore.

PRESENT VALUES OF FUNDED DEBTS AT 5 PER CENT

(In dollars, 000 omitted)

Country	Debt Prior to Funding	Present Value of Funded Debt on the Basis of a 5 Per Cent Interest Rate	*Percentage of Cancellation*
Finland	9,190	6,452	*29.8*
Hungary	1,984	1,388	*30.0*
Poland	182,324	127,643	*30.0*
Esthonia	14,143	9,915	*29.9*
Latvia	5,893	4,137	*29.8*
Lithuania	6,216	4,322	*30.5*
Czechoslovakia	123,854	77,985	*37.0*
Rumania	46,945	29,507	*37.1*
Belgium	483,426	191,766	*60.3*
France	4,230,777	1,681,369	*60.3*
Yugoslavia	66,164	15,919	*75.9*
Italy	2,150,150	426,287	*80.2*
Total	7,321,066	2,576,690	64.8
Great Britain	4,715,310	3,296,948	*30.1*
Grand Total	12,036,376	5,873,638	51.2

The extent of cancellation in the case of the first six countries shown in this table, is about 30 per cent. For Czechoslovakia and Rumania, the cancellation is about 37 per cent; for Belgium and France, about 60 per cent; for Yugoslavia about 76 per cent; and for Italy it is a fraction over 80 per cent. For the 12 Continental debtors combined the extent of cancellation is 64.8 per cent.

The cancellation of the British debt, shown separately in the table, is 30 per cent. But the amount of Great Britain's indebtedness bulks so large in the total for the 13 debtors, that the extent of cancellation for all the debtors combined works out at only 51.2 per cent.

The above percentages represent the maximum cancellation that can be figured on the basis of the settlements as negotiated. In the case of commercial obligations between private parties, the rate originally stipulated would, of course, be regarded as the one and only rate to be considered. But in the case of the war loans, it was taken for granted that 5 per cent was merely a provisional rate and subject to reconsideration at the time of funding operations. In view of the fact that the later Liberty Loans of the United States government were floated at 4.25 per cent, Congress, in the act creating the Debt Commission, fixed 4.25 per cent as the minimum, though not necessarily the actual, rate at which the obligations should be refunded. This rate is perhaps a fairer basis on which to compute the extent of the cancellation that has occurred.

The table on page 99 gives the present values of the funded settlements on the basis of a 4.25 per cent interest rate, and the consequent percentages of cancellation. This is the basis used by the Debt Commission in reporting to Congress the results of its negotiations.[4]

---

[4] Hearings before the Ways and Means Committee of the House of Representatives, May 20, 1926.

PRESENT VALUES OF FUNDED DEBTS AT 4.25 PER CENT

(In dollars, 000 omitted)

Country	Debt Prior to Funding	Present Value of the Funded Debts on the Basis of a 4.25 Per Cent Interest Rate	Percentage of Cancellation
Finland	9,190	7,413	19.3
Hungary	1,984	1,596	19.6
Poland	182,324	146,825	19.5
Esthonia	14,143	11,392	19.5
Latvia	5,893	4,755	19.3
Lithuania	6,216	4,967	20.1
Czechoslovakia	123,854	91,964	25.7
Rumania	46,945	35,172	25.1
Belgium	483,426	225,000	53.5
France	4,230,777	1,996,509	52.8
Yugoslavia	66,164	20,030	69.7
Italy	2,150,150	528,192	75.4
Total	7,321,066	3,073,815	58.0
Great Britain	4,715,310	3,788,470	19.7
Grand Total	12,036,376	6,862,285	43.0

The extent of cancellation as indicated by this table is considerably smaller than the percentages in the table on page 97. For the Continental debtors combined, the cancellation on this basis is 58 per cent; and for Great Britain it is 19.7 per cent. The cancellation on the aggregate amount of the 13 debts works out at 43 per cent.

Still another way of looking at the question of cancellation has been suggested by the Debt Commission. In the above computations cancellation

PERCENTAGES OF DEBTS CANCELLED BY FUNDING AGREEMENTS

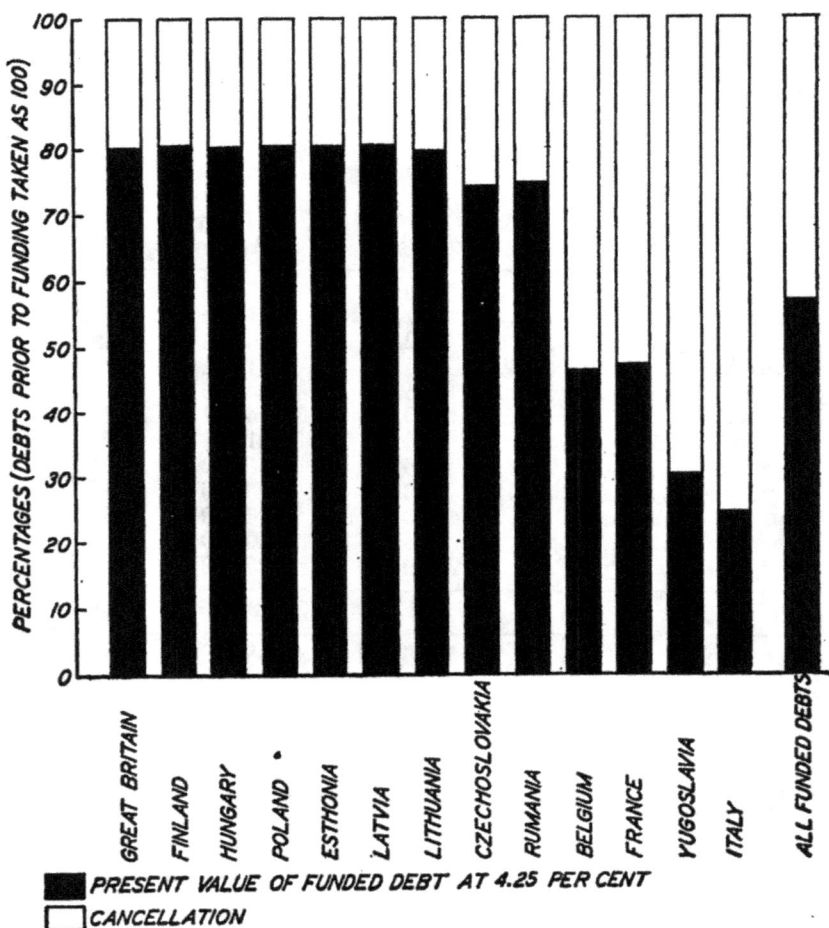

PRESENT VALUE OF FUNDED DEBT AT 4.25 PER CENT
CANCELLATION

has been considered as the reduction from the
amounts which the United States Treasury would
have received if the debt settlements had been made
strictly on the terms prescribed by Congress. Cancellation may, however, be considered as the difference between the rates of interest at which the

various debts have been funded and the cost of borrowing to the Treasury during the period of payments.

No one, of course, can predict with any degree of certainty the average rate of interest that the Treasury will have to pay during the next 62 years. However, Secretary Mellon considers that the average cost of Treasury borrowing during this period ought to be in the neighborhood of 3 per cent.[5] On this basis the cancellation on the aggregate indebtedness works out at as low a figure as 20 per cent. But if, as Secretary Mellon implies, 3 per cent is a proper rate on which to base the computations, then it follows that Great Britain and those countries which have settled substantially on the British terms are paying more than the full amount of their indebtedness. Belgium, France, Yugoslavia, and Italy, however, would still be paying considerably less. Such a method of computation is obviously of value only for hypothetical purposes.

PROVISIONS GOVERNING ANNUAL PAYMENTS

From the standpoint of arrangements affecting annual payments the settlements may be divided into three groups. The agreements with Great Britain, Finland, Hungary, Poland, Esthonia, Latvia, and Lithuania provide for practically uniform payments during the first 10 years, and somewhat

[5] See Secretary Mellon's statement on the French debt in Appendix B.

larger, but again practically uniform, payments during the remaining 52 years. The uniformity is attained by increasing the sums attributable to principal as the interest charges decrease. Poland, Esthonia, and Latvia, however, have the option, during the first 10 years, of postponing a part of their annual payments to later dates.

Czechoslovakia and Rumania may be placed in the second group. With both of these countries special concessions were made in the instalments of the early years, a portion of the sums nominally due being deferred to later years. In the case of Czechoslovakia, this preliminary period extends for 18 years, and the payments actually required are uniform in amount. In the case of Rumania, the preliminary period is 11 years, and the payments required begin at a very low figure and rise fairly rapidly until the full amount nominally due is reached in the twelfth year. They become uniform in amount after the fourteenth year.

In the third group—Belgium, France, Yugoslavia, and Italy—there are no deferments, the sums which are to be required in each year being regarded as the full amounts prescribed. Belgium's payments are graduated upward for the first 10 years and are practically uniform thereafter. French payments are graduated upward for the first 16 years and are then rigidly uniform until the very last year of the payment period. Yugoslavia's payments are graduated upward for 35 years before they become uniform.

PAYMENTS TO BE MADE TO THE TREASURY, 1926-1955

(Totals for five-year periods, in dollars)

Country	1926-1930	1931-1935	1936-1940	1941-1945	1946-1950	1951-1955
Finland	1,573,360	1,701,635	1,785,665	1,783,780	1,781,820	1,779,300
Hungary	337,968	356,567	381,492	381,798	383,872	383,727
Poland	31,243,750	33,625,875	34,963,750	34,765,000	34,972,500	35,571,625
Esthonia	2,419,270	2,612,710	2,740,200	2,739,790	2,739,515	2,739,315
Latvia	1,008,600	1,088,525	1,142,120	1,142,085	1,142,175	1,142,780
Lithuania	1,050,700	1,080,635	1,198,120	1,197,225	1,197,350	1,196,410
Czechoslovakia	15,000,000	15,000,000	15,000,000	20,765,634	29,408,700	29,408,250
Rumania	2,000,000	5,100,000	9,845,680	11,229,690	11,228,990	11,229,080
Belgium	24,290,000	42,300,000	63,571,000	63,426,000	63,483,500	63,387,500
France	160,000,000	305,000,000	520,000,000	620,000,000	625,000,000	625,000,000
Yugoslavia	1,000,000	1,375,000	2,285,500	4,467,110	5,012,495	5,591,140
Italy	25,000,000	74,653,500	85,341,250	111,393,500	125,313,000	164,355,000
Total	264,923,648	483,894,447	738,254,777	873,291,612	901,663,917	941,784,127
Great Britain	803,820,000	869,380,000	915,450,000	913,485,000	907,025,000	907,950,000
Grand Total	1,068,743,648	1,353,274,447	1,658,704,777	1,786,776,612	1,808,688,917	1,849,734,127

Finally, Italy's instalments increase year by year throughout the entire period of payments, beginning with 5 million and running up to 80 million dollars.[6]

The table on p. 103 shows the aggregate amounts to be received by the United States Treasury by

PAYMENTS TO THE TREASURY ON FOREIGN DEBTS, 1926–1955.

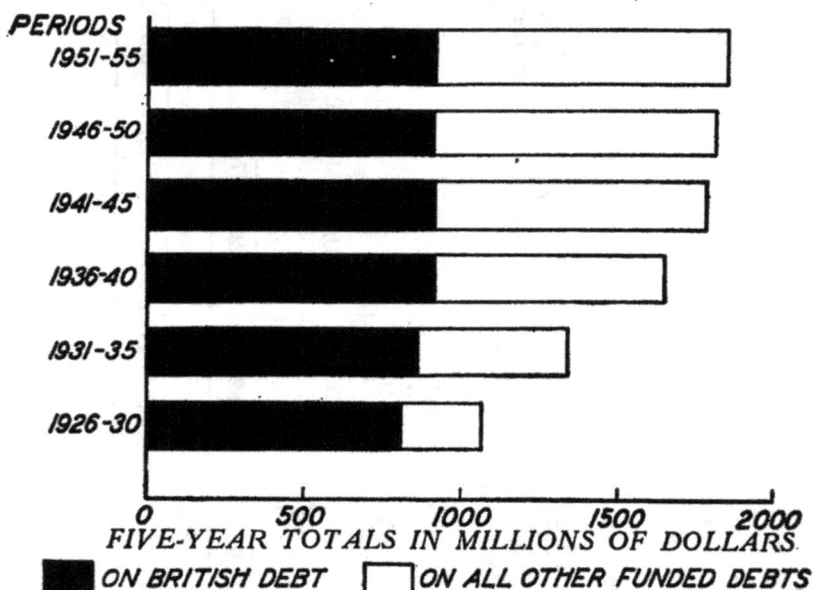

FIVE-YEAR TOTALS IN MILLIONS OF DOLLARS
■ ON BRITISH DEBT   □ ON ALL OTHER FUNDED DEBTS

five-year periods from 1926 to 1955, inclusive. The British payments are shown separately in order to indicate their relative importance in the totals.

During the five years from 1926 to 1930 the Treasury will receive on account of interest and principal

[6] For detailed figures see the schedules of payments attached to each of the agreements in Appendix B.

a little over one billion dollars, of which almost four-fifths will come from Great Britain. The total funded debt of the 12 Continental debtors is one and one-half times the total of the British debt, yet their combined payments will, during the next five years, be only a little more than one-fourth of the British payments.[7] In the years 1931 to 1935 Great Britain will still contribute about two-thirds of the total. It is not until the period 1951-55 that the combined payments of the Continental debtors will exceed those of Great Britain.

[7] These figures represent the full payments as provided for in the settlements. If the options which some of these countries possess are exercised, the Continental payments during the first five years would be slightly smaller than the above figures indicate.

CHAPTER IX

CHANGING POLICIES

PUBLIC attitudes and policies with reference to the war debts have been undergoing more or less constant change ever since the Armistice. Perhaps the most striking fact is the difference in the rate and extent to which official opinion has moved in the three countries most actively connected with the problem—Great Britain, France, and the United States. This shifting opinion applies alike to reparation obligations and to the inter-allied debts.

SHIFTING VIEWS ON THE REPARATION PROBLEM

The official attitude of all the Allied countries with reference to reparations, immediately after the war, was that the defeated countries should make complete restitution. This included recompense to the Allies for damages sustained as a result of enemy aggression by land, by sea, and from the air, and provision for pensions and separation allowances which would otherwise have devolved upon the Allied governments. The bill of claims which was finally presented to Germany at the London Conference of 1921 had been drawn up by the Reparation Commission without reference to Germany's capacity to pay, though it was no doubt assumed that the sums involved were within Germany's ability.

It was, however, repeatedly stated by Allied spokesmen that finding the ways and means of payment was Germany's problem and no concern of the Allies. There was no recognition of the fact that capacity to pay was conditioned upon a foreign trade surplus. Since the principle of restitution for damages and provision for pensions had been incorporated in the peace treaty, the matter was a closed issue. Germany was held to be under solemn obligation to meet the full payments stipulated, whatever the effect of such payments upon her financial and trade situation. The penalty for failure to fulfill the obligations was the seizure and occupation of her territory.

Both public and official sentiment in Great Britain, however, changed rapidly after 1921. The whole trend of economic events was such as to strengthen the growing British conviction that the procedure which was being followed in connection with enforcing reparation payments was fundamentally unsound and economically detrimental to all concerned. The British spokesmen as early as 1922 were expressing themselves in favor of a thoroughgoing modification of the reparation terms, and the British representative on the Reparation Commission voted against the occupation of the Ruhr in January, 1923. The British government, it may be recalled, also refused to participate in the occupation, and it played an important rôle in the events which brought about the so-called Dawes Plan.

The official attitude of France remained unchanged until near the very end of the Poincaré régime when, under pressure of the United States and Great Britain,[1] consent was given to the appointment of the expert committees to investigate the German economic situation. While many individual Frenchmen, and even some in official positions, were seriously doubting the wisdom of the policy that had been pursued, it remains true that the French official position underwent practically no change from the end of the war until the autumn of 1923.

As one of the leading participants in the framing of the peace treaty, the United States acquiesced in the reparation clauses which imposed upon Germany the obligation to make full restitution and provide pensions. Although the Versailles treaty was not ratified by the United States Senate, the treaty of peace which was finally signed between the United States and Germany reserved for us all the rights and privileges under the Versailles treaty. However, this country has never attempted to validate these rights and privileges, the only claim for participation in the reparation receipts being in connection with the costs of the army of occupation. And, under legislation now pending in Congress, there may be substituted even for these claims the

[1] See Hughes and Curzon notes, Appendix A.

awards to American citizens by the German-American Claims Commission.

The United States government, so far as any published documents disclose, took no official position with reference to the reparation discussion prior to 1922. It is, however, of record that Mr. Boyden, the American unofficial observer on the Reparation Commission, was openly in sympathy with the British rather than the French position.

America's active participation in the reparation discussion may be said to have begun with Secretary Hughes' New Haven address, made in December, 1922, in which he announced the readiness of the United States to assist the Allies in every way possible in finding a solution for the reparation tangle, on condition, however, that all the reparation creditors of Germany express their willingness to face frankly a thorough consideration of the whole problem, and that the question of the interallied debts be kept out of the discussion. France was at the time, however, apparently committed to the occupation of the Ruhr, which came within a few weeks of Secretary Hughes' proposal. Officially the whole matter then remained in abeyance until the autumn of 1923 when at last France consented to a reconsideration of the reparation question. Accordingly, on November 30, the expert committees which eventually formulated the Dawes Plan were appointed by the Reparation Commission.

Since the inauguration of the Dawes Plan on August 30, 1924, the differences in attitude among the different countries as respects the reparation problem have largely disappeared. All are now united in waiting for the full results of the experiment to be manifested.

The significant change that has occurred is that the original view that Germany's capacity was of no concern to the Allies has undergone a complete modification. It is now recognized, and incorporated as a part of the Dawes Plan, that the total of Germany's annual payments must depend upon her capacity to make the payments without the disintegration of her economic and financial system. Of particular significance is the belated recognition of the fact that the extent of Germany's payments will in the long run be measured by her capacity to develop an export surplus. Indeed, under the terms of the Dawes Plan Germany's responsibility ceases when the sums collected internally have been paid into the reparation account, the administrators of the plan, acting for the creditors, being responsible for the transfer of these funds to Allied Treasuries.

CONFLICTING NATIONAL ATTITUDES ON INTER-ALLIED DEBTS

With inter-allied debts, as with reparations, marked differences in official attitudes have characterized the leading countries concerned. Immediately after the war official discussion of the debts was in all countries held in abeyance. For the first two or three years it appears to have been the general assumption of the peoples of Europe that the debts would be largely, if not wholly, remitted. While public opinion in the United States during these years was more or less apathetic on the subject of debts, it was doubtless assumed by the great majority of people that these obligations would, as a matter of course, be honored and paid in full. In any event, it is certain that there never was any serious movement in this country in favor of a complete remission of the war debts.

The attitude of the American people was finally crystallized in the Act of Congress (approved February 9, 1922) creating the World War Foreign Debt Commission, which laid down the guiding principles that were to govern the negotiations of debt settlements. After empowering the Commission, with the approval of the President, to fund the war and relief obligations of the various foreign governments to the United States, "in such form and on such terms, conditions, date or dates of maturity, and rate or rates of interest, and with such security, if any, as shall be deemed to the best interest of the United States of America," it was provided: [2]

That nothing contained in this Act shall be construed to authorize or empower the Commission to extend the time of the maturity of any such bonds or other obligations due the United States of America by any foreign

[2] For the full text of the Act see Appendix B.

government beyond June 15, 1947, or to fix the rate of interest at less than four and one-quarter per cent *per annum.*

It was also provided "that this Act shall not be construed to authorize the exchange of bonds or other obligations of any foreign government for those of any other foreign government, or cancellation of any part of such indebtedness except through payment thereof." In other words, the principal was to be paid in full in a period of 25 years, the interest rate should not be less than the average rate at which we floated our Liberty Bonds, and there should be no washing out of debts, through the transference to the United States of reparation obligations or other foreign government bonds held by our debtors.

It is of importance to note that the American policy by this Act became a policy not only of essentially literal fulfillment of the original obligations but also one of negotiating with each nation separately. Moreover, under this policy the amount of reparation or debt payments which any particular debtor to the United States might receive from its own debtors was to have no bearing upon the amount that should be paid to us. Debts and reparations were regarded as separate and distinct problems. Each country had borrowed from the United States certain definite sums, and each country was therefore obligated to return that amount with interest.

This definite formulation of American policy

brought to a close the informal discussion with regard to the inter-allied debts that have been taking
place more or less continuously since the war. It
naturally then became necessary for Great Britain,
as the other great creditor country, to state her
position with reference to the settlement of the war
debts. The Balfour Note addressed to the French
Ambassador in London and also to the diplomatic
representatives of Italy, Yugoslavia, Rumania,
Portugal, and Greece, was accordingly issued from
the Foreign Office on August 1, 1922.[3]

The Balfour Note stated the British policy in the
following terms:

The policy favored by His Majesty's Government is
that of surrendering their share of German reparation,
and writing off, through one great transaction, the whole
body of interallied indebtedness. But, if this be found
impossible of accomplishment, we wish it to be understood that we do not in any event desire to make a
profit out of any less satisfactory arrangement.

The British government contended, however,
that it would be impossible to meet British obligations in accordance with the American plan "without profoundly modifying the course, which in different circumstances, they would have wished to
pursue. They cannot treat the payment of the
Anglo-American loan as if it were an isolated incident in which only the United States of America
and Great Britain had any concern. It is but one

[3] For the full text of the note see Appendix C.

of a connected series of transactions in which this country appears sometimes as debtor, sometimes as creditor, and, if our undoubted obligations as a debtor are to be enforced, our no less undoubted rights as a creditor cannot be left wholly in abeyance." Accordingly, Great Britain adopted the following principle to govern collections from her own debtors:

In no circumstances do we propose to ask more from our debtors than is necessary to pay to our creditors, and, while we do not ask for more, all will admit that we can hardly be contented with less.

The Balfour Note showed very clearly that British official opinion had been headed in a different direction from that of American official opinion. Great Britain recognized, however, that the American debt-funding Act definitely closed the door to any possibility—at least for a long time to come—of a general cancellation or offsetting of reparation and debt claims. The die was now cast in favor of separate negotiations and settlements; and Great Britain was the first to recognize the new situation and to send a debt-funding commission to the United States for the purpose of negotiating a settlement.

THE TREND AWAY FROM LITERAL FULFILLMENT

The British-American debt settlement [4] was regarded here as representing but a slight departure

[4] For the details of the agreement see Chapter IV and Appendix B.

from the principles in the Act which created the World War Foreign Debt Commission. The principal and accrued interest were to be paid in full, with interest at 3 per cent for the first 10 years and 3.5 per cent for the remaining period. The departures from the principles laid down consisted in cutting the interest rate somewhat below 4.25 per cent and in extending the payments over a period of 62 years instead of only 25 years. The American official attitude toward the settlement was expressed by President Harding on February 7, 1923, in the following words:

The call of the world today is for integrity of agreements, the sanctity of covenants, the validity of contracts. Here is the first clearing of the war-clouded skies in a debt-burdened world, and the sincere commitment of one great nation to validate its financial pledges and discharge its obligations in the highest sense of financial honor.

There is no purpose to report that your commission has driven a hard bargain with Great Britain or to do a less seemly thing in proclaiming a rare generosity in settlement.. Amid widespread clamor for the cancellation of World War debts as a fancied but fallacious contribution toward peace . . . the British commission came to make acknowledgment of the debt, to put fresh stamp of approval upon its validity and agree upon terms for its repayment.

It was manifest from the beginning that Great Britain could not undertake any program of payment which would conform to the limitations of time and interest rates which the commission had been authorized to grant. But here was a great nation acknowledging its obligations and seeking terms in which it might repay. So your commission proceeded to negotiate in a business way for a fair and just settlement. Such a settlement had to take into consideration the approximately normal interest rates payable, as the commission suggests, "by strong governments over a long term of years," with a temporary interest rate and suitable options adjusted to the tremendous problems of readjustment and recuperation. Your commission went so far as it believed the American sense of fair play would justify.

It is clear enough that the reduction of the rate of interest from 4.25 to 3.5 per cent was regarded as only fair in view of the fact that 3.5 per cent was then the prevailing rate in Great Britain and the United States and was likely to be close to the normal peace time rate on government loans. It obviously amounted, however, to an appreciable reduction of the debt. Congressional approval of the departures from the original terms was expressed in an amendment to the Act creating the debt commission.[5]

At the time the American debt-funding Act was passed the principle of payments in accordance with capacity was not in any way considered. It had been taken for granted that all of the European debtors could pay in full if they really desired to do so. However, even the British settlement represented a departure from the policy of literal fulfillment. This departure was not due to a desire to remit any portion of the debt; it was caused rather by an emerging appreciation of the problem of paying capacity. While the principal, with accrued

[5] For text of the amendment see Appendix B.

interest on the debt was to be paid in full, the current interest rate was shaded to 3 per cent for the
first 10 years during the period of "readjustment
and recuperation." Moreover, the provision permitting the payments to be spread over a period of 62
years, rather than 25 years, was a recognition that
there were limits to the amount that might be paid
annually. Nevertheless, the principle that the debt
settlements should be made strictly in accordance
with capacity to pay was not officially recognized
by the debt-funding commission until two years
later.

The terms of the settlement with Britain became
the basis of eight other agreements. The settlements with Finland, Hungary, Poland, Lithuania,
Latvia, Esthonia, Czechoslovakia, and Rumania followed this general model, with some modifications
as to the payments during the first few years in the
case of the last two.[6] In each case the principal is
to be paid in full together with accrued interest at
the rate of 4.25 per cent up to December 15, 1922,
and at the rate of 3 per cent from that date until
the date of settlement. The period of payment in
each case is 62 years. The rate of current interest
for the first 10 years is 3 per cent and for the remaining 52 years 3.5 per cent, the average interest
rate over the whole period being 3.3 per cent.

The first really important special concession was
made in the case of the Belgian settlement, con-

[6] See pp. 83-4.

cluded in August, 1925. Again the principal is paid in full, but no interest, either accrued or current, is charged on the pre-Armistice debt, while the post-Armistice debt is funded on the British basis, with the exception that the current interest during the first 10 years is lower than 3 per cent and gradually rises up to the 3.5 per cent rate which becomes effective in 1936. As a result of this the average rate of interest paid by Belgium during the whole 62-year period of payments is only 1.8 per cent.

These concessions with reference to the pre-Armistice debt were in recognition of the commitments made at the time of the peace conference and of Belgium's heroic sacrifices during the war. They were not the result of any estimate of Belgium's paying capacity. A reference to paying capacity is, however, found in connection with the provision for a graduated rate of interest on the post-war debt during the first 10 years, this concession being granted because of the temporary trade and financial difficulties with which Belgium is confronted.

DEFINITE RECOGNITION OF THE PRINCIPLE OF CAPACITY TO PAY

It was not until September, 1925, when the French Debt Commission headed by M. Caillaux began its negotiations in Washington, that the principle of capacity to pay was given official recognition as a determining consideration in working out the settlement. In a statement issued by the American Commission on October 1, 1925, this recognition is expressed in the following terms:

We believe it is fully recognized by the Commissions that the only basis of negotiations fair to both peoples is the principle of the capacity of France to pay. The nub of the difficulty of the two Commissions arises from a difference in judgment as to the future capacity of France to pay without, as we have stated, undermining her economic and social fabric; and this difficulty narrows itself to the future rather than to the present, for we are prepared to accept the views of the French Commission as to the immediate difficulties of France.

Here we have for the first time a clearly expressed admission on the part of the American Commission that the debtor may have a limited paying capacity throughout the entire period of payments as well as during the first few years of reconstruction and recuperation. In all of the earlier settlements the question was not considered as to whether a 3.5 per cent interest rate over the whole of the last 52 years of payment would be within the paying capacity of the debtor countries.

In the negotiations with the Italian Debt Commission in November, 1925, the question of capacity to pay moved into the very foreground of the discussion, and the settlement which was concluded was worked out with much more regard to the economic factors in the situation both as regards the earlier and the later years than had been the case in any of the earlier settlements. For the first five years there is no interest at all and the instalments on account of principal are much lower than those of subsequent years.[7]

In the negotiations with France, in April, 1926, which resulted in the signing of an agreement, the principle that payment should be fixed in accordance with capacity to pay was taken for granted. Indeed, the French plenipotentiary who negotiated the settlement entitled the memorandum which he presented to the American Commission "France's Capacity to Pay." The terms of the settlement, as was noted on page 43, moreover, indicate that the American conception of French capacity had undergone considerable change in the six months that had elapsed since the first negotiation in September, 1925.[8]

PAYING CAPACITY AND REPARATION RECEIPTS

The recognition that the settlements should be based upon capacity to pay automatically created a serious difficulty in connection with the enforcement of the American principle that debts and reparations were distinct and separate problems. This difficulty first arose in connection with the Belgium settlement. Under the terms of the treaty of Versailles the total of the Belgian war debt was to be included in the German reparation obligations.

[7] For the details of the Italian settlement see Chapter V and Appendix B.
[8] See Chapter IV.

Belgium was thus to be freed from her foreign debts contracted prior to the Armistice by the transference of these obligations to Germany.

In the course of their negotiations with our Debt Commission the Belgian delegation attempted to obtain the consent of our Commission to a similar scheme for a transference of Belgian reparation claims to the United States in exchange for the pre-Armistice debt. They failed, however, of achieving this object. But while the American Commission stated that they could not agree to any linking up of Belgian reparation receipts with Belgian payments to the United States, they nevertheless took the position that "under the circumstances the United States should not ask for more than the repayment of the principal of the pre-Armistice debt."

This difficulty again hovered like a specter over the ill-fated French negotiations conducted by M. Caillaux in September, 1925. The French delegates held that France's capacity to pay the sums asked for would depend in no small degree upon the ultimate receipts of France from Germany on reparation account. The French Commission was therefore anxious to write into the agreement some sort of safeguard clause which would make French commitments to some extent contingent upon French receipts from Germany. The American Commission, however, refused to accede to any such arrangement, still clinging to the view enunciated in the Act creating the war debt commission; namely, that the inter-allied debts and the reparation payments are two separate and distinct problems which are not to be confounded in any of the American debt settlements.

Yet, as early as December, 1922, Secretary Hughes, in his New Haven address, had fully recognized the bearing of reparation receipts by the Allies upon their capacity to pay the United States.[9]   He said:

The matter is plain enough from our standpoint. The capacity of Germany to pay is not at all affected by any indebtedness of any of the Allies to us.   That indebtedness does not diminish Germany's capacity, and its removal would not increase her capacity. . . . So far as the debtors to the United States are concerned, they have unsettled credit balances, and their condition and capacity to pay cannot be properly determined until the amount that can be realized on these credits for reparations has been determined.

Nevertheless, in his reply to the communication of the British Chargé d'Affaires in Washington, October 15, 1923, Secretary Hughes said:

The government of the United States has consistently maintained the essential difference between the questions of Germany's capacity to pay and of the practical methods to secure reparations from Germany, and payment by the Allies of their debts to the United States, which constitute distinct obligations.

The American Debt Commission has invariably followed this policy of maintaining that the inter-

[9] For the text of Secretary Hughes' address see Appendix A.

allied debts and the reparation payments are two separate and distinct problems so far, at least, as the American debt settlements are concerned. Hence their refusal to permit a "safeguard clause" of the sort desired by the French delegates to be written into the French agreement.[10]

GREAT BRITAIN'S POLICY AND CAPACITY TO PAY

Great Britain, the other great creditor on account of war debts, has been adhering to the policy set down in the Balfour Note of 1922. It is her avowed determination to collect from her debtors only sufficient sums to cover her own payments to the United States, and Great Britain is thus, in effect, only a transfer agency between her debtors and the United States. Great Britain's policy was designed to establish and maintain a close inter-relationship between all the international debts, including reparation obligations. This policy is, however, not in accord with the principle of payments in proportion to capacity.

The fact that Great Britain has undertaken to pay the United States some 160 million dollars a year does not mean that her Continental debtors will have a capacity to pay like sums to Great Britain. Her Continental debtors might be able to pay more than this sum and they might be able to pay less. It is true that Great Britain recognizes her own obligation outright and has agreed to pay,

[10] For further discussion of this point see pp. 130-3.

whether or not her debtors fulfill their obligations to Great Britain. Nevertheless, it remains true that the Balfour principle establishes the minimum which Great Britain's debtors are expected to pay and this minimum is in no sense arrived at by considerations of capacity to pay. However, in Great Britain's negotiations with her Continental debtors, she has, like the United States, been drifting toward a recognition of the principle that payments must be determined by the capacity of the debtors.

The act of February 9, 1922, creating the World War Foreign Debt Commission, may be taken as representing the general opinion in this country at that time—namely, that the problem of paying the war debts would present no real difficulty, provided the various debtors would only recognize their obligations and begin at once the task of setting their financial houses in order. As with the German reparation problem, the main thing necessary was supposed to be the disposition to pay.

It must be pointed out, however, that in administrative circles efforts had been made to secure the passage of legislation that would give the Treasury wide latitude in negotiating settlements. Even after the Act was passed the administration still sought from time to time to be relieved of the stringent restrictions of the law. For example, President Harding in a letter to Senator Lodge, December 27, 1922, said:

If Congress really means to facilitate the task of the government in dealing with the European situation, the first practical step would be to free the hands of the Commission so that helpful negotiations may be undertaken.

The desire of the administration to have the hands of the Debt Commission left free did not, however, mean that there was any clear conception among government officials generally of the basic economic issues involved. What the administration was mainly concerned with was the limitations upon its powers of negotiation. It was not until very much later that there came to be any consensus of official opinion to the effect that the settlements should be negotiated strictly in accordance with capacity to pay and that considerations of paying capacity required, in some cases at least, substantial reductions in the total payments.

CHAPTER X

ISSUES IN SUSPENSE

HAVING traced the history of the debt-funding negotiations we may now take note of some of the questions that may still be regarded as in the nature of unsettled issues. Although the reparation problem was ostensibly disposed of by the inauguration of the Dawes Plan, and although the various debt agreements that have been negotiated nominally appear as final settlements, nevertheless there are a number of important issues which still await solution.

UNFIXED TOTAL OF THE REPARATION DEBT

The total reparation obligation still officially stands at the sum fixed at the London Conference of 1921, namely, 132 billion gold marks.[1] The annual payments stipulated under the Dawes Plan, namely, 2.5 billion marks a year, do not, however, fully cover the 6 per cent interest and sinking fund charges even on the 50 billions of A and B bonds

---

[1] Minus credits for payments already made for reparation, plus the Belgian war debt estimated at four billions, plus certain other obligations incidental to the fulfillment of the treaty.

provided for under the London agreement.[2] If the interest on the rest of the debt should accumulate, it will be seen that the total German obligation would increase year by year rather than decrease. As matters now stand, Germany is obligated to pay 2.5 billion gold marks indefinitely without any chance of getting out of debt; on the contrary, instead of liquidating her indebtedness in the process, she would be going ever more deeply into debt.

It is obvious that in due course the amount originally fixed must be scaled down to a sum that would make possible its eventual liquidation out of the annual instalments, or else the number of years that the annuities are to run must be fixed. The latter procedure would be in accordance with the principle followed in connection with the debt settlements.

RELATION OF NEW BORROWINGS TO REPARATION AND WAR DEBT PAYMENTS

In preceding chapters attention was called to the new loans that have been granted to European countries in the course of the past few years. The large and growing volume of this new indebtedness presents a problem of primary importance in connection with the meeting of reparation and war debt obligations.

[2] The settlement provided for 12 billion marks of Class A bonds; 38 billion marks of Class B bonds; and 82 billions of Class C bonds. The Class C bonds were not to be issued until Germany had demonstrated her capacity to meet the payments on account of the 50 billions of A and B bonds.

Since the inauguration of the Dawes Plan, Germany has been a huge borrower in foreign markets. The 800 million gold mark reconstruction loan provided for under the plan constitutes an obligation of the German government that is prior to the reparation obligation itself. But the mass of loans and credits that have since been extended to German industrial, commercial, financial, public utility, and municipal enterprises, do not have any *legal* priority as against the reparation debt. The official policy that has been pursued by the administrators of the Dawes Plan has been to regard such loans as no affair of theirs—being merely private transactions between the citizens of Germany and of other countries.

In actual practice these borrowers will attempt to procure, and probably will succeed in procuring, foreign bills of exchange with which to meet their obligations. Thus, we may be confronted with a situation in which, with a favorable balance of trade, the Agent General for Reparation Payments may yet be unable to procure the bills of exchange necessary for remittance on reparation account, for the simple reason that private interests had already appropriated the excess of bills in the market, using them in meeting private obligations incurred since the inauguration of the Dawes Plan.

The issue here presented has thus far not arisen since Germany has not as yet had to meet her external obligations out of her own resources. For the first year and a half of the Plan, new German foreign borrowings have been more than twice as large as the sums which the Agent General has had to transfer on reparation account. The issue can ultimately be escaped, however, only in the event that Germany actually develops an export surplus of sufficient size to meet both the reparation and the new private obligations.

The Allied debt settlements are also closely connected with new borrowing operations. The more recent agreements have been followed by the flotation in the United States of government as well as of private loans. Indeed the debt settlements have been very closely linked with loan negotiations, notwithstanding the fact that the new loans are not made by the United States government but by private interests. That is to say, private banking interests have co-operated with the government by making the flotation of new loans in this country contingent upon the conclusion of satisfactory debt settlements.

In some cases, moreover, the aggregate volume of new loans has greatly exceeded the amounts to be paid under the debt settlements during the first few years. For example, after Italy agreed to pay a total of 25 million dollars to the United States Treasury in the first five years, the Italian government was able to float a loan in this country of 100 million dollars.

The status of these new debts owed to private

investors in relation to the war debts owed to foreign governments has already given rise to no little discussion. Is interest on the funded government debt to have precedence over the interest on these new loans floated through ordinary investment channels—in the event that the debtor country does not prove to have sufficient capacity to take care of the charges on both sets of obligations? In any case, how will it be possible in practice to protect the interests of the United States government as against the interests of the owners of the new European securities both public and private? The fact that the interest rates on the war loans have been fixed very low, whereas the new loans floated through private channels yield very high returns, is in itself the subject of acrimonious discussion.

RELATION BETWEEN REPARATION AND DEBT PAYMENTS

Another subject of continuing controversy is the linking of reparation receipts with Allied debt payments. The official position of the United States government, as has been noted in preceding chapters, is that the reparation problem is one thing and the debt problem quite a different matter. Accordingly, the United States has been willing to go only so far (in some of its debt settlements) as to work out the annual instalments with implied reference to expected reparation receipts.[3]

[3] See, for example, pp. 42 and 51.

The European debtors, on the other hand, continue to insist that their capacity to pay is directly dependent upon reparation receipts. While the Balfour principle does not stipulate that Great Britain's capacity to pay is dependent upon reparation receipts, or for that matter upon her receipts from reparation and war debts combined, it does link reparation obligations and inter-allied debts together through the provision that Great Britain will not seek to collect an aggregate amount from her debtors greater than the sums she is to pay the United States. The British policy applies only to the amount that Great Britain will collect from each one of her debtors, and does not imply any acceptance of the idea that each debtor's capacity to pay Great Britain is in any way connected with reparation receipts.

This fact is clearly shown in the correspondence between the British Chancellor of the Exchequer, Mr. Winston Churchill, and the French Minister of Finance, M. Caillaux, in connection with the Franco-British debt settlement negotiated in July, 1926. M. Caillaux' statement is as follows:

In assuming the responsibility of signing the agreement for the settlement of the French war debt to Great Britain and thereby accepting payment of the annuities fixed on the sole credit of France, I feel bound to explain that the payments of the amounts required to assure fulfillment of the debt settlements with the United States and Great Britain inevitably depend largely on the continued transfer of receipts from Germany under the

Dawes Plan. If, therefore, for reasons outside of the control of France, such receipts should cease completely, or to an extent greater than one-half, a new situation would be created and the French Government reserves the right in such an event of asking the British Government to reconsider the question in the light of all the circumstances then prevailing. It is subject to this express reservation that I am ready to sign the agreement which we have drawn up.

To which Mr. Churchill replied:

His Majesty's Government must maintain that the position of the settlement which we have arrived at of the French war debt to this country depends, like that of the debt itself, on the sole credit of France. You will realize that in the hypothetical circumstances you mention Great Britain would already have suffered a diminution of receipts from the Dawes scheme, which we have taken into account in arriving at the various debt settlements, and this is one of the factors which would have to be borne in mind in the event of any reconsideration of the question being desired by the French Government. Subject to this I do not object to the statement that you make.

In the event of any modification being made I should expect, in order to secure equal treatment among creditors, that the other creditors of France would take into consideration a corresponding modification of the debts due to them.

Mr. Churchill makes it entirely clear that France is expected to pay the sums stipulated irrespective of her receipts from Germany. Indeed, it is pointed out to M. Caillaux that, in the event that reparation payments should fall below expectations, Great Britain may, in case the French settlement were to be reconsidered, have to insist upon even larger payments from France because of the reduction of her own receipts from Germany—this strictly in accordance with the Balfour principle. The last paragraph, however, implies that in the event that subsequent modifications of the French terms should be found advisable Great Britain would be willing to go as far as other creditors, which means, of course, for all practical purposes, as far as the United States.

The whole controversy is not, however, as significant as the discussion centered around it would indicate. Viewed strictly from the standpoint of capacity to pay, there is no sound reason for making the payments of the Allied debtors depend directly upon the amount of the reparation receipts. The Allied nations may have a capacity to pay out of their own resources, as has been notably the case with Great Britain; and, on the other hand, even with some reparation receipts, a particular country might not be able to make any payments without unsettling its general financial situation. In a word, reparation receipts constitute but one item in a nation's ledger of accounts, and accordingly cannot be made the sole key to capacity to pay. Nevertheless, as a result of the developments of recent years, proposals for linking debt payments directly with reparation receipts will doubtless remain a subject of vigorous and widespread controversy for no little time to come.

PROPOSED SALE OF GERMAN RAILROAD AND INDUSTRIAL BONDS

It has been suggested from time to time, and from various quarters, that a solution of the reparation and war debt problem may be found in the sale in world markets of the 16 billion marks of German railroad and industrial securities which have been pledged under the Dawes Plan. The bonds would be offered for sale by the Reparation Commission and the proceeds paid into Allied Treasuries in whole or in partial fulfillment of German reparation obligations. As to the manner in which this transaction would affect the inter-allied debt situation there is some divergence of opinion. The thought in the minds of some is that the receipt of 16 billion marks by Allied countries would place their finances definitely on a sound basis and thus enable them henceforth to meet, without difficulty, their instalments on the war debts. This would indirectly link the liquidation of reparation obligations with debt payments.

The thought in the minds of others is that the sums realized from the sale of the German marks might be directly utilized in liquidating a part of the Allied debts. Some even go so far as to urge that this financial operation should be regarded as liquidating the entire reparation and inter-allied indebtedness, leaving practically a clean slate so far as inter-governmental obligations are concerned.

The bulk of this four billion dollars' worth of German bonds would, of course, have to be sold in the American investment market if they were to be sold at all. Thus the transaction if carried through would really mean that private investors in the United States would furnish the funds required to liquidate, in turn, both reparation obligations and the war debts to the United States government. The American investor, would, for his part, possess the bonds of German railroads and industries. His security would obviously depend upon Germany's capacity to pay, just as the value of the reparation bonds held by Allied governments depends upon Germany's capacity to raise revenues and to transfer them beyond her frontiers. It is no part of our purpose here to discuss either the merits or the feasibility of such proposals. They are mentioned merely because of their bearing on the general discussion of the inter-relations of debt and reparation obligations.

THE COMMERCIALIZATION OF THE WAR DEBTS

The proposal for the sale of German industrial and railroad bonds, which has just been discussed, involves what is commonly called the commercialization of inter-governmental debts. That is to say, governments are replaced as creditors by private investors, and the debts cease to be political and become commercial in character. In all of the

American debt settlements a clause has been inserted making it within the rights of the United States to call for the delivery of bonds of marketable denominations. It would then be possible for the United States Treasury to sell to private citizens the bonds which it receives from foreign governments, utilizing the proceeds in liquidating its own Liberty Bonds. The foreign governments would thenceforth pay interest to private citizens in this country or elsewhere rather than to the Treasury of the United States.

This provision, which is Clause 7 in all of the settlements,[4] has been vigorously opposed by some of the European governments concerned, notably France. The objection from the point of view of the debtors is that the transfer of bonds from the government of the United States to private channels would impair their general credit position, and would, moreover, practically close the door to any subsequent revision of the debt settlements. The French have insisted upon the exclusion of this clause from the American agreement, but the American Debt-Funding Commission is opposed to its removal, not because there is any disposition to make use of the provision, or any real possibility of disposing of such bonds at anything like their face value, but because all of the other settlements have been negotiated on that basis. France has, therefore, been asked to take the assurance of the present

[4] Except in the British agreement where it is Clause 9.

administration that over a period of 62 years no administration will be disposed to make use of this clause.

DEVICES FOR GAUGING CAPACITY TO PAY

While the principle that payments should be regulated according to the capacity of the debtor has, as we have seen, come to be increasingly recognized in the later debt agreements, none of these agreements has thus far set up any devices for gauging capacity to pay. The really significant feature of the Dawes Plan is that it provides machinery which will regulate the amount of German payments in accordance with demonstrated capacity. No more is to be collected or transferred than can be collected or transferred without producing budgetary instability and disorganization of the exchange and currency system.

But in the case of the inter-allied debts neither Great Britain nor the United States has been willing to accept the guiding economic principles that have been set forth, and acclaimed, in connection with the German and Hungarian reparation plans. The principle that an indispensable minimum of domestic expenditures must be provided for before foreign obligations can be met has not been recognized, nor has the extent of the international trade and financial surplus been admitted as a definite index to the amount that can be transferred. On the contrary, definite schedules of payments have been worked out extending over a period of two generations, and the only reductions that are permitted are the partial deferments of the instalments during the first few years.

No body of men can, however, prophesy with any degree of accuracy what the minimum budget and international surplus of each of these countries will be during the next 62 years. In the words of Secretary Mellon:[5] "The capacity of a nation to pay over a long period of time is not subject to mathematical determination. It is and must be largely a matter of opinion." The soundness of this contention is well illustrated by the Secretary's statement, referred to on p. 43, that the annual instalments required of France in the earlier years were reduced in the agreement reached with France in April, 1926, as compared with the terms discussed in September, 1925, because France's fiscal position had deteriorated in the intervening months. If the economic position of the country cannot be predicted six months ahead, it obviously cannot be estimated for a period of more than half a century.

It was because capacity to pay cannot be appraised with any degree of accuracy over a long period of time that the Dawes Plan made provision for adjusting the amount of the annual payments in accordance with the demonstrated eco-

[5] Secretary Mellon's statement to the Ways and Means Committee of the House of Representatives, January 4, 1926; see Appendix B.

nomic capacity from year to year. Whether the principles which underlie the Dawes Plan in this regard could be utilized in connection with debt payments without setting up control machinery similar to that which has been devised in connection with reparation payments is a question which need not here be discussed. Nor are we interested in advocating that such control machinery should be adopted. We are merely concerned in pointing out that one of the issues remaining to be settled is the extent to which devices provided in connection with the reparation plan may be used as a model in connection with inter-allied debt payments.

WAR DEBTS AND INTERNATIONAL TRADE

The relationship of war debt payments to foreign trade has been the subject of no little discussion. From the standpoint of the United States it is contended, on the one hand, that the maintenance of a high tariff is evidence of American unwillingness to allow the European creditors to pay by means of an increase of exports to this country. At the same time, it is observed that the United States desires to maintain its export trade and is thus not eager to see Europe increase her paying capacity by curtailing her purchases in the United States. In short, it is pointed out that the commercial policy of the United States is directed toward maintaining, if not increasing, the surplus of exports, rather than toward having the balance run in the opposite direction. Those who argue in this fashion conclude that American trade and debt policies are incompatible and that one or the other of them ought to be modified.

On the other hand, there are those who hold that American trade and debt policies need not be in conflict. They point out that the United States may receive additional imports in non-competitive lines—rubber, for example,—and that such imports do not need to come to the United States directly from Europe, but may come through triangular trading operations. They also contend that by means of credit operations the United States can get paid without suffering any reduction of exports. Indeed, it is upon these foreign loans that reliance is chiefly placed for reconciling the apparent conflict between our commercial and debt policies.

American export trade has undoubtedly been aided very materially by the new credits which the United States has been extending to Europe and the rest of the world since 1923. The aggregate of new American loans has, in fact, been much larger than the aggregate sums which we have been receiving on account of war debt settlements. In one sense, and in a very real sense, the purpose of the later settlements has been to make it possible for the United States to increase its foreign loans and thus to maintain the export trade. It is obvious that until the various European debtors had recognized and funded their existing obligations investors in this country could not be expected to look with favor upon large additional credit extensions. Debt settlements were thus naturally regarded as a prerequisite to further credit operations.[6]

The significance of the debt payments from the point of view of American trade was emphasized by Secretary Mellon in discussing the Italian settlement before the Ways and Means Committee of the House of Representatives, as follows:[7]

Only from these private loans during the past year have the countries abroad been able to pay for their wheat and cotton. It is these new loans which make our exports possible. . . . The settlements are made in the real interests of those American producers who must have a foreign market able to pay. The American producer needs these debt settlements. *The entire foreign debt is not worth as much to the American people in dollars and cents as a prosperous Europe as a customer.* (Italics ours.)

It will be noted that two principal considerations are involved in this statement. The first is that foreign loans have been regarded as necessary for the maintenance of our export trade to the continent of Europe, even during a period when the burden of debt payments has been negligible. The second is that in the long run the gains to the Treasury resulting from large debt collections might

[6] It will be recalled that the failure of the Soviet government to accept legal liability for the war and pre-war debts of Russia is still regarded as a bar to the negotiation of new Russian credits.
[7] For the full text of Secretary Mellon's statement see Appendix B.

be more than counterbalanced by trade losses resulting from restricted European purchasing power.

Credit extensions for the purpose of maintaining American export trade, however, merely obscure and do not obviate the essential conflict between American commercial and American debt policy. The volume of new foreign loans extended annually can only temporarily exceed the volume of debt payments due to the United States. Interest charges steadily increase, on account of the new loans as well as because of the increasing instalments on the war debts, and it is only for a few years at the most that these credit operations can obviate the necessity of significant shifts in the currents of trade.

A cycle of debt discussion and negotiation has now been completed. With the exception of the Russian debts, practically all of the international obligations bequeathed by the war have been funded and thus formally settled. But the primary economic issues which have been involved from the beginning have not been resolved.

Considerations such as those discussed in this chapter are responsible for the view now commonly held, even in official circles, that the whole reparation and debt problem will have to be reconsidered within a very few years. The terms of the Dawes Plan and the later debt settlements have been so worked out that there has been created what may be considered as a five-year trial period—more or less. Within this period will come the test—both of the capacity of the debtors to pay and of the willingness of the creditors to receive the amounts that have tentatively been fixed.

APPENDIX A

REPARATION DOCUMENTS

I. THE SPA PROTOCOL *

(Signed July 16, 1920)

Agreement Between the Allies for the Settlement of Certain Questions as to the Application of the Treaties of Peace and Complementary Agreements with Germany, Austria, Hungary, and Bulgaria, Signed at Spa, July 16, 1920.

The Governments of Belgium, France, Great Britain, Italy, Japan and Portugal respectively represented by the undersigned, recognizing that it is in the general interest to effect an immediate settlement between themselves of certain problems arising from the application of the Treaties of Peace and the complementary agreements, have agreed upon the following:

PART I

ARTICLE 1

In pursuance of Article 237 of the Treaty of Versailles, sums received from Germany under the head of reparation shall be divided in the following proportions:

* Text from the British Parliamentary Papers, Cmd. 1615.

	Per Cent
British Empire	22
France	52
Italy	10
Japan	0.75
Belgium	8
Portugal	0.75

6.5 per cent shall be reserved for Greece, Roumania, and Serb-Croat-Slovene State, and for the other Powers entitled to reparation which are not signatories of this Agreement.

ARTICLE 2

The aggregate amount received under the head of reparation from Austria, Bulgaria and Hungary, together with the sums received from Italy, the Czecho-Slovak State, Roumania and the Serb-Croat-Slovene State under the agreements made on September 10 and December 8, 1919, shall be divided as follows:

(a) One-half shall be divided between the Allied Governments mentioned in Article 1 in the proportion fixed by the said Article.

(b) Of the other half, Italy shall receive 40 per cent., and 60 per cent is reserved for Greece, Roumania, the Serb-Croat-Slovene State, and for other Powers entitled to reparation which are not signatories of this Agreement.

PART II

ARTICLE 3

The Allied Governments recognize that it is in the general interest to determine the total amount due by

Germany under Articles 231 and 232 of the Treaty of Versailles, and to make provision for the method of payment on the basis of an agreement embodying:

(1) The fixing of annuities to be paid by Germany;
(2) The faculty for her to free herself at an earlier date by discounting some or all of these annuities;
(3) The issue by Germany of loans destined for the internal requirements of the country and the prompt discharge of its debt to the Allied Powers.

The Allied Governments declare their readiness to take among themselves such measures as they may deem appropriate to facilitate an agreement of this kind.

PART III

ARTICLE 4

(1) For each of the Allied Powers the Reparation Commission will draw up, as on May 1, 1921, a statement in the following form:

May 1, 1921

Creditor	Debtor
(a) Cost to May 1, 1921, of Armies of Occupation.	(d) Receipts on account of Armies of Occupation.
(b) Sums advanced to Belgium before November 11, 1918, with interest to May 1, 1921.	(e) Value of deliveries in kind up to May 1, 1921, excluding restitutions under Article 238 under the Treaty of Versailles.
(c) Present value of share in reparation.	(f) Receipts to be credited to Germany under Article 243 of the said Treaty excluding final balances

150

under Sections III and IV of Part X (Economic Clauses), and sums applied in accordance with Article 5(a) of this agreement below towards the satisfaction of the Belgian priority.

If the payments to be made by Germany consist of annuities, or periodical payments which can be discounted, the credit for the present value of the share in reparation referred to in (c) above for each Power shall be fixed by discounting at 5 per cent the share attributed to that Power in the annuities or periodical payments unless the said share has been, as an exception, fixed at a capital sum.

Where the receipts to be credited under (f) have not been definitely ascertained when the statement is drawn up, the Reparation Commission will estimate the receipts to be credited. The Commission will make such subsequent adjustments in the accounts as may be necessary when the amount is definitely ascertained.

(2) If the above statement shows that a Power has received under (d), (e) and (f) more than the aggregate totals of (a), (b) and (c), the Reparation Commission will notify the amount of the excess to the Power in question, and it shall be paid to the Reparation Commission by that Power within three months from the date of the notification.

(3) In all cases, even where the repayment provided for above has been made, any excess of the sums debited under (d), (e) and (f) over the sums credited under (a) shall be retained for the following purposes:

(a) In the case of Belgium, the excess shall be regarded as a payment on account of her priority of 2½ milliards of gold francs.

(b) In the case of each of the Allied Powers other than Belgium, it shall be treated as an advance repayable in the manner indicated below, and bearing interest of 5 per cent., which shall be placed to the credit of the special interest account referred to in paragraph 4.

The amounts so treated as an advance shall constitute contingent reserves for the purpose of enabling the Reparation Commission to meet, during the ensuing five years, the service of the whole or part of the German loans referred to in Article 3 (3) in the event of default by Germany.

For this purpose, the amount for each Power shall be divided into five equal parts, one of which shall be attributable to each of the five years. If, in any year, the part attributable to that year is not required for the service of the German loans, it shall be applied for the following purposes in the order named:

(i) In discharge of sums then due by Germany to that Power in respect of the cost of the Army of Occupation.

(ii) In satisfaction of sums, either capital or interest, due by Belgium to the Power in question for monies advanced before November 11, 1918.

(iii) Towards the annuities, if any, due by Germany to the Power concerned.

(iv) As regards Italy and Japan, towards the payment by anticipation of future instalments of the annuities due to those Powers (beginning with the earlier instalments) at such rates of discount not being less than 5 per cent (five) as may from time to time be agreed between those Powers and the Reparation Commission.

Any balance not required for the above purpose shall be paid to the Reparation Commission for division among the Powers in the proportions laid down in Article 1.

(4) A special interest account shall be drawn up for each Power, and in it shall be included after May 1, 1921, the interest on the advances referred to in paragraph 3. The credit balance on the account shall be divided among the Powers, other than Belgium, in proportion to the percentages laid down in Article 1.

ARTICLE 5

In consideration of the sacrifice made in the general interest by all the Powers which are creditors of Germany in order to ensure the success of the loans referred to in Article 3, and with a view to avoiding all difficulty in inter-allied financial adjustments, Belgium consents, and it is hereby agreed, that the sum of 2½ milliards of gold francs, to which she is entitled in priority under the Agreement of June 16, 1919, should be ensued as follows:

Belgium retains, as laid down in Article 4 of this Agreement, the excess of the deliveries in kind and the transfer of German rights and interests received before May 1, 1921. The remainder of the 2½ milliards of gold francs shall, after payment of the costs of the Armies of Occupation which have not been paid as provided in Article 4, and until the priority granted to her is satisfied, be paid:

(a) Up till May 1, 1921, out of any cash payments received by the Reparation Commission under Article 243, and, in particular, from sums received under the following heads:—

(1) Reimbursements to be effected under the conditions specified in Article 4 by any Allied Power which has received deliveries in kind or transfers of German rights or interests referred to in Article 243 of the Treaty of Versailles, to a value in excess of her credits with Germany on account of the cost, if any, of her Armies of Occupation, of her reparation for damage, and of the sums. if any, to be reimbursed to her in respect of advances to Belgium up to November 11, 1918.

(2) Receipts in respect of final balances in favour of Germany from the clearing houses provided for in Article 296 of the Treaty of Versailles and of the proceeds of the liquidation of German property, rights and interests seized by the Allied Powers in their respective territories, and paid to the Reparation Commission in conformity with the provisions of Article 297, paragraph (h) of the said Treaty.

(3) Any payments under Article 254 of the Treaty of Versailles in respect of the assumption of part of the debt of the German Empire, or of a German State, by Denmark (Schleswig), Czecho-Slovakia, or the Free City of Danzig.

(4) The value under Article 256 of the Treaty of Versailles of the assets and properties of the German Empire and States in the territories transferred by Germany received from Denmark (Schleswig), Czecho-Slovakia and the Free City of Danzig.

(5) The acquisition under Article 260 of the Treaty of Versailles of the value of German rights or interests in public utility undertakings or concessions in the countries and territories referred to in that Article.

(6) The sale of arms, munitions, war material and machinery which is to be destroyed in accord-

ance with Article 169 of the Treaty of Versailles.

(7) Sale to Luxemburg of German coal delivered in execution of paragraph 5 of Annex V of Part VIII (Reparation) of the Treaty of Versailles.

(8) Distribution or sale by the Reparation Commission of dyestuffs and chemical drugs delivered by Germany under the conditions laid down in Annex VI of Part VIII (Reparation) of the Treaty of Versailles.

(b) After May 1, 1921, subject to the payment in priority of the cost of the armies of occupation, the value of all deliveries or payments made by Germany, and any other receipts of the Reparation Commission available for distribution.

(c) To the extent specified below, the proceeds of the first German loan, and contingently, the proceeds of the following loans, Belgium recognises that, in order to ensure the success of the loans it is proper to interest the largest number of Germany's creditors in their success, and not to reserve to one Power practically the whole proceeds. After deducting that part of the proceeds of these loans which is reserved for Germany, Belgium will receive, if necessary, up to 50 per cent of the proceeds.

(d) If the payment of the amounts due by Germany for Reparation is provided for in the form of annuities, sums paid to Belgium by reason of her right of priority will be deducted from her share of the annuities, or from her share of the proceeds of the annuities if all or any of them are discounted. This deduction must be so arranged as to ensure that Belgium's share in the present value of the receipts from Germany shall coincide with the percentage allotted to her in Article 1 of this Agreement.

ARTICLE 6

(1) Germany, by Annex III of Part VIII (Reparation) of the Treaty of Versailles, and Austria and Hun-

gary, by the corresponding provisions of the Treaty of St. Germain and the Treaty of Trianon, having recognized the right of the Allied and Associated Powers to the replacement, ton for ton and class for class, of all merchant ships and fishing boats lost or damaged owing to the war, and in view of the great difficulty of fixing a fair value for the ships surrendered except after the actual sale of the greater portion of such ships, it is agreed as follows:

The sale of the ships allotted to the British Empire shall be made before May 1, 1921, by the Reparation Commission on the British market and shall be made to British nationals.

The amount to be credited to the ex-Enemy Powers and debited to the British Empire in respect of merchant vessels and fishing craft allotted to it, or subsequently transferred to it under Inter-Allied Agreements, shall, subject to adjustments rendered necessary by repairs or the expenses of delivery be the actual price realized by such sales.

In the case of other Powers, the amount to be debited in respect of merchant vessels and fishing craft allotted to them, or subsequently transferred to them under Inter-Allied Agreements, shall be the average amounts, subject to similar adjustments, realized by the sale of similar ships of each class on the British market.

The value so ascertained shall be debited to the Allied Power and credited to the ex-Enemy Power concerned as on the following dates. In the case of Germany, on January 10, 1920, or the date of the delivery of the vessel which ever may be later; in the case of Austria and Hungary on the respective dates of the coming into force of the Treaties of Peace with those countries.

Interest at 5 per cent per annum from the above dates up till the date of sale or up to May 1, 1921, if the ships are not sold before that date shall be debited to the British Empire in respect of ships allotted or transferred to it and shall be credited to the special interest account referred to in Article 4.

In the case of each of the other Powers a lump sum shall be debited in respect of interest and credited to the said special account. This sum shall bear the same proportion to the total amount debited to the British Empire in respect of interest as the value of the total amount of tonnage allotted or transferred to that Power bears to the value of the total amount of tonnage allotted or transferred to the British Empire.

(2) No charge shall be debited to any Allied Power to which ships have been allotted for the use of such ships after the coming into force of the several Treaties of Peace.

(3) In the case of ships transferred, the hire of such ships, until transferred, shall be paid over to the transferring power by the Power to which ships are transferred. Such payments shall be effected by deducting the amount of the hire, plus interest at 5 per cent per annum from the date of the transfer of the ships, from the first percentage payment, other than payments in kind or services rendered, received either from Germany, Austria, or Hungary, whichever may be the earliest, by the Power to which the ship is transferred, and adding it to the first percentage payment received by the transferring Power.

(4)   After the final allotment of tonnage by the Reparation Commission, there shall be transferred to Belgium out of the shares of the other Powers sharing in the distribution of tonnage, such an amount of tonnage as will make up for ton for ton allotment to a total equivalent to the tonnage of the vessels condemned after the Armistice in the Belgian Prize Court. Such tonnage shall be approximately the same age, type and value as the condemned ships. The contribution of each of the transferring Powers shall be in proportion to their approved claims for the ton for ton allotment of ex-Enemy tonnage.

The value of the vessels allotted to Belgium, and also of those transferred to her as above, will be debited to the transferring Powers in the same proportions as they contribute the transferred ships.

The condemnation of the above vessels in the Belgian Prize Court not being recognized by the Allied Powers, Belgium, while maintaining the validity of these decisions, agrees, in consideration of the tonnage transferred to her under this paragraph (4), not to claim any interest in these vessels by reason of their condemnation.

ARTICLE 7

No sum shall be credited to Germany for the light cruisers, floating docks or the material handed over, or to be handed over under the Protocol of January 10, 1920, as compensation for the warships which were sunk.

As regards sunk German ships which have been, or may be, salved, a Power to which they have been, or may be, allotted, will be chargeable with the cost of the salvage incurred by the Power which has borne them.

ARTICLE 8

No sum shall be credited to Germany in respect of the proceeds of the sale of warships and naval war material surrendered under the Naval Clauses of the Treaty of Versailles, including the value of the arisings from naval war material which may have been, or may be, sold by the Reparation Commission at the request of the Supreme Council. These sums shall be divided between the Allied Powers in the same proportions as were approved by the Supreme Council for the material surrendered under the Protocol of January 10, 1920.

ARTICLE 9

Italy shall, in priority to all other Allied Powers, be entitled to retain and set off against the amounts due to her by Austria, Bulgaria and Hungary in respect of the Armies of Occupation and reparation a sum equal to the amount for which she may be adjudged by the Reparation Commission to be liable to account to the Reparation Commission in respect of the value of property transferred and services rendered up to May 1, 1921, under Article 189 and Annexes III, IV, and V to Part VIII (Reparation) of the Treaty of St. Germain, and of the corresponding provisions of the Treaty of Trianon and also of the sum provided for in the agreement relating to Italy with respect to the Reparation contribution signed at St. Germain on September 10, 1919, as modified at Paris on December 8, 1919. Italy will in consequence only be obliged to issue the bonds referred to in Article 4 of the said Agreement if and so far as her debt is not covered by the set off provided for above.

ARTICLE 10

The provisions of the present Agreement do not apply to Poland. The right of Poland to reparation for damage suffered by her, as an integral part of the former Empire of Russia, is reserved in accordance with Article 116 of the Treaty of Versailles and Article 87 of the Treaty of St. Germain.

The sums to be credited to Germany and Austria under Articles 92 and 243 of the Treaty of Versailles, and Article 189 of the Treaty of St. Germain, shall be entered provisionally in suspense accounts carrying interest at 5 per cent per annum.

ARTICLE 11

The stipulations of the present Agreement shall not affect the operation of the provisions of Article 232, paragraph 3, of the Treaty of Versailles.

The amount of the sums borrowed by Belgium up till November 11, 1919, including interest at 5 per cent per annum up till the date of payment, shall rank immediately after the payment of 2½ milliard of gold francs referred to in Article 5 and be distributed as equally as possible over the sums paid each year by Germany before May 1, 1926.

Sums paid in advance by Germany shall not be applied for the purpose of discounting this part of her yearly payments.

ARTICLE 12

Nothing in this Agreement shall prejudice the right of the Allied Powers to repayment of the relief credits afforded by them to the ex-Enemy Powers.

ARTICLE 13

The question of the reduction of the cost of the Armies of Occupation to a uniform basis for all the Allied and Associated Powers is reserved in order that it may be discussed with the United States of America.

BELGIUM	(Signed)	LEON DELACROIX.
FRANCE	(Signed)	A. MILLERAND.
GREAT BRITAIN	(Signed)	D. LLOYD GEORGE.
ITALY	(Signed)	C. SFORZA.
JAPAN	(Signed)	S. CHINDA.
PORTUGAL	(Signed)	ALFONSO COSTIA.

Spa,

JULY 16th, 1920.

Le Secretaire-Général de la Conference de Spa.

(Signed)   ROLIN JACQUEMYNS.

II. THE LONDON SCHEDULE OF PAYMENTS *

(Dated May 5, 1921, accepted by Germany May 11, 1921)

Prescribing the time and manner for securing and discharging the entire obligation of Germany for reparation under articles 231, 232, and 233 of the treaty of Versailles.

The Reparation Commission has, in accordance with article 233 of the treaty of Versailles, fixed the time and manner for securing and discharging the entire obligation

* Text from "Official Documents Relative to the Amount of Payment to be Effected by Germany under Reparation Account." Reparation Commission, 1922.

of Germany for reparation under articles 231, 232, and 233 of the treaty as follows. (this determination is without prejudice to the duty of Germany to make restitution under article 238 or to other obligation under the treaty):

ARTICLE 1. Germany will perform in the manner laid down in this schedule her obligation to pay the total fixed in accordance with articles 231, 232, and 233 of the treaty of Versailles by the commission, viz., 132 milliards of gold marks less (a) the amount already paid on account of reparation, (b) sums which may from time to time be credited to Germany in respect of State properties in ceded territory, etc., and (c) any sums received from other enemy or ex-enemy powers in respect of which the commission may decide that credit should be given to Germany, plus the amount of the Belgian debt to the Allies, the amounts of these deductions and addition to be determined later by the commission.

ART. 2. Germany shall create and deliver to the commission in substitution for bonds already delivered or deliverable under paragraph 12 (c) of Annex II of Part VIII (Reparation) of the treaty of Versailles the bonds thereafter described.

A. Bonds for an amount of 12 milliards of gold marks. These bonds shall be created and delivered at latest on July 1, 1921.

There shall be an annual payment from funds to be provided by Germany as prescribed in this schedule in each year from May 1, 1921, equal in amount to 5 per cent of the nominal value of the issued bonds, out of which there shall be paid interest at 5 per cent per annum payable half yearly on the bonds outstanding at any time, and the balance to sinking fund for the redemption of the bonds by annual drawings at par. These bonds are hereinafter referred to as bonds of series A.

B. Bonds for a further amount of 38 milliards of gold marks. These bonds shall be created and delivered at the latest on November 1, 1921.

There shall be an annual payment from funds to be provided by Germany as prescribed in this schedule in each year from November 1, 1921, equal in amount to 6 per cent of the nominal value of the issued bonds, out of which there shall be paid interest at 5 per cent per annum payable half-yearly on the bonds outstanding at any time and the balance to sinking fund for the redemption of the bonds by annual drawings at par. These bonds are hereinafter referred to as bonds of series B.

C. Bonds for 82 milliards of gold marks, subject to such subsequent adjustment by creation or cancellation of bonds as may be required under article 1.

These bonds shall be created and delivered to the Reparation Commission, without coupons attached, at latest on November 1, 1921; they shall be issued by the commission as and when it is satisfied that the payments which Germany is required to make in pursuance of this schedule are sufficient to provide for the payment of interest and sinking fund on such bonds. There shall be an annual payment from funds to be provided by Germany as prescribed in this schedule in each year from the date of issue by the Reparation Commission equal in amount to 6 per cent of the nominal value of the issued bonds, out of which shall be paid interest at 5 per cent per annum payable half-yearly on the bonds outstanding at any time, and the balance to sinking fund for the redemption of the bonds by annual drawings at par.

The German Government shall supply to the commission coupon sheets for such bonds as and when issued by the commission. These bonds are hereinafter referred to as bonds of series C.

ART. 3. The bonds provided for in article 2, shall be .signed German Government bearer bonds, in such form and in such denominations as the commission shall prescribe for the purpose of making them marketable, and shall be free of all German taxes and charges of every description, present or future.

Subject to the provisions of articles 248 and 251 of the treaty of Versailles, these bonds shall be secured on the whole of the assets and revenues of the German Empire and the German States, and in particular on the assets and revenues specified in article 7 of this schedule. The service of the bonds of series A, B, and C shall be a first, second, and third charge, respectively, on the said assets and revenues and shall be met by the payments to be made by Germany under this schedule.

ART. 4. Germany shall pay in each year until the redemption of the bonds provided for in article 2, by means of the sinking funds attached thereto, (1) a sum of 2 milliard gold marks; (2) (a) a sum equivalent to 25 per cent of the value of her exports in each period of 12 months starting from May 1, 1921, as determined by the commission, or (b) alternatively an equivalent amount as fixed in accordance with any other index proposed by Germany and accepted by the commission; (3) a further sum equivalent to 1 per cent of the value of her exports as above defined or alternatively an equivalent amount fixed as provided in (b) above. Provided always that when Germany shall have discharged all her obligations under this schedule, other than her liability in respect of outstanding bonds, the amount to be paid in each year under this paragraph shall be reduced to the amount required in that year to meet the interest and sinking fund on the bonds then outstanding.

Subject to the provisions of article 5 the payments to be made in respect of paragraph (1) above shall be made quarterly on or before January 15, April 15, July 15, and October 15 each year, and the payments in respect of paragraphs (2) and (3) above shall be made quarterly on or before February 15, May 15, August 15, and November 15, and calculated on the basis of the exports in the last quarter but one preceding that quarter, the first payment to be made on or before November 15, 1921, to be calculated on the basis of the exports in the three months ending July 31, 1921.

ART. 5. Germany shall pay within 25 days from this notification one milliard gold marks in gold or approved foreign currencies or approved foreign bills or in drafts at three months on the German treasury indorsed by approved German banks and payable in pounds sterling in London, in francs in Paris, in dollars in New York, or any currency in any other place designated by the commission. These payments will be treated as the two first quarterly instalments of the payments provided for in article 4 (1).

ART. 6. The commission will within 25 days from this notification, in accordance with paragraph 12 A (d), Annex II, of the treaty as amended, establish the special subcommission to be called the committee of guaranties.

The committee of guaranties will consist of representatives of the Allied Powers now represented on the Reparation Commission, including a representative of the United States of America in the event of that Government desiring to make the appointment.

The committee shall co-opt not more than three representatives of nationals of other powers whenever it shall appear to the commission that a sufficient portion of the bonds to be issued under this schedule is held by nationals of such powers to justify their representation on the committee of guaranties.

ART. 7. The committee of guaranties will be charged with the duty of securing the application of articles 241 and 248 of the treaty of Versailles. It shall supervise the application to the service of the bonds provided for in article 2 of the funds assigned as security for the payments to be made by Germany under article 4. The funds to be so assigned shall be: (a) The proceeds of all German maritime and land customs duties, and in particular the proceeds of all import and export duties; (b) the proceeds of a levy of 25 per cent on the value of all exports from Germany, except those exports upon which a levy of not less than 25 per cent is applied under the legislation referred to in article 9; (c) the proceeds of such direct or indirect taxes or any other funds as may be proposed by the German Government and accepted by the committee of guaranties in addition to or in substitution for the funds specified in (a) or (b) above.

The assigned funds shall be paid to accounts to be opened in the name of the committee and supervised by it, in gold or in foreign currencies approved by the committee. The equivalent of the 25 per cent levy referred to in paragraph (b) shall be paid in German currency by the German Government to the exporter.

The German Government shall notify to the committee of guaranties any proposed action which may tend to diminish the proceeds of any of the assigned funds and shall, if the committee demand it, substitute some other approved funds.

The committee of guaranties shall be charged further with the duty of conducting on behalf of the commission the examination provided for in paragraph 12 (b) of Annex II to Part VIII of the treaty of Versailles and of verifying on behalf of the commission and, if necessary, of correcting the amount declared by the German Government as the value of German exports for the purpose of the calculation of the sum payable in each year or quarter under article 4 (2) and the amounts of the funds assigned under this article to the service of the bonds. The committee shall be entitled to take such measures as it may deem necessary for the proper discharge of its duties. The committee of guaranties is not authorized to interfere in German administration.

ART. 8. In accordance with paragraph 9 (2) of Annex II as amended, Germany shall on demand, subject to the prior approval of the commission, provide such material and labor as any of the Allied Powers may require toward the restoration of the devastated areas of that power, or to enable any Allied power to proceed with the restoration or development of its industrial or economic life. The value of such material and labor shall be determined in each case by a valuer appointed by Germany and a valuer appointed by the power concerned, and, in default of agreement, by a referee nominated by the commission.

This provision as to valuation does not apply to deliveries under Annexes III, IV, V, and VI to Part VIII of the treaty.

ART. 9. Germany shall take every necessary measure of legislative and administrative action to facilitate the operation of the German reparation recovery act, 1921, in force in the United Kingdom, and of any similar legislation enacted by any Allied power, so long as such legislation remains in force. Payments effected by the operation of such legislation shall be credited to Germany on account of the payments to be made by it under article 4 (2).

The equivalent in German currency shall be paid by the German Government to the exporter.

ART. 10. Payments for all services rendered, all deliveries in kind, and all receipts under article 9 shall be made to the Reparation Commission by the Allied power receiving the same in cash or current coupons within one month of the receipt thereof, and shall be credited to Germany on account of the payments to be made by her under article 4.

ART. 11. The sum payable under article 4 (3) and any surplus receipts by the commission under article 4 (1) and (2) in each year, not required for the payment of interest and sinking fund on bonds outstanding in that year, shall be accumulated and applied so far as they will extend, at such times as the commission may think fit, by the commission in paying simple interest not exceeding 2½ per cent per annum, from May 1, 1921, to May 1, 1926, and thereafter at a rate not exceeding 5 per cent on the balance of the debt not covered by the bonds then issued.

The interest on such balance of the debt shall not be cumulative. No interest thereon shall be payable otherwise than as provided in this paragraph.

ART. 12. The present schedule does not modify the provisions securing the execution of the treaty of Versailles, which are applicable to the stipulations of the present schedule.

III. SECRETARY HUGHES ON THE REPARATION PROBLEM *

Concluding section of the address delivered by the Secretary of State before the Annual Meeting of the American Historical Association at New Haven, Conn., December 29, 1922.

The economic conditions in Europe give us the greatest concern. They have long received the earnest consideration of the Administration. It is idle to say that we are not interested in these problems, for we are deeply interested from an economic standpoint, as our credits and markets are involved, and from a humanitarian standpoint, as the heart of the American people goes out to those who are in distress. We cannot dispose of these problems by calling them European, for they are world problems and we cannot escape the injurious consequences of a failure to settle them.

They are, however, European problems in the sense that they cannot be solved without the consent of Euro-

* From the authorized text published in *Current History*, February, 1923.

pean Governments. We cannot consent for them. The key to the settlement is in their hands, not in ours.

The crux of the European situation lies in the settlement of reparations. There will be no adjustment of other needs, however pressing, until a definite and accepted basis for the discharge of reparations claims has been fixed. It is futile to attempt to erect any economic structure in Europe until the foundation is laid.

How can the United States help in this matter? We are not seeking reparations. We are indeed asking for the reimbursement of the costs of our army of occupation; and, with good reason, for we have maintained our army in Europe at the request of the Allies and of Germany, and under an agreement that its cost with like army costs should be a first charge upon the amounts paid by Germany. Others have been paid and we have not been paid.

But we are not seeking general reparations. We are bearing our own burden and through our loans a large part of Europe's burden in addition. No demands of ours stand in the way of a proper settlement of the reparation question.

Of course we hold the obligations of European Governments and there has been discussion abroad and here with respect to them. There has been a persistent attempt ever since the armistice to link up the debts owing to our Government with reparations or with projects of cancellation. This attempt has been resisted in a determined manner under the former Administration and under the present Administration. The matter is plain enough from our standpoint. The capacity of Germany to pay is not at all affected by any indebtedness of any of the Allies to us. That indebtedness does not diminish Germany's capacity, and its removal would not increase her capacity. For example, if France had been able to finance her part in the war without borrowing at all from us, that is, by taxation and internal loans, the problem of what Germany could pay would be exactly the same. Moreover, so far as the debtors to the United States are concerned, they have unsettled credit balances, and their condition and capacity to pay cannot properly be determined until the amount that can be realized on these credits for reparations has been determined.

The Administration must also consider the difficulty arising from the fact that the question of these obligations which we hold, and what shall be done with them, is not a question within the province of the Executive. Not only may Congress deal with public property of this sort, but it has dealt with it. It has created a commission and instead of giving that commission broad powers such as the Administration proposed, which quite apart from cancellation might permit a sound discretion to be exercised in accordance with the facts elicited, Congress has placed definite restrictions upon the power of the Commission in providing for the refunding of these debts.

But what is our attitude toward the question of reparations, standing as it does as a distinct question and as one which cannot be settled unless the European Governments concerned are able to agree?

We have no desire to see Germany relieved of her responsibility for the war or of her just obligations to make reparation for the injuries due to her aggression. There is not the slightest desire that France shall lose any part of her just claims. On the other hand, we do not wish to see a prostrate Germany. There can be no economic recuperation in Europe unless Germany recuperates. There will be no permanent peace unless economic satisfactions are enjoyed. There must be hope, and industry must have promise of reward if there is to be prosperity. We should view with disfavor measures which instead of producing reparations would threaten disaster.

Some of our own people have suggested that the United States should assume the rôle of arbiter. There is one sufficient answer to this suggestion, and that is that we have not been asked to assume the rôle of arbiter. There could be no such arbitrament unless it were invited, and it would be an extraordinary and unprecedented thing for us to ask for such an invitation.

I do not think that we should endeavor to take such a burden of responsibility. We have quite enough to bear without drawing to ourselves all the ill feeling which would result from disappointed hopes and a settlement which was viewed as forced upon nations by this country which at the same time is demanding the payment of its debts.

But the situation does call for a settlement upon its merits. The first condition of a satisfactory settlement is that the question should be taken out of politics. Statesmen have their difficulties, their public opinion, the exigencies which they must face. It is devoutly to be hoped that they will effect a settlement among themselves, and that the coming meeting at Paris will find a solution. But if it does not, what should be done? The alternative of forcible measures to obtain reparations is not an attractive one. No one can foretell the extent of the serious consequences which might ensue from such a course. Apart from political results, I believe that the opinion of experts is that such measures will not produce reparation payments, but might tend to destroy the basis of those payments which must be found in economic recuperation.

If, however, statesmen cannot agree and such an alternative is faced, what can be done? Is there not another way out? The fundamental condition is that in this critical moment the merits of the question, as an economic one, must alone be regarded. Sentiment, however natural, must be disregarded; mutual recriminations are of no avail; reviews of the past, whether accurate or inaccurate, promise nothing; assertions of blame on the one hand and excuses on the other come to naught.

There ought to be a way for statesmen to agree upon what Germany can pay, for no matter what claims may be made against her that is the limit of satisfaction. There ought to be a way to determine that limit and to provide a financial plan by which immediate results can be obtained, and the European nations can feel that the foundation has been laid for their mutual and earnest endeavors to bring about the utmost prosperity to which the industry of their people entitles them.

If statesmen cannot agree, and exigencies of public opinion make their course difficult, then there should be called to their aid those who can point the way to a solution.

Why should they not invite men of the highest authority in finance in their respective countries—men of such prestige, experience and honor that their agreement upon the amount to be paid, and upon a financial plan for working out the payments, would be accepted throughout the world as the most authoritative expression obtainable? Governments need not bind themselves in advance to accept the recommendations, but they can at least make possible such an inquiry with their approval and free the men who may represent their country in such a commission from any responsibility to Foreign Offices and from any duty to obey political instructions. In other words, they may invite an answer to this difficult and pressing question from men of such standing and in such circumstances of freedom as will insure a reply prompted only by knowledge and conscience. I have no doubt that distinguished Americans would be willing to serve in such a commission. If Governments saw fit to reject the recommendation upon which such a body agreed, they would be free to do so, but they would have the advantage of impartial advice and of an enlightened public opinion. Peoples would be informed, the question would be rescued from assertion and counter-assertion, and the problem put upon its way to solution.

I do not believe that any general conference would answer the purpose better, much less that any political conference would accomplish a result which Premiers find it impossible to reach. But I do believe that a small group, given proper freedom of action, would be able soon to devise a proper plan. It would be time enough to consider forcible measures after such an opportunity had been exhausted. Such a body would not only be expert, but friendly. It would not be bound by special official obligations; it would have no animus and no duty but to find and state the truth. In a situation which requires an absence of technicality and immunity from interference,

I hope that the way may soon be found for a frank discussion and determination of what is essentially an economic problem.

The United States has the most friendly and disinterested purpose in this matter, and wishes to aid in any practicable way. But it is idle to make suggestions which arouse false hopes and are so impracticable that they cannot bear fruit. On the other hand, there lies open a broad avenue of opportunity if those whose voluntary action is indispensable are willing to take advantage of it. And, once this is done, the avenues of American helpfulness cannot fail to open hopefully.

IV. TELEGRAM FROM LORD CURZON TO THE BRITISH CHARGE D'AFFAIRES IN WASHINGTON *
(Dated October 12, 1923)

The information which reaches America will have acquainted the American Government with the extremely critical economic position that has arisen in Europe owing to the failure to find any solution for the reparations problem, which daily becomes more acute as the financial and political condition of Germany grows worse. There does not appear to be among the European Powers that unity of thought which either renders common action feasible or will be successful in finding an early solution. His Majesty's Government have during the past nine months made a series of proposals to their Allies for meeting these difficulties, none of which has been so fortunate as to meet with a measure of acceptance sufficient to bring about common action. And yet without such action not merely Germany but Europe appears to

* Text from *The London Times*, October 26, 1923.

be drifting into economic disaster. In these circumstances His Majesty's Government have for long entertained the belief that the cooperation of the United States Government is an essential condition of any real advantage toward settlement. America, by reason of her position and history, is more disinterested than any of the European Powers. At the same time she is directly and vitally concerned with the solution of the European problem, if for no other reason because in it is involved the question of the inter-Allied debt.

When Mr. Hughes made his declaration in December last both Great Britain and Germany made it clear that they would warmly welcome the proffered assistance; and whenever the suggestion has been revived it has met with the hearty approval of His Majesty's Government. The French Government have hitherto taken a different view. This lack of unanimity is, so far as His Majesty's Government are aware, the sole reason why the proposal has not been proceeded with.

His Majesty's Government were already engaged in formulating an inquiry to the United States Government as to the manner in which, in the opinion of the latter, the united action, which is the common desideratum, could best be brought about when they read in the press yesterday morning a declaration, reported to have been made by President Coolidge, that the American Government rest on their proposal of December last. His Majesty's Government warmly welcome this declaration and hope that they are justified in deducing from it that if the European Powers will join in such an inquiry America will render the promised cooperation.

If His Majesty's Government have rightly interpreted

the statement of the President, and if they may count upon an encouraging reception being given to such a proceeding, they will not hesitate to invite the immediate cooperation of their Allies in Europe in an invitation to the United States Government to assist in the proposed inquiry by deputing a delegate, whether official or unofficial, to take part in it. If, on the other hand, it were proposed to hold such an inquiry, although complete unanimity had not been forthcoming at this end, might His Majesty's Government and the majority of the Allies still hope for American cooperation? Alternatively, if it were proposed that such an inquiry should be intrusted to the Reparation Commission or to a body appointed by it, would America still be willing to participate?

It is in the firm belief that the American Government have it in their power to render a great service to the security and peace of the world that His Majesty's Government, speaking in the name of the whole British Empire as represented in the imperial conference now assembled in London, desire to associate themselves with the renewed proposal of the President, and they will be glad to receive from the American Government any suggestion that the latter may be disposed to offer in reply to the questions which I have ventured to put.

V. SECRETARY HUGHES'S REPLY TO THE COMMUNICATION OF THE BRITISH CHARGE D'AFFAIRES *

DEPARTMENT OF STATE,
Washington, October 15, 1923.

In reply to the communication of His Majesty's chargé d'affairs of October thirteenth, the Secretary of State

* Text from the Department of State press release, dated October 25, 1923.

desires again to express the deep interest of the United States in the economic situation in Europe and its readiness to aid in any practicable way to promote recuperation and a reestablishment of economic stability. The Government of the United States has viewed with deep concern the lack, as His Majesty's Government expresses it, of that unity of thought on the part of the European Powers essential to common action. The views of the Government of the United States as to the importance of agreement among the Allies and the relations of the Government of the United States to the questions involved were set forth in the statement of the Secretary of State to which His Majesty's Government refers, and these views are still held. It is observed that His Majesty's Government states that Great Britain and Germany made it clear that the proffered assistance would be warmly welcomed by them, and that His Majesty's Government has always heartily approved the suggestion, then made by the Secretary of State whenever it has been revived, and that so far as His Majesty's Government is aware the sole reason why the proposal has not been proceeded with has been lack of unanimity among the interested Powers.

It is believed that present conditions make it imperative that a suitable financial plan should be evolved to prevent economic disaster in Europe, the consequences of which would be world-wide. It is hoped that existing circumstances are propitious for the consideration of such a plan inasmuch as the abandonment of resistance on the part of the German Government will present a freer opportunity and an immediate necessity for establishing an economic program. The Government of the

United States is therefore entirely willing to take part in an economic conference, in which all the European Allies chiefly concerned in German reparations participate, for the purpose of considering the questions of the capacity of Germany to make reparation payments and an appropriate financial plan for securing such payments. It is deemed advisable, however, to emphasize the following points:

1. Confirming what was said by the Secretary of State in his statement of last December to which you refer, the Government of the United States has no desire to see Germany relieved of her responsibility for the war or of her just obligations. There should be no ground for the impression that a conference, if called, should have any such aim or that resistance to the fulfillment of Germany's obligations has any support. It should be evident that in the effort to attain the ends in view regard must be had to the capacity of Germany to pay and to the fundamental condition of Germany's recuperation, without which reparation payments will be impossible.

2. Such a conference should be advisory, not for the purpose of binding governments who would naturally be unwilling to pledge their acceptance in advance, but to assure appropriate recommendations by a thoroughly informed and impartial body intent upon the solution of the difficult pending problems upon their merits.

3. The Secretary of State notes the observation in the communication of His Majesty's Government that the European problem is of direct and vital interest to the United States "if for no other reason because the question of inter-Allied debt is involved therein." The Govern-

ment of the United States has consistently maintained the essential difference between the questions of Germany's capacity to pay and of the practicable methods to secure reparation payments from Germany and the payment by the Allies of their debts to the United States, which constitute distinct obligations. In the statement of the Secretary of State, to which His Majesty's Government refers, it was said:

"The matter is plain enough from our standpoint. The capacity of Germany to pay is not at all affected by any indebtedness of any of the Allies to us. That indebtedness does not diminish Germany's capacity, and its removal would not increase her capacity. For example, if France had been able to finance her part in the war without borrowing at all from us—that is, by taxation and internal loans—the problem of what Germany could pay would be exactly the same. Moreover, so far as the debtors to the United States are concerned, they have unsettled credit balances, and their condition and capacity to pay can not be properly determined until the amount that can be realized on these credits for reparations has been determined.

"The Administration must also consider the difficulty arising from the fact that the question of these obligations which we hold, and what shall be done with them, is not a question within the province of the Executive. Not only may Congress deal with public property of this sort but it has dealt with it. It has created a commission, and instead of giving that commission broad powers such as the Administration proposed, which, quite apart from cancellation, might permit a sound discretion to be exercised in accordance with the facts elicited, Congress has placed definite restrictions upon the power of the commission in providing for the refunding of these debts."

It is hardly necessary to add, as it has frequently been stated by the Government of the United States, that while the American people do not favor cancellation of the debts of the Allies to the United States or of the transfer to the people of the United States of the burden of Germany's obligations, directly or indirectly, the Government of the United States has no desire to be oppressive or to refuse to make reasonable settlements as to time and terms of payment, in full consideration of the circumstances of the Allied debtors. It may be added that the establishment of sound economic conditions in Europe, the serious reduction of military outlays, and the demonstration of a disposition of European peoples to work together to achieve the aims of peace and justice will not fail to have their proper influence upon American thought and purpose in connection with such adjustments.

In further reply to the communication of His Majesty's Government it may be said that the Government of the United States is not in a position to appoint a member of the Reparation Commission, inasmuch as such an appointment can not be made without the consent of the Congress. The Secretary of State has no doubt, however, that competent American citizens would be willing to participate in an economic inquiry, for the purposes stated, through an advisory body appointed by the Reparation Commission, to make recommendations, in case that course after further consideration should be deemed preferable.

As to the further question whether American cooperation in an inquiry for the purposes described in the communication of His Majesty's Government could be hoped for in case unanimity of the European Powers could not be had, the Government of the United States must again express the view that the questions involved can not be finally settled without the concurrence of the European Governments directly concerned. Other governments can not consent for them, and it would manifestly be extremely difficult to formulate financial plans of such importance and complexity without the participation of those whose assent is necessary to their fulfillment. In view of the existing exigencies it is hoped that the project of such an inquiry as is contemplated, of an advisory nature, might commend itself to all these Powers, and that the question suggested will not arise. But if it should arise, through lack of unanimity on the part of the European Powers, the Government of the United States must reserve decision as to its course of action in order that the developments in such a contingency may be fully considered and that course taken which will give best promise of ultimate success in securing the desired end of reestablishing the essential conditions of European peace and economic restoration. To the attainment of that end it may be repeated the Government of the United States desires to lend its assistance in any manner that may be found feasible.

VI. FINAL PROTOCOL OF THE LONDON CONFERENCE *
(Dated August 16, 1924)

The representatives of the Belgian Government, the British Government (with the Governments of Canada,

* Official text. For the text of the plan drawn up by the Committee of Experts, which was the basis of this agreement,

Australia, New Zealand, South Africa, and India), the French Government, the Greek Government, the Italian Government, the Japanese Government, the Portuguese Government, the Rumanian Government, the Serb-Croat-Slovene Government, and the German Government, accompanied by the representatives of the Government of the United States of America, with specifically limited powers, and the representatives of the Reparation Commission, being assembled at the foreign office under the chairmanship of the Right Honorable James Ramsay MacDonald, Prime Minister and Secretary of State for Foreign Affairs, on the conclusion of the proceedings of the London conference on the application of the plan presented to the Reparation Commission on April 9, 1924, by the first committee of experts appointed by it on November 30, 1923, the president states that all the governments concerned and the Reparation Commission have confirmed their acceptance of the plan and have agreed to its being brought into operation, and that in the course of the proceedings of the conference certain agreements which are necessary to enable the plan to be brought into operation have been drawn up or already signed by the parties concerned. It is understood that these agreements, which have now been signed or initialled *ne varietur* (except as regards the dates laid down in the agreement forming Annex III hereto, which will be extended by 17 days) and are annexed hereto, are mutually interdependent. The representatives of the parties concerned will meet in London on the thirtieth

see Dawes, Rufus G., *The Dawes Plan in the Making*, 1925; also Moulton, Harold G., *The Reparation Plan* (Investigations in International Economic Reconstruction, Institute of Economics, Washington), 1924.

of August next in order to effect at one and the same session the formal signature of the documents which affect them and have not already been signed. On this occasion a certified copy of the agreement concluded between the Allied Governments will be communicated to the German Government.

The statement of the president having been approved unanimously by the representatives of the Governments concerned and of the Reparation Commission, the president declares the proceedings of the conference at an end.

ANNEX 1

AGREEMENT BETWEEN THE REPARATION COMMISSION AND
THE GERMAN GOVERNMENT

The contracting parties, being desirous of carrying into effect the plan for the discharge of the reparation obligations and other pecuniary liabilities of Germany under the treaty of Versailles proposed to the Reparation Commission on April 9, 1924, by the first committee of experts appointed by the commission (which plan is referred to in this agreement as the experts' plan) and of facilitating the working of the experts' plan by putting into operation such additional arrangements as may hereafter be made between the German Government and the Allied Governments at the conference now being held in London, in so far as the same may lie within the respective spheres of action of the Reparation Commission and the German Government;

And the Reparation Commission, acting in virtue not only of the powers conferred upon it by the said treaty but also of the authority given to it by the Allied Governments represented at the said conference in respect of all payments by Germany dealt with in the experts' plan, but not comprised in Part VIII of the said treaty, hereby agree as follows:

I. The German Government undertakes to take all appropriate measures for carrying into effect the experts' plan and for ensuring its permanent operation, and in particular—

(a) It will take all measures necessary with a view to the promulgation and enforcement of the laws and regulations required for that purpose (specially the laws on the bank, the German railways, and the industrial debentures) in the form approved by the Reparation Commission.

(b) It will apply the provisions contained in Annex I hereto as to the control of the revenues assigned as security for the annuities under the experts' plan and other matters.

II. The Reparation Commission undertakes on its side to take all appropriate measures for carrying into effect the experts' plan and for ensuring its permanent operation, and in particular—

(a) For facilitating the issue of the German loan contemplated in the experts' plan.

(b) For making all financial and accounting adjustments necessary to give full effect to the experts' plan.

III. The Reparation Commission and the German Government agree—

(a) To carry into effect in so far as the same may lie within their respective spheres of action such additional arrangements as may hereafter be made between the German Government and the Allied Governments at the said conference now being held in London, including any provisions which may be so agreed for carrying into effect the experts' plan or for the introduction of modifications of detail in the working of the said plan. The said additional arrangements when concluded shall be added in the form of a second schedule to this document and shall be identified by the signatures of two members of the Reparation Commission on behalf of that body and of two duly authorized representatives of the German Government.

(b) Any dispute which may arise between the Reparation Commission and the German Government with regard to the interpretation either of the present agreement and its schedules or of the experts' plan or of the German legislation enacted in execution of that plan, shall be submitted to arbitration in accordance with the methods to be fixed and subject to the conditions to be determined by the London conference for questions of the interpretation of the experts' plan.

This provision shall be without prejudice to the arbitration clauses included in the experts' plan or in the said German legislation or in any of the annexes hereto.

IV. If no agreement shall be reached at the London conference between the Allied Governments and the German Government for the purpose of carrying into effect the experts' plan, this agreement shall be void.

Signed for the Reparation Commission:

Louis Barthou.	Salvago Raggi.
John Bradbury.	Leon Delacroix.

Signed for the German Government:

Marx.

London, *August 9, 1924.*

ANNEX II

AGREEMENT BETWEEN THE ALLIED GOVERNMENTS AND THE
GERMAN GOVERNMENT CONCERNING THE AGREEMENT OF
AUGUST 9, 1924, BETWEEN THE GERMAN GOVERNMENT
AND THE REPARATION COMMISSION

The representatives of the Governments assembled in London, having taken note of the provisions of the agreement signed in London on August 9, 1924, between the German Government and the Reparation Commission and of the questions of which under Article III of the said agreement the settlement must be completed, agree that the following clauses shall be embodied in the said agreement:

CLAUSE 1. The procedure for the settlement of disputes contemplated in Article III (b) of the said agreement of August 9, 1924, shall be as follows:

Subject to the powers of interpretation conferred upon the Reparation Commission by paragraph 12 of Annex II to Part VIII of the treaty of Versailles and subject to the provisions as to arbitration existing elsewhere, and in particular in the experts' plan or in the German legislation enacted in execution of that plan, all disputes which may arise between the Reparation Commission and Germany with regard to the interpretation either of the agreement concluded between them, the experts' plan, or the German legislation enacted in execution of that plan, shall be submitted for decision to three arbitrators appointed for five years; one by the Reparation Commission, one by the German Government, and the third, who shall act as president, by agreement between the Reparation Commission and the German Government, or failing such agreement, by the president for the time being of the Permanent Court of International Justice.

Before giving a final decision and without prejudice to the questions at issue, the President, on the request of the first party applying therefor, may order any appropriate provisional measures in order to avoid an interruption in the regular working of the plan and to safeguard the respective rights of the parties.

Subject to any decision of the arbitrators to the contrary the procedure shall be governed by the provisions of the convention of The Hague of October 18, 1907, on the pacific settlement of international disputes.

CLAUSE 2. The German Government declares:

(a) That it recognizes that the transfer committee is free, subject to the conditions of the report of the experts, to employ the funds at its disposal in the payment for deliveries on customary commercial conditions of any commodities or services provided for in the program from time to time prescribed by the Reparation Commission after consultation with the transfer committee or by the arbitral commission provided for in paragraph (d) below, including in particular coal, coke, and dyestuffs and any other commodities specially provided for in the treaty of Versailles, even after the fulfilment of the treaty obligations in regard to these commodities.

(b) That it recognizes that the programs laid down by the Reparation Commission, after consultation with the transfer committee, or by the arbitral commission, provided for in paragraph (d) below, for deliveries to be made under ordinary commercial conditions, shall not be subject, as regards the nature of the products, to the limitations fixed by the treaty of Versailles for the deliveries which the Reparation Commission can demand from Germany thereunder; but they shall be fixed with due regard to the possibilities of production in Germany, to the position of her supplies of raw materials and to her domestic requirements in so far as is necessary for the maintenance of her social and economic life and also with due regard to the limitations set out in the experts' report.

(c) That it will facilitate as far as possible the execution of the programs for all deliveries under either the treaty or the experts' report by means of commercial contracts passed under ordinary commercial conditions; and that in particular, it will not take, nor allow to be taken, any measure which would result in deliveries being unobtainable under ordinary commercial conditions.

The Allied Governments on their side each undertake, so far as it is concerned, to prevent as far as possible the reexportation of the deliveries received from Germany, except in accordance with the provisions of Article V of annex 6 of the experts' report.

(d) The German Government further declares that it agrees to the following additional provisions in regard to the fixation and execution of programs for the deliveries of the undermentioned products after the fulfilment of the treaty obligations in regard to such products.

(i) In default of agreement as regards the programs of deliveries of these products, either between the members of the Reparation Commission or between the Reparation Commission, acting unanimously, and the German Government, programs which take due account of ordinary commercial custom shall be laid down for periods to be determined by the special committee referred to in clause 3 of this agreement by an arbitral commission consisting of three independent and impartial arbitrators. The members of this arbitral commission shall be appointed in advance for a definite period by agreement between the Reparation Commission, acting unanimously, and the German Government, or, in default of agreement, by the president for the time being of the Permanent Court of International Justice at the Hague. The chairman of the commission shall be a citizen of the United States of America.

(ii) In laying down the program the arbitral commission shall take into account the possibilities of production in Germany, the position of her supplies of raw materials, and her domestic requirements, in so far as necessary for the maintenance of her social and economic life, and also of the conditions set out in the experts' report, nor shall it exceed the limits fixed by the transfer committee with a view to the maintenance of the German exchange.

(iii) The decision of the arbitral commission fixing the programs shall be final.

(iv) The Allied Governments and nationals shall make every effort to obtain the delivery of the full amounts fixed by these programs by means of direct commercial contracts with the German suppliers.

(v) If any Allied Government considers that it or its nationals have not been able to make commercial contracts to the full amount of the program owing to measures of wilful discrimination or wilful obstruction on the part of the German Government or its nationals, it may submit a reasoned claim to the arbitral commission, and the commission, after hearing the parties, shall decide, as a matter of equity, taking into account the conditions referred to in paragraph (ii) above, whether there have in fact been measures of wilful discrimination or wilful obstruction on the part of the German Government or of German suppliers.

(vi) In the event of the arbitral commission deciding this question in the affirmative, it shall require the German Government to ensure the delivery of such quantities as it shall decide and under such conditions, particularly as regards price, as it shall fix.

(vii) Any disputes which may arise as to the interpretation of the decisions of the arbitral commission shall be submitted to it for final judgment.

(viii) Nothing in this clause shall affect in any way the powers of the transfer committee as set out in the experts' report.

The above procedure will apply to the following products:

(i) Coal, coke, and lignite briquettes.

(ii) Sulphate of ammonia prepared by synthetic processes and other synthetic-nitrogenous products. These last-named products can only be called for simultaneously with synthetic sulphate of ammonia and up to a quantity corresponding to the proportion in which these products are manufactured as compared with sulphate of ammonia in the same period of manufacture.

(iii) Products referred to in paragraph 5 of Annex VI of Part VIII of the treaty of Versailles (English text) with the exception, as regards chemical products, of specialties manufactured by a single "concern,"

As regards the products falling under (iii), the special provisions of paragraph (d) will cease to apply on the 15th August, 1928. As regards the products falling under (ii) and (iii) above, the special committee provided for in clause 3 will draw up a more detailed list. For certain among them it may fix maximum quantities as regards either weight or value; it may also exclude certain of them, if it is shown that they are indispensable for the protection of German national economy.

CLAUSE 3. The German Government agrees to the appointment of a special committee, not exceeding six members, composed of an equal number of Allied and German representatives, who shall be appointed by the Reparation Commission and the German Government, respectively, with the power in the event of difference to co-opt an additional member of neutral nationality, to be chosen by the Allied and German members in agreement, or in default of agreement to be appointed by the Reparation Commission. This committee will be charged with the duty of—

1. Determining the procedure for placing orders and the conditions for carrying out deliveries in kind so as to ensure the satisfactory working of such deliveries, adhering as closely as possible to ordinary commercial usage.

2. Examining the best means of ensuring the fulfilment of the undertakings to be given by the German Government in accordance with clause 2, paragraphs (c) and (d), of this agreement, in particular by providing for the reference to arbitration of any disagreements which may arise thereon between the interested parties;

the decision of the arbitrator or arbitrators being binding on such parties.

3. Examining the best means of applying the provisions of the experts' report relative to the limitation of deliveries to those which are not of an anti-economic character, and to recommend the measures to be taken against any persons who may infringe the prohibition against reexportation of deliveries.

The members of the committee may be assisted by such experts as they may consider necessary. The work of this committee is not in any way to delay the bringing into operation of the experts' plan, and its decisions are not to encroach in any way on the powers of the transfer committee to be set up under that plan. Its decisions must accordingly, before being carried out, be approved by the Reparation Commission and by the transfer committee in so far as the latter is concerned. It is understood that the conclusions of this committee will not be modified without the consent of the German Government.

CLAUSE 4. If differences of opinion should arise between the transfer committee and the German Government on any of the following points relating to the execution of Article VI of annex 6 of the experts' report, viz, (1) the inclusion of any particular class of property in the list, (2) any modification in the list, (3) the scope of any class so included, or (4) the measures to be taken to secure that investments to be purchased by this procedure shall not be of a temporary character, such difference shall be referred, at the request of either party, to an arbitrator (who, if the German Government so desire, shall be a national of a country not interested.

in German reparation payments) to be chosen by agreement between the two parties; or in default of agreement, to be nominated by the president for the time being of the Permanent Court of International Justice at The Hague. The arbitrator shall decide whether any claim made or objection raised is justified or not, and in so doing shall in particular give consideration to the principles set out in Article VI, viz, (1) that the investment must not be of a temporary character, and (2) that the German Government is required to have due regard to the necessity for making maximum payments to its creditors, but is also entitled to have regard to maintaining its control of its own internal economy.

The Allied Governments agree that the transfer committee should only transfer marks for purchases under the operation of the said Article VI if and when the accumulated funds exceed the amounts which the bank of issue will accept as short-term deposits.

CLAUSE 5. If the transfer committee is equally divided in regard to the question whether concerted financial maneuvers have been set on foot within the meaning of Article VIII of annex 6 of the experts' report, the question shall be referred to an independent and impartial arbitrator, who shall hear the views of each of the members of the committee and decide between them. The arbitrator shall be a financial expert selected by the members of the transfer committee in agreement, or, in default of an agreement, by the president for the time being of the Permanent Court of International Justice at The Hague. On all other questions, if the transfer committee is equally divided, the chairman shall have a casting vote.

If the funds at the disposal of the Agent General for Reparation Payments are at any time accumulated in Germany up to the limit of 5 milliards of gold marks referred to in paragraph (a) of Article X of annex 6 of the experts' report, or such lower figure as may be fixed by the transfer committee under paragraph (b) of that article, and the committee has, by a majority, decided that concerted financial maneuvers within the meaning of Article VIII of that annex have not taken place, or that certain measures to defeat maneuvers contemplated in that article should not be taken, any member of the minority of the committee may, within eight days, appeal against such decision to an arbitral tribunal, whose decision on the matters before them shall be final. The arbitral tribunal shall consist of three independent and impartial financial experts, including a citizen of the United States of America, who shall act as chairman, such experts to be selected by the committee unanimously, or, failing unanimity, to be appointed by the president for the time being of the Permanent Court of International Justice at The Hague.

CLAUSE 6. If any Government interested (Allied or German) considers that a defect exists in the technical working of the experts' plan so far as it relates to the collection of German payments or the control of the securities therefor, which can be remedied without affecting the substantial principles of that plan, it may submit the question to the Reparation Commission, which will transmit it forthwith for inquiry and advice to a committee consisting of the Agent General for Reparation Payments, the trustee or trustees for the railway and industrial mortgage bonds, the railway commissioner, the bank commissioner, and the commissioner of controlled revenues.

This committe will, as soon as possible, transmit to the Reparation Commission either a unanimous report or majority and minority reports, including, if necessary, proposals for the removal of any defect to which attention may have been drawn.

If the Reparation Commission arrives at a unanimous decision, it shall invite the German Government to adhere to it, and if an agreement is reached with the German Government on the subject the necessary measures shall be carried into effect without delay. If the Reparation Commission is not unanimous, or if any decision taken unanimously is not accepted by the German Government, any of the parties interested, may submit the question to a committee of three independent and impartial experts chosen by agreement between the Reparation Commission deciding unanimously and the German Government, or, in default of such agreement, by the president for the time being of the Permanent Court of International Justice at The Hague. The decision of this committee shall be final.

It is understood that this provision shall not apply to any question in regard to the disposal of the funds paid to the account of the Agent General for Reparation Payments, or to any other matter which falls solely within the competence of the transfer committee.

Done at London the —— day of August, 1924, in a single copy which will remain deposited in the archives of His Britannic Majesty's Government, which will transmit a certified copy to the Reparation Commission for inclusion in the agreement of August 9, 1924, and to each of the signatory Governments.

ANNEX III

AGREEMENT BETWEEN THE ALLIED GOVERNMENTS AND GERMANY

The Royal Government of Belgium, the Government of His Britannic Majesty (with the Governments of the Dominion of Canada, the Commonwealth of Australia, the Dominion of New Zealand, the Union of South Africa, and India), the Government of the French Republic, the Government of the Greek Republic, the Royal Government of Italy, the Imperial Government of Japan, the Government of the Portuguese Republic, the Royal Government of Rumania, and the Royal Government of the Serb-Croat-Slovene State, of the one part, and the Government of the German Republic of the other part, animated with the desire to bring into being as soon as possible as regards matters affecting them, the plan presented to the Reparation Commission on April 9, 1924, by the first committee of experts appointed by it on November 30, 1923, "to consider the means of balancing the budget and the measures to be taken to stabilize the currency of Germany," approved by the commission and accepted by each of the interested powers, have resolved to conclude an agreement for this purpose, and, therefore, the undersigned duly authorized have agreed as follows:

ARTICLE 1. (A) The experts' plan of April 9, 1924, will be considered as having been put into execution, except as regards measures to be taken by the Allied Governments, when the Reparation Commission has declared that the measures prescribed by it in its decision No. 2877 (4) of July 15, 1924, have been taken, that is to say:

1. That Germany has taken the following measures: (a) The voting by the Reichstag in the form approved by the Reparation Commission of the laws necessary to the working of the plan, and their promulgation; (b) the installation with a view to their normal working of all the executive and controlling bodies provided for in the plan; (c) the definitive constitution, in conformity with the provisions of the respective laws, of the banks and the German Railway Company; (d) the deposit with the trustees of certificates representing the railway bonds and such similar certificates for the industrial debentures as may result from the report of the organization committee.

2. That contracts have been concluded assuring the subscription of the loan of 800 million gold marks as soon as the plan has been brought into operation and all the conditions contained in the experts' report have been fulfilled.

(B) The fiscal and economic unity of Germany will be considered to have been restored in accordance with the experts' plan when the Allied Governments have taken the following measures:

1. The removal and cessation of all vetoes imposed since January 11, 1923, on German fiscal and economic legislation; the reestablishment of the German authorities with the full powers which they exercised in the occupied territories before January 11, 1923, as regards

the administration of customs and taxes, foreign commerce, woods and forests, railways (under the conditions specified in article 5), and, in general, all other branches of economic and fiscal administration; the remaining administrations not mentioned above will operate in every respect in conformity with the Rhineland agreement; the formalities regarding the admission or readmission of German officials will be applied in such a manner that the reestablishment of the German authorities, in particular the customs administration, may take place with the least possible delay; all this without other restrictions than those stipulated in the treaty of Versailles, the Rhineland agreement and the experts' plan.

2. The restoration to their owners of all mines, cokeries and other industrial, agricultural, forest and shipping undertaking exploited under Allied management or provisionally leased by the occupying authorities since January 11, 1923.

3. The withdrawal of the special organizations established to exploit the pledges and the release of requisitions made for the working of those organizations.

4. The removal, subject to the provisions of the Rhineland agreement, of restrictions on the movement of persons, goods, and vehicles.

5. In general, the Allied Governments, in order to insure in the occupied territories the fiscal and economic unity of Germany, will cause the Inter-Allied Rhineland High Commission to proceed, subject to the provisions of the Rhineland agreement, to an adjustment of the ordnances passed by the said commission since January 11, 1923.

ART. 2. The experts' plan will be put into execution

with the least possible delay. For this purpose the measures indicated in article 1 will be taken as rapidly as possible; in particular, the laws necessary for the working of the plan will be promulgated immediately after they have been voted.

ART. 3. (1) Every effort shall be made to bring the experts' plan into full operation not later than October 5, 1924. (2) On August 15, 1924, at the latest, the Reparation Commission ought to be in a position to announce that the German laws necessary for the working of the plan have been promulgated in the terms approved by it, and also that the Agent General for Reparation Payments has taken up his duties. (3) Within five weeks (35 days) from the date of this first announcement (i. e., not later than September 20, 1924), the commission should be in a position to announce that the other measures prescribed in its decision of July 15, 1924, mentioned in article 1, have been fulfilled.

The Reparation Commission shall have power if necessary to advance these dates if circumstances permit, or to postpone them so far as may be deemed indispensable for the complete fulfillment of the above provisions.

The French and Belgian Governments undertake to fulfil within a fortnight after the date of the second announcement (i. e., by October 5, 1924), the program laid down in article 1 for the restoration of Germany's fiscal and economic unity. They will notify the Reparation Commission of such fulfillment. The decision that the program has been fully executed will be taken by the Reparation Commission.

ART. 4. (a) As soon as the first announcement referred to in article 3 (2) has been made (i. e., on August 15,

1924), and during the transition period between the first and second announcements (i. e., between August 15 and September 20, 1924), without waiting for the complete execution of the measures prescribed by the Reparation Commission in its decision of July 15, 1924, the French and Belgian Governments, being desirous of restoring in a large measure Germany's fiscal and economic unity as soon as possible, will take the following steps:

Eight days after the first announcement (i. e., August 23, 1924) the levy of duties on the eastern customs line (i. e., the customs barrier between occupied and unoccupied Germany) will cease.

Twenty days after the first announcement (September 5), and earlier if possible, the Allied authorities will reduce as far as possible the restrictions imposed since January 11, 1923, on the movements of persons, goods, and vehicles, especially between occupied and unoccupied Germany. Within the same period the French and Belgian Governments will have established the said eastern customs line and will apply solely the legislation and tariffs in force in unoccupied Germany to collections and charges of all kinds levied by them in the occupied territories, as well as to the régime for external trades, except so far as concerns the Franco-Belgian Railway Régie, which will continue to apply its own tariffs.

(b) The aforesaid Governments will continue to levy the collections and charges thus adjusted, but will hand over to the Agent General for Reparation payments the receipts accruing to them after the first announcement (August 15, 1924) from the application of the new régime, including the net profits from the Franco-Belgian Railway Régie, but less the monthly deduction of a lump sum of two million gold marks to cover the cost of collection during the transition period.

(c) On its side the German Government will pay over to the Agent General for Reparation Payments during the transition period such monthly installments as, added to the receipts above provided for, shall place at his disposal each month an amount equal to one-twelfth of the first annuity under the experts' plan, less the estimated receipts during the month from the operation of the British reparation recovery act or corresponding measures which may be adopted by the other Allied Governments and the paper marks supplied to the armies of occupation. It is understood that the monthly burden to fall upon Germany during the transition period shall be one-twelfth of the first annuity of the global payment incumbent on Germany, as such global payment is defined in Section IX of the experts' plan; to such monthly burden is to be added each month during the transition period the two million of gold marks mentioned above.

(d) Payments toward the above-mentioned monthly sums will be made every ten days.

The first payment by Germany will take place on the date of the first announcement (August 15, 1924).

The first payment by the French and Belgian Governments will be made ten days later (August 25, 1924).

The first and second payments by Germany will amount to twenty million gold marks each. The third payment will consist of the balance of the payment to be made by Germany during the first month.

The subsequent payments by Germany shall be fixed by the Agent General for Reparation Payments and shall be such as to place at the disposal of the Agent General during each period of ten days one-third of the monthly installment stipulated above, taking into account the payments made by the French and Belgian Governments and the receipts from the reparation recovery acts, etc.

The payments by the French and Belgian Governments will only fall due in so far as the German Government has on its part effected its payments.

(e) With the resources thus placed at his disposal the Agent General for Reparation Payments shall provide for the payment of reparation and other treaty charges during the transition period, in conformity with the decisions as to distribution which will be taken by the Allied and Associated Governments.

In particular he shall place at the disposal of the interested Governments the sums necessary—

1. To ensure the complete financing of all agreements concerning deliveries in kind continued or entered into by them or by their representatives during the transition period, including the cost of the transport of the said deliveries, as provided by the treaty of Versailles.

2. To cover the working expenses of mines and cokeries under Allied management, including the cost of transport to the frontiers.

As a consequence of the above provisions and in order that the period during which German payments are made at the rate prescribed for the first annuity shall not exceed one year, the period corresponding to the first annuity in the experts' plan will be reduced by a period equal to that of the transition period, and the second annuity will begin immediately thereafter (i. e., August 15, 1925).

ART. 5. Upon the second announcement (September 20, 1924), the railway system of the Reich will be transferred to the new company contemplated by the experts' plan. As from that date the operation of all the lines now worked by the Deutsche Reichsbahn will pass to the said company. As from a fortnight after the second announcement (October 5, 1924), the lines now operated by the Régie will be worked on account of the company under the control of the railway organization committee.

As soon as the present agreement has been signed, the organization committee will place itself in communication with the Régie in order to arrange the details of the transfer. The actual transfer from the Régie to the company will be made step by step under the control of the organization committee with as little delay as is compatible with an orderly transfer. It shall be completed within a period of six weeks (by November 20, 1924), the organization committee, however, having authority to grant extensions of time for the arrangement of details.

ART. 6. The detailed measures to be applied and the machinery to be set up in order to carry out the provisions of articles 1B, 2, 3, and 4 (a) will be studied by technical conferences between the representatives of the interested Allied authorities and the German departments concerned. These conferences will begin at Coblenz and Dusseldorf immediately after the London conference. The measures to be applied as well as transitional measures shall be put into force in the occupied territories in the customary form.

ART. 7. In order to bring about mutual conciliation and in order to wipe out the past to the utmost possible extent, the Allied Governments and the German Government have agreed on the following stipulations, it being understood that, as regards future incidents, the jurisdiction and legislation of Germany, notably in the matter of the security of the State, and the jurisdiction and the legislation of the occupying authorities, notably in the matter of their security, will respectively follow their normal course in conformity with the treaty of peace and the Rhineland agreement:

1. No one shall, under any pretext, be prosecuted, disturbed or molested or subjected to any injury, whether material or moral, either by reason of acts committed exclusively or principally for political reasons or by reason of his political attitude in the occupied territories from January 11, 1923, up to the putting into force of the present agreement, or by reason of his obedience or disobedience to orders, ordinances, decrees, or other injunctions issued by the occupying authorities or the German authorities respectively and relating to events which have taken place within the same period, or by reason of his relations with the said authorities.

2. The German Government and the Allied Governments concerned will remit all sentences and penalties, judicial or administrative, imposed for the above facts from January 11, 1923, up to the putting into force of the present agreement. It is understood that fines or other pecuniary penalties, whether judicial or administrative, already paid will not be reimbursed.

3. The provisions of paragraphs (1) and (2) do not

apply to crimes committed against the life of persons and resulting in death.

4. The offences to which the amnesty provided for in the stipulations of paragraphs (1) and (2) do not apply and which are at the present moment subject to the jurisdiction of the occupying authorities by reason of the creation of special organizations which are to be suppressed under the terms of the present agreement, will be transferred to the German tribunals.

5. The Governments concerned will each take, so far as they are concerned, the measures necessary to assure the fulfillment of this article. If need arise, this fulfillment will be amicably arranged by the Governments concerned, and if necessary by means of mixed commissions set up by common agreement.

ART. 8. German-allied commissions of arbitration, similar to those appointed in 1920, charged with the duty of deciding any disputes which the change of régime may give rise to between Allied merchants and the German authorities, shall be set up by the Governments concerned.

ART. 9. The suppression of the Bad-Ems subcommittee on October 5, 1924, shall not prejudice the full execution of articles 264 to 267 of the treaty of Versailles.

ART. 10. All disputes which may arise between the Allied Governments or one of them on the one side and Germany on the other side with regard to the present agreement shall, if they can not be settled by negotiation, be submitted to the Permanent Court of International Justice.

ART. 11. The present agreement, of which the French

and English texts are both authentic, shall come into force from the moment of signature.

Done at London the —— day of August, 1924, in a single copy which will remain deposited in the archives of His Britannic Majesty's Government, which will transmit certified copies to each of the parties.

ANNEX IV

INTER-ALLIED AGREEMENT

The Royal Government of Belgium, the Government of His Britannic Majesty (with the Governments of the Dominion of Canada, the Commonwealth of Australia, the Dominion of New Zealand, the Union of South Africa, and India), the Government of the French Republic, the Government of the Greek Republic, the Royal Government of Italy, the Imperial Government of Japan, the Government of the Portuguese Republic, the Royal Government of Rumania, and the Royal Government of the Serb-Croat-Slovene State, anxious to provide for the complete fulfillment, so far as they are concerned, of the plan presented to the Reparation Commission on April 9, 1924, by the first committee of experts appointed by it on November 30, 1923, "to consider the means of balancing the budget and the measures to be taken to stabilize the currency of Germany," the said plan being approved by the commission and accepted by each of the interested Powers, and having resolved to conclude an agreement for this purpose, the undersigned, duly authorized, have agreed as follows:

ARTICLE 1. The Governments represented upon the

Reparation Commission acting under paragraph 22 of Annex II to Part VIII (reparation) of the treaty of Versailles will modify the said Annex II by the introduction of the following paragraphs 2 A and 16 A, and by the amendment of paragraph 17 as set out below.

Paragraph 2 A. "When the Reparation Commission is deliberating on any point relating to the report presented on April 9, 1924, to the Reparation Commission by the first committee of experts appointed by it on November 30, 1923, a citizen of the United States of America appointed as provided below shall take part in the discussions and shall vote as if he had been appointed in virtue of paragraph 2 of the present annex.

"The American citizen shall be appointed by unanimous vote of the Reparation Commission within thirty days after the adoption of this amendment.

"In the event of the Reparation Commission not being unanimous, the appointment shall be made by the president for the time being of the Permanent Court of International Justice at The Hague.

"The person appointed shall hold office for five years, and may be reappointed. In the event of any vacancy the same procedure shall apply to the appointment of a successor.

"Provided always that if the United States of America are officially represented by a delegate on the Reparation Commission, any American citizen appointed under the provisions of this paragraph shall cease to hold office and no fresh appointment under these provisions shall be made as long as the United States are so officially represented."

Paragraph 16 A. "In the event of any application that

Germany be declared in default in any of the obligations contained either in this part of the present treaty as put into force on January 10, 1920, and subsequently amended in virtue of paragraph 22 of the present annex or in the experts' plan dated April 9, 1924, it will be the duty of the Reparation Commission to come to a decision thereon. If the decision of the Reparation Commission granting or rejecting such application has been taken by a majority, any member of the Reparation Commission who has participated in the vote may within eight days from the date of the said decision appeal from that decision to an arbitral commission composed of three impartial and independent persons whose decision shall be final. The members of the arbitral commission shall be appointed for five years by the Reparation Commission deciding by a unanimous vote, or failing unanimity by the president for the time being of the Permanent Court of International Justice at The Hague. At the end of the five-year period or in case of vacancies arising during such period the same procedure will be followed as in the case of the first appointments. The president of the arbitral commission shall be a citizen of the United States of America."

Paragraph 17. "If a default by Germany is established under the foregoing conditions, the commission will forthwith give notice of such default to each of the interested powers and may make such recommendations as to the action to be taken in consequence of such default as it may think necessary."

ART. 2. In accordance with the provisions of the experts' plan, sanctions will not be imposed on Germany in pursuance of paragraph 18 of Annex II to Part VIII (reparation) of the treaty of Versailles unless a default within the meaning of Section III of Part I of the report of the said committee of experts has been declared under the conditions laid down by the said annex as amended in conformity with this agreement.

In this case the signatory Governments, acting with the consciousness of joint trusteeship for the financial interests of themselves and of the persons who advance money upon the lines of the said plan, will confer at once on the nature of the sanctions to be applied and on the method of their rapid and effective application.

ART. 3. In order to secure the service of the loan of 800 million gold marks contemplated by the experts' plan, and in order to facilitate the issue of that loan to the public, the signatory Governments hereby declare that, in case sanctions have to be imposed in consequence of a default by Germany they will safeguard any specific securities which may be pledged to the service of the loan.

The signatory Governments further declare that they consider the service of the loan as entitled to absolute priority as regards any resources of Germany so far as such resources may have been subjected to a general charge in favor of the said loan and also as regards any resources that may arise as a result of the imposition of sanctions.

ART. 4. Any dispute between the signatory Governments arising out of articles 2 or 3 of the present agreement shall, if it can not be settled by negotiation, be submitted to the permanent Court of International Justice.

ART. 5. Unless otherwise expressly stipulated in the

preceding articles of this agreement all the existing rights of the signatory Governments under the treaty of Versailles read with the report of the experts referred to in article 2 are reserved.

ART. 6. The present agreement, of which the French and English texts are both authentic, shall come into force from the moment of signature.

Done at London, the —— day of August, 1924, in a single copy, which will remain deposited in the archives of His Britannic Majesty's Government, which will transmit certified copies to each of the parties.

VII. HUNGARIAN REPARATION PROGRAM *

A. DECISION OF THE REPARATION COMMISSION, EXCEPTING SPECIFIED ASSETS IN VIEW OF HUNGARIAN LOANS RENDERED FEBRUARY 21, 1924.

THE REPARATION COMMISSION:

Considering the present state of Hungarian finances;

Taking note of the plan of the League of Nations for the reconstruction of Hungary transmitted to the Reparation Commission by the Hungarian Committee of the Council of the League as the plan asked for in the resolution of the Commission of the 17th October 1923 as the said plan is set forth in the draft Protocols Nos. I and II and the report of the Financial Committee of the League dated the 20th December 1923;

And considering that, under the said plan, it is proposed that Hungary should raise a reconstruction loan

* Text from *The Monthly Summary* of the League of Nations, Supplement for May, 1924.

the net proceeds of which should not exceed 250,000,-000 gold crowns and which is to be repaid in a period of 20 years and also possibly short-term loans which are to be repaid out of the yield of the principal reconstruction loan as soon as the latter has been issued;

Hereby in exercise of the power conferred by Article 180 of the Treaty of Trianon to make exceptions to the first charge created by that Treaty on the assets and revenues of Hungary for the cost of reparation and other costs:

Excepts from the charge created by the said Article 180 for the cost of reparation by Hungary and any other costs arising under the Treaty of Trianon or any Treaties or Agreements supplementary thereto or any Arrangements concluded by Hungary with the Allied and Associated Powers during the Armistice signed on the 3rd November 1918 and from any and every other charge to which the powers of the Commission extend and so that this exception shall take effect for a period of 20 years from the date of this decision:

1. The gross receipts of the Customs;
2. The gross receipts from the tobacco monopoly;
3. The net receipts of the salt monopoly;
4. The gross receipts of the sugar tax;
5. Such of the other revenues and receipts of the Hungarian Government, other than the State railways and the revenues thereof, as may from time to time be duly required under the conditions mentioned in the said plan for the service of the reconstruction long-term loan to Hungary therein referred to;

And whereas this release is intended to permit of the repayment of the said reconstruction loan within the period for which the said release takes effect, the Reparation Commission agrees that if, at the end of the said period, any part of the said reconstruction loan or the interest thereon has not been completely discharged, such part of the loan or interest shall until completely discharged have priority in respect of the revenues and receipts above excepted over the said first charge for the cost of reparations and other costs under Article 180 of the said Treaty;

And the Reparation Commission makes this exception and temporary waiver of priority on certain Hungarian assets upon the express conditions that, without prejudice to the rights of the holders of Hungarian Relief Bonds, (1) no portion of the revenues and receipts so excepted be applied, in priority to the said first charge for the costs of reparations and other Treaty charges, to any purpose other than the service of the said projected loans, and (2) that the said short-term loans, if any, shall (if not already otherwise repaid) be discharged out of the proceeds of the said reconstruction loan;

Provided always and it is hereby declared that, if the said Protocols Nos. I and II shall not have been signed by or on behalf of all the Governments named therein respectively on or before the 31st March 1924, or if before the 31st December 1924 the League of Nations, taking into consideration the figure reached by the subscriptions to the said principal reconstruction loan, has not notified the Reparation Commission that it undertakes the responsibility to complete the reconstruction plan contained in the said Protocols, this decision shall be void and of no effect, but so that any short-term loans, to be repaid out of the yield of the principal loan, which may have been issued after the signature of the Protocols of the plan of the League of Nations and in conformity with those Protocols, shall be repaid in priority to reparations.

The Reparation Commission takes this decision upon the understanding that the Council of the League of Nations will declare before the 31st March next that it interprets Articles II and VII of the said Protocol II as meaning that it will, in conformity with the said plan of reconstruction, re-establish the control of Hungarian finances if and when it finds that any payment or delivery prescribed by the Schedule to Decision No. 2797 of the Reparation Commission which fixes the reparation payments of Hungary has not been made and this Decision shall take effect only if the Council has made such a declaration before that date.

B. DECISION OF THE REPARATION COMMISSION, AS TO AMOUNT OF TREATY CHARGES TO BE IMPOSED UPON HUNGARY FOR A PERIOD OF TWENTY YEARS

THE REPARATION COMMISSION:

Considering the present state of Hungarian finances;

Taking note of the plan of the League of Nations for the financial reconstruction of Hungary transmitted to the Reparation Commission by the Hungarian Committee of the Council of the League as the plan asked for in the resolution of the Commission of the 17th October 1923 and consisting of the Protocols Nos. I and II and the report of the Financial Committee of the League dated the 20th December 1923;

Considering also that it is essential in the interest of Hungary and the States creditors of Hungary on reparation account that the projected loan to Hungary for financial reconstruction as contemplated by the said plan be adequately subscribed, but that it is not practicable before the date proposed for the issue of any such loan to determine the amount of the damage for which compensation is to be made by Hungary, to assign to her a part of the debt, and draw up a schedule of payments for securing and discharging the part so assigned pursuant to Article 163 of the Treaty of Trianon;

Recognising further that subscriptions to the said projected loan will be made upon the understanding that the recommendations as to the external obligations of Hungary, reparations and the powers of the Commissioner-General, contained in the said plan, receive the approval of the Reparation Commission and, therefore, that the burden to be imposed on Hungary on account of reparation and other charges under the Treaty of Trianon (other than such burdens, if any, as may arise under the said Treaty in respect of the obligations of Hungary or her nationals which existed before the Treaty) shall not for a period of twenty years from the date of this decision exceed the amounts mentioned in the Annex hereto and shall be subject to the conditions contained in the said plan;

And taking note of the engagement of the Hungarian Government dated the 21st February 1924, consenting and agreeing to make the payment of the said amounts on the dates prescribed:

Decides that the payments and deliveries to be made by Hungary from the 1st January 1924 to the 31st December 1943 in respect of her liability to make reparation shall, in pursuance of the said plan and subject to the conditions contained therein, be those set out in the Annex hereto, but so that if, during the said period of twenty years, Hungary shall, with the approval of the Reparation Commission, make any payment or delivery under the said Treaty (not being a payment or delivery in respect of obligations of Hungary or her nationals which existed before the war, as for example the obligations contained in Articles 186 and 231 and any such obligations as are contained in Article 232) otherwise than on account of reparation, such payment or the value of any such delivery shall not exceed the figure fixed by the schedule for the period in which it takes place and shall be deducted from the obligations of Hungary fixed in the schedule for that period;

And further, if the payments fixed in the schedule for the years 1927 to 1943 added to the value of the deliveries or payments made in the years 1924, 1925 and 1926 do not amount to 200,000,000 gold crowns, the deficiency shall be paid or delivered during 1940, 1941, 1942 and 1943 in addition to the payments or deliveries fixed for those years, one-fourth of the deficiency being allotted to each year, and, similarly, if those payments added to that value exceed 200,000,000 gold crowns, the excess shall in like manner be deducted from the payments or deliveries fixed for the same last years;

Provided also and it is hereby declared that, if the said Protocols I and II shall not have been duly signed by or on behalf of all the Governments named therein respectively on or before the 31st March 1924 or if before' the 31st December 1924 the League of Nations, taking into consideration the figure reached by the subscriptions to the said principal reconstruction loan, has not notified the Reparation Commission that it undertakes the responsibility to complete the reconstruction plan contained in the said protocols, this decision shall be void and of no effect.

The Reparation Commission takes this decision upon the understanding that the Council of the League of Nations will declare before the 31st March next that it interprets Articles II and VII of the said Protocol II as meaning that it will, in conformity with the said plan of reconstruction, re-establish the control of Hungarian finances if and when it finds that any payment or delivery prescribed by the schedule to this decision has not been made pursuant to this decision and this decision shall take effect only if the Council has made such a declaration before that date.

ANNEX REFERRED TO IN THE ABOVE DECISION
PAYMENTS OR DELIVERIES
(Value expressed in gold crowns)

Period: From January 1st, 1924, to December 31st, 1926	Such deliveries in kind or payments as may from time to time be authorised by the Reparation Commission to an amount corresponding to the value of 880 tons of coal per working day.	
June 30th, 1927..............	2,500,000	
December 31st, 1927..........	2,500,000	5,000,000
June 30th, 1928..............	2,500,000	
December 31st, 1928...........	2,500,000	5,000,000
June 30th, 1929..............	3,000,000	
December 31st, 1929..........	3,000,000	6,000,000
June 30th, 1930..............	3,500,000	
December 31st, 1930..........	3,500,000	7,000,000
June 30th, 1931..............	4,000,000	
December 31st, 1931..........	4,000,000	8,000,000
June 30th, 1932..............	4,500,000	
December 31st, 1932..........	4,500,000	9,000,000
June 30th, 1933..............	5,000,000	
December 31st, 1933..........	5,000,000	10,000,000
June 30th, 1934..............	5,500,000	
December 31st, 1934..........	5,500,000	11,000,000
June 30th, 1935..............	6,000,000	
December 31st, 1935..........	6,000,000	12,000,000
June 30th, 1936..............	6,500,000	
December 31st, 1936..........	6,500,000	13,000,000
June 30th, 1937..............	6,500,000	
December 31st, 1937..........	6,500,000	13,000,000
June 30th, 1938..............	6,500,000	
December 31st, 1938..........	6,500,000	13,000,000
June 30th, 1939..............	6,500,000	
December 31st, 1939..........	6,500,000	13,000,000
June 30th, 1940..............	6,500,000	
December 31st, 1940..........	6,500,000	13,000,000
June 30th, 1941..............	6,500,000	
December 31st, 1941..........	6,500,000	13,000,000
June 30th, 1942..............	7,000,000	
December 31st, 1942..........	7,000,000	14,000,000
June 30th, 1943..............	7,000,000	
December 31st, 1943..........	7,000,000	14,000,000

APPENDIX B

UNITED STATES DEBT SETTLEMENTS

I. ACT OF CONGRESS CREATING THE WORLD WAR FOREIGN DEBT COMMISSION *

(Approved February 9, 1922)

An Act to Create a Commission Authorized under Certain Conditions to Refund or Convert Obligations of Foreign Governments Held by the United States of America and for Other Purposes

Be it enacted by the Senate and House of Representatives of the United States of America in Congress assembled. That a World War Foreign Debt Commission is hereby created consisting of five members, one of whom shall be the Secretary of the Treasury, who shall serve as chairman, and four of whom shall be appointed by the President, by and with the advice and consent of the Senate.

Sec. 2. That, subject to the approval of the President, the commission created by section 1 is hereby authorized to refund or convert, and to extend the time of payment of the principal or the interest, or both, of any obligation of any foreign Government now held by the United States of America, or any obligation of any foreign Government hereafter received by the United States of America (including obligations held by the United States Grain Corporation, the War Department, the Navy Department, or the American Relief Administration), aris-

---

* Official text (Public—No. 139—67th Congress, 42 Stat. L., 363).

221

ing out of the World War, into bonds or other obligations of such foreign Government in substitution for the bonds or other obligations of such Government now or hereafter held by the United States of America, in such form and of such terms, conditions, date or dates of maturity, and rate or rates of interest, and with such security, if any, as shall be deemed for the best interests of the United States of America: *Provided*, That nothing contained in this Act shall be construed to authorize or empower the commission to extend the time of maturity of any such bonds or other obligations due the United States of America by any foreign Government beyond June 15, 1947, or to fix the rate of interest at less than $4\frac{1}{4}$ per centum per annum: *Provided further*, That when the bond or other obligation of any such Government has been refunded or converted as herein provided, the authority of the commission over such refunded or converted bond or other obligation shall cease.

SEC. 3. That this Act shall not be construed to authorize the exchange of bonds or other obligations of any foreign Government for those of any other foreign Government, or cancellation of any part of such indebtedness except through payment thereof.

SEC. 4. That the authority granted by this Act shall cease and determine at the end of three years from the date of the passage of this Act.

SEC. 5. That the annual report of this commission shall be included in the Annual Report of the Secretary of the Treasury on the state of the finances, but said commission shall immediately transmit to the Congress copies of any refunding agreements entered into, with the approval of the President, by each foreign Government

upon the completion of the authority granted under this
Act.

II. AMENDMENT TO THE DEBT COMMISSION ACT RELATIVE TO THE BRITISH SETTLEMENT *
(Approved February 28, 1923)

AN ACT TO AMEND THE ACT ENTITLED "AN ACT TO CRE-
ATE A COMMISSION AUTHORIZED UNDER CERTAIN CON-
DITIONS TO REFUND OR CONVERT OBLIGATIONS OF
FOREIGN GOVERNMENTS HELD BY THE UNITED STATES
OF AMERICA, AND FOR OTHER PURPOSES," APPROVED
FEBRUARY 9, 1922.

Be it enacted by the Senate and House of Representatives of the United States of America in Congress assembled, That the first proviso of section 2 of the Act entitled "An Act to create a commission authorized under certain conditions to refund or convert obligations of foreign governments held by the United States of America, and for other purposes," approved February 9, 1922, is amended to read as follows:

"*Provided,* That the settlement of indebtedness of the United Kingdom of Great Britain and Ireland to the United States, as given below. (See p. 224.)

"The principal of the bonds shall be paid in annual installments on a fixed schedule, subject to the right of the British Government to make these payments in three-year periods. The amount of the first year's installment will be $23,000,000 and these annual installments will increase with due regularity during the life of the bonds until, in the sixty-second year, the amount of the in-

* Official text (Public—No. 455—67th Congress, 42 Stat. L., 1325).

Principal of notes to be refunded.............	$4,074,818,358.44
Interest accrued and unpaid up to December 15th, 1922, at the rate of 4¼ per cent.......	629,836,106.99
	4,704,654,465.43
Deduct payments made October 16, 1922, and November 15, 1922, with interest at 4¼ per cent thereon to December 15, 1922..........	100,526,379.69
	4,604,128,085.74
To be paid in cash..........................	4,128,085.74
Total principal of indebtedness as of December 15, 1922, for which British Government bonds are to be issued to the United States Government at par......	4,600,000,000.00

stallment will be $175,000,000, the aggregate installments being equal to the total principal of the debt.

"The British Government shall have the right to pay off additional amounts of the principal of the bonds on any interest date upon ninety days' previous notice.

"Interest is to be payable upon the unpaid balances at the following rates, on December 15 and June 15 of each year: At the rate of 3 per cent per annum payable semiannually from December 15, 1922, to December 15, 1932, thereafter at the rate of 3½ per cent per annum payable semiannually until final payment.

"For the first five years one-half of the interest may be deferred and added to the principal, bonds to be issued therefor similar to those of the original issue.

"Any payment of interest or of principal may be made in any United States Government bonds issued since April 6, 1917, such bonds to be taken at par and accrued interest—is hereby approved and authorized, and settlements with other governments indebted to the United States are hereby authorized to be made upon such terms as the commission, created by the Act approved February 9, 1922, may believe to be just, subject to the approval of the Congress by Act or joint resolution."

Sec. 2. That the first section of the Act entitled "An Act to create a commission authorized under certain conditions to refund or convert obligations of foreign governments held by the United States of America, and for other purposes," approved February 9, 1922, is amended to read as follows:

"That a World War Foreign Debt Commission is hereby created consisting of eight members, one of whom shall be the Secretary of the Treasury, who shall serve as chairman, and seven of whom shall be appointed by the President, by and with the advice and consent of the Senate. Not more than four members so appointed shall be from the same political party."

Sec. 3. That the provisions of section 2 of this Act shall not affect the tenure of office of any person who is a member of the World War Foreign Debt Commission at the time this Act takes effect.

III. DEBT SETTLEMENT WITH GREAT BRITAIN *

Agreement dated June 19, 1923. Approved on the part of the United States by Act of Congress of February 28, 1923. It was not necessary to have the agreement ratified by the British Parliament.

* Official text as issued by the Treasury Department.

A PROPOSAL,

Dated the eighteenth day of June, 1923, by HIS
  BRITANNIC MAJESTY'S GOVERNMENT, hereinafter called GREAT BRITAIN, to the GOVERN-
  MENT OF THE UNITED STATES OF AMERICA,
  hereinafter called the UNITED STATES, regarding
  the funding of the debt of GREAT BRITAIN to the
  UNITED STATES.

Whereas Great Britain is indebted to the United States
as of 15th December, 1922, upon demand obligations in
the principal amount of $4,074,818,358.44, not including
obligations in the principal amount of $61,000,000, repre-
senting advances deemed to have been made to cover
purchases of silver under the Act of Congress approved
23rd April, 1918, of which $30,500,000 has been repaid
in April and May, 1923, and the balance is to be repaid
in 1924, pursuant to an agreement already made between
the parties, and Great Britain is further indebted to the
United States, as of 15th December, 1922, on account of
interest accrued from 15th April and 15th May, 1919, on
said $4,074,818,358.44, principal amount of demand
obligations:

And whereas Great Britain has power under the War
Loan Act, 1919 (9 and 10 Geo. 5, cap 37) to issue
securities in exchange for maturing securities issued under
the War Loan Acts, 1914 to 1918:

And whereas the demand obligations now held by the
United States Treasury were so issued, and will become
payable upon the request of the United States Treasury
for their payment:

Now therefore Great Britain proposes, in the exercise of the powers above recited and in consideration and in faith of the statements, conditions, premises and mutual covenants herein contained, to issue to the United States, in exchange for the demand obligations now held by the United States Treasury, securities which shall be in their terms and conditions in accordance with the following provisions:

1. *Amount of Indebtedness.*

The total amount of indebtedness to be funded is $4,600,000,000, which has been computed as follows:

Principal amount of demand obligations to be funded.........		$4,074,818,358.44
Interest accrued thereon from 15th April and 15th May, 1919, respectively, to 15th December, 1922, at the rate of 4¼ per cent per annum...............	$629,836,106.99	
Less—Payments made by Great Britain on 16th October and 15th November, 1922, on account of interest, with interest thereon at 4¼ per cent per annum from said dates, respectively, to 15th December, 1922	100,526,379.69	529,309,727.30
Total principal and interest, accrued and unpaid, as of 15th December, 1922		4,604,128,085.74
Paid in cash by Great Britain, 15th March, 1923..........		4,128,085.74
Total indebtedness to be funded into bonds of Great Britain....		4,600,000,000.00

2. *Issue of Long-Time Obligations.*

The securities, which it is proposed to issue at par as promptly as possible, shall be obligations in the principal amount of \$4,600,000,000, in the form of bonds to be dated 15th December, 1922, maturing 15th December, 1984, with interest payable semi-annually on 15th June and 15th December in each year at the rate of 3 per cent per annum from 15th December, 1922, to 15th December, 1932, and thereafter at the rate of 3½ per cent per annum until the principal thereof shall have been repaid.

3. *Method of Payment.*

The bonds shall be payable as to both principal and interest in United States gold coin of the present standard of weight and fineness, or its equivalent in gold bullion, or, at the option of Great Britain, upon not less than thirty days' advance notice indicating the minimum amount which it is contemplated to pay at next due date in gold, cash or available funds, in any bonds of the United States issued or to be issued after 6th April, 1917, to be taken at par and accrued interest to the date of payment hereunder: *provided, however,* that Great Britain may at its option, upon not less than ninety days' advance notice, pay up to one-half of any interest accruing between 15th December, 1922, and 15th December, 1927, on any British bonds proposed to be issued hereunder, in bonds of Great Britain, maturing 15th December, 1984, dated and bearing interest from the respective dates when the interest to be paid thereby becomes due and substantially similar in other respects to the original bonds proposed to be issued hereunder.

All payments to be made by Great Britain on account of the principal or interest of any bonds proposed to be issued hereunder shall be made at the Treasury of the United States in Washington or, at the option of the

Secretary of the Treasury of the United States, at the Federal Reserve Bank of New York and, if in cash, shall be made at the option of Great Britain in gold coin of the United States or in gold bullion or in immediately available funds (or, if in bonds of the United States, shall be in form acceptable to the Secretary of the Treasury of the United States). Appropriate notation of all payments on account of principal shall be made on the bonds proposed to be issued hereunder which may be held by the United States: *provided, however*, that all payments in respect of any marketable obligations issued under paragraph 9 of this proposal shall be made at the office of the fiscal agents of the British Government in the City of New York.

4. *Exemption from Taxation.*

The principal and interest of all bonds issued or to be issued hereunder shall be exempt from all British taxation, present or future, so long as they are in the beneficial ownership of the United States or of a person, firm, association, or corporation neither domiciled nor ordinarily resident in the United Kingdom.

5. *Form of Bonds.*

All bonds proposed to be issued hereunder to the United States shall be payable to the United States of America, or order, shall be issued, so far as possible, in denominations of $4,600,000 each, and shall be substantially in the form set forth in the exhibit annexed hereto, and marked "Exhibit A." The bonds shall be signed for Great Britain by the Counsellor of His Britannic Majesty's Embassy at Washington.

6. *Repayment of Principal.*

To provide for the repayment of the total principal of the debt before maturity of the $4,600,000,000 principal amount of bonds to be issued, it is proposed that the bonds shall contain provisions the effect of which shall be that Great Britain shall make to the United States payments, on account of the original principal amount of the bonds to be issued, in the amounts and on the dates named in the following table: (See schedule on p. 239).

Provided, however, that Great Britain may at its option, upon not less than ninety days' advance notice, postpone any payment of principal falling due as hereinabove provided to any subsequent 15th June or 15th December, not more than two years distant from its due date, but only on condition that, if Great Britain shall at any time exercise this option as to any payment of principal, the payment falling due in the next succeeding year cannot be postponed to any date more than one year distant from the date when it becomes due, unless and until the payment previously postponed shall actually have been made, and the payment falling due in the second succeeding year cannot be postponed at all unless and until the payment of principal due two years previous thereto shall actually have been made.

In the event of Great Britain issuing bonds to the United States in payment of interest accruing between 15th December, 1922, and 15th December, 1927, as proposed in paragraph 3 above, the bonds so issued shall contain provision for the payment of their principal before maturity through annual instalments on account of principal corresponding substantially to the schedule of payments on account of principal appearing in the table hereinabove set forth.

7. *Payments before Maturity.*

Great Britain may at its option, on any interest date or dates upon not less than ninety days' advance notice, make advance payments of principal, in addition to the payments required to be made by the provisions of the bonds in accordance with paragraph 6 of this proposal. Any such additional payments shall first be applied to the principal of any bonds which shall have been issued hereunder on account of interest accruing between 15th December, 1922, and 15th December, 1927, and then to the principal of any other bonds which shall have been issued hereunder. Any payments made to the United States under this provision shall be in amounts of $1,000,-000 or multiples thereof.

8. *Calculation of Interest.*

Notwithstanding anything herein contained, the interest payable from time to time on the bonds proposed to be issued shall be computed on the amount of the principal outstanding on the previous interest date, with adjustments in respect of any payment on account of principal which may have been made since the previous interest date.

9. *Exchange for Marketable Obligations.*

Great Britain will issue to the United States at any time or from time to time, at the request of the Secretary of the Treasury of the United States, in exchange for any or all of the bonds proposed to be issued hereunder and held by the United States, definitive engraved bonds in form suitable for sale to the public, in such amounts and denominations as the Secretary of the Treasury of the United States may request, in bearer form, with provision for registration as to principal, and/or in fully registered form, and otherwise on the same terms and conditions, as to dates of issue and maturity, rate or rates of interest, exemption from taxation, payment in bonds of the United States issued or to be issued after 6th April, 1917, payment before maturity, and the like, as the bonds surrendered on such exchange, except that the bonds shall carry such provision for repayment of principal as shall be agreed upon; provided that, if no agreement to the contrary is arrived at, any such bonds shall contain separate provision for payments before maturity, conforming substantially to the table of repayments of principal prescribed by paragraph 6 of this proposal and in form satisfactory to the Secretary of the Treasury of the United States, such payments to be computed on a basis to accomplish the retirement of any such bonds by 15th December, 1984, and to be made through annual drawings for redemption at par and accrued interest. Any payments of principal thus made before maturity on any such bonds shall be deducted from the payments required to be made by Great Britain to the United States in the corresponding years under the terms of the table of repayments of principal prescribed in paragraph 6 of this proposal.

Great Britain will deliver definitive engraved bonds to the United States in accordance herewith within six months of receiving notice of any such request from the Secretary of the Treasury of the United States, and pending the delivery of the definitive engraved bonds will, at the request of the Secretary of the Treasury of the United States, deliver temporary bonds or interim receipts in a form to be agreed upon within three months of the receipt of such request. The United States, before offering any such bonds or interim receipts for sale in Great Britain, will first offer them to Great Britain for purchase at par and accrued interest and Great Britain shall likewise have the option, in lieu of issuing to the United States any such bonds or interim receipts, to make advance redemption, at par and accrued interest, of a corresponding amount of bonds issued hereunder and held by the United States.

10. *Cancellation and Surrender of Demand Obligations.*

Upon the delivery to the United States of the $4,600,-000,000 principal amount of bonds proposed to be issued hereunder, the United States will cancel and surrender to Great Britain, through the British Ambassador at Washington, or his representative, at the Treasury of the United States in Washington, the demand obligations of Great Britain in the principal amount of $4,074,-818,358.44 described in the preamble to this proposal.

11. *Notices.*

Any notice, request or consent under the hand of the Secretary of the Treasury of the United States shall be deemed and taken as the notice, request, or consent of the United States, and shall be sufficient if delivered at the British Embassy at Washington or at the office of the Permanent Secretary of the British Treasury in London; and any notice, request, or election from or by

Great Britain shall be sufficient if delivered to the American Embassy in London or to the Secretary of the Treasury of the United States at the Treasury of the United States in Washington. The United States in its discretion may waive any notice required hereunder, but any such waiver shall be in writing and shall not extend to or affect any subsequent notice or impair any right of the United States to require notice hereunder.

Signed on behalf of the Lords Commissioners of His Majesty's Treasury, this eighteenth day of June, 1923.

Washington. A. GEDDES,
His Britannic Majesty's Ambassador
Extraordinary and Plenipotentiary.

EXHIBIT "A."

(Form of Bond)

THE GOVERNMENT OF THE UNITED KINGDOM

Sixty-two year 3-3½ per cent Gold Bond
Dated 15th December, 1922. Maturing 15th December, 1984.

$ No.

The Government of the United Kingdom, hereinafter called Great Britain, for value received, promises to pay to the United States of America, hereinafter called the United States, or order, on the 15th day of December, 1984, the sum of Four Million Six Hundred Thousand Dollars ($4,600,000), less any amount which may have been paid upon the principal hereof as endorsed upon the back hereof, and to pay interest upon said principal sum semiannually on the fifteenth day of June and December in each year at the rate of three per cent per annum from 15th December, 1922, to 15th December, 1932, and at the rate of three and one-half per cent per annum thereafter until the principal hereof shall have been paid. All payments on account of principal and/or interest shall be made at the Treasury of the United States in Washington, or, at the option of the Secretary of the Treasury of the United States, at the Federal Reserve Bank of New York. This bond is payable as to both principal and interest in gold coin of the United States of America of the present standard of weight and fineness or in its equivalent in gold bullion, or, at the option of Great Britain, upon not less than thirty days' notice indicating the minimum amount which it is contemplated to pay at next due date in gold, cash or available funds, in any bonds of the United States issued or to be issued after 6th April, 1917, to be taken at par and accrued interest to the date of payment hereunder; *provided, however,* that Great Britain may at its option, upon not less than ninety days' notice, pay up to one-half of any interest accruing hereon between 15th December, 1922, and 15th December, 1927, in bonds of Great Britain dated and bearing interest from the respective dates when the interest to be paid thereby becomes due, and substantially similar in maturity and other respects to this bond.

The principal and interest of this bond shall be exempt from all British taxation, present or future, so long as it is in the beneficial ownership of the United States, or of a person, firm, association or corporation neither domiciled nor ordinarily resident in the United Kingdom.

In order to provide for the repayment of the principal of this bond before maturity, Great Britain will make to the United States payments of principal in the amounts, and on the dates shown in the following table:

Date 15th December:	Annual Instalments to Be Paid on Account of Principal	Date 15th December	Annual Instalments to Be Paid on Account of Principal
1923	$ 23,000	1955	64,000
1924	23,000	1956	64,000
1925	24,000	1957	67,000
1926	25,000	1958	70,000
1927	25,000	1959	72,000
1928	27,000	1960	74,000
1929	27,000	1961	78.000
1930	28,000	1962	78,000
1931	28,000	1963	83,000
1932	30,000	1964	85,000
1933	32,000	1965	89,000
1934	32,000	1966	94,000
1935	32,000	1967	96,000
1936	32,000	1968	100,000
1937	37,000	1969	105,000
1938	37,000	1970	110,000
1939	37,000	1971	114,000
1940	42,000	1972	119,000
1941	42,000	1973	123,000
1942	42,000	1974	127,000
1943	42,000	1975	132,000
1944	46,000	1976	136,000
1945	46,000	1977	141,000
1946	46,000	1978	146,000
1947	51,000	1979	151,000
1948	51,000	1980	156,000
1949	51,000	1981	162,000
1950	53,000	1982	167,000
1951	55,000	1983	175,000
1952	57,000	1984	175,000
1953	60,000		
1954	64,000	Total	$4,600,000

Provided, however, that Great Britain may, at its option, upon not less than ninety days' advance notice, postpone any payment of principal falling due, as hereinabove provided, to any subsequent 15th June or 15th December, not more than two years distant from its due date, but only on condition that if Great Britain shall at any time exercise this option as to any payment of principal, the payment falling due in the next succeeding year cannot be postponed to any date more than one year distant from the date when it becomes due unless and until the payment previously postponed shall actually have been made, and the payment falling due in the second succeeding year cannot be postponed at all unless and until the payment of principal due two years previous thereto shall actually have been made.

This bond may be paid on any interest date before maturity in whole or in part, in amounts of $1,000,000, or multiples thereof, at the option of Great Britain, on not less than ninety days' advance notice.

This bond is issued by Great Britain pursuant to the proposal, dated the 18th day of June, 1923, and to the Acceptance of proposal, dated the 19th day of June, 1923.

IN WITNESS WHEREOF, Great Britain has caused this bond to be executed in its behalf by the Counsellor of His Britannic Majesty's Embassy at Washington, thereunto duly authorized.

For the United Kingdom:

Dated 15th December, 1922.

(Back)

The following amounts have been paid upon the principal amount of this bond:

Date.   Amount paid.

ACCEPTANCE.

JUNE 19, 1923.

The Right Honorable,
  Sir AUCKLAND GEDDES, G. C. M. G., K. C. B.,
    Ambassador Extraordinary and Plenipotentiary,
      The British Embassy,
        Washington, D. C.

MY DEAR MR. AMBASSADOR: I have the honor to acknowledge the receipt of your note of June 18, 1923, transmitting the proposal dated the 18th day of June, 1923, by His Britannic Majesty's Government to the Government of the United States of America regarding the funding of the debt of Great Britain to the United States. This proposal is agreeable to the World War Foreign Debt Commission, and I am writing for the Commission and by its authority to advise you that the proposal is hereby accepted on behalf of the United States of America, pursuant to the authority conferred by the Act of Congress approved February 9, 1922, as amended by the Act of Congress approved February 28, 1923. In accordance therewith I am writing to ask that the bonds as contemplated thereby may be delivered as soon as possible to the Secretary of the Treasury of the United States in exchange for the demand obligations amounting to $4,074,818,358.44 now held by him which are otherwise now payable.

Very truly yours,

A. W. Mellon,

Secretary of the Treasury, and Chairman of the World War Foreign Debt Commission.

Approved:

Warren G. Harding,

President.

June 19, 1923.

B. Schedule of British Payments

Principal	Annual Interest Payments	Annual Principal Payments	Total Annual Payments	Year
$4,600,000,000	$ 138,000,000	$ 23,000,000	$ 161,000,000	1—1923
4,577,000,000	137,310,000	23,000,000	160,310,000	2—1924
4,554,000,000	136,620,000	24,000,000	160,620,000	3—1925
4,530,000,000	135,900,000	25,000,000	160,900,000	4—1926
4,505,000,000	135,150,000	25,000,000	160,150,000	5—1927
4,480,000,000	134,400,000	27,000,000	161,400,000	6—1928
4,453,000,000	133,590,000	27,000,000	160,590,000	7—1929
4,426,000,000	132,780,000	28,000,000	160,780,000	8—1930
4,398,000,000	131,940,000	28,000,000	159,940,000	9—1931
4,370,000,000	131,100,000	30,000,000	161,100,000	10—1932
4,340,000,000	151,900,000	32,000,000	183,900,000	11—1933
4,308,000,000	150,780,000	32,000,000	182,780,000	12—1934
4,276,000,000	149,660,000	32,000,000	181,660,000	13—1935
4,244,000,000	148,540,000	32,000,000	180,540,000	14—1936
4,212,000,000	147,420,000	37,000,000	184,420,000	15—1937
4,175,000,000	146,125,000	37,000,000	183,125,000	16—1938
4,138,000,000	144,830,000	37,000,000	181,830,000	17—1939
4,101,000,000	143,535,000	42,000,000	185,535,000	18—1940
4,059,000,000	142,065,000	42,000,000	184,065,000	19—1941
4,017,000,000	140,595,000	42,000,000	182,595,000	20—1942
3,975,000,000	139,125,000	42,000,000	181,125,000	21—1943
3,933,000,000	137,655,000	46,000,000	183,655,000	22—1944
3,887,000,000	136,045,000	46,000,000	182,045,000	23—1945
3,841,000,000	134,435,000	46,000,000	180,435,000	24—1946

B. Schedule of British Payments—*Continued*

Principal	Annual Interest Payments	Annual Principal Payments	Total Annual Payments	Year
$3,795,000,000	$132,825,000	$51,000,000	$183,825,000	25—1947
3,744,000,000	131,040,000	51,000,000	182,040,000	26—1948
3,693,000,000	129,255,000	51,000,000	180,255,000	27—1949
3,642,000,000	127,470,000	53,000,000	180,470,000	28—1950
3,589,000,000	125,615,000	55,000,000	180,615,000	29—1951
3,534,000,000	123,690,000	57,000,000	180,690,000	30—1952
3,477,000,000	121,695,000	60,000,000	181,695,000	31—1953
3,417,000,000	119,595,000	64,000,000	183,595,000	32—1954
3,353,000,000	117,355,000	64,000,000	181,355,000	33—1955
3,229,000,000	115,115,000	64,000,000	179,115,000	34—1956
3,225,000,000	112,875,000	67,000,000	179,875,000	35—1957
3,158,000,000	110,530,000	70,000,000	180,530,000	36—1958
3,088,000,000	108,080,000	72,000,000	180,080,000	37—1959
3,016,000,000	105,560,000	74,000,000	179,560,000	38—1960
2,942,000,000	102,970,000	78,000,000	180,970,000	39—1961
2,864,000,000	100,240,000	78,000,000	178,240,000	40—1962
2,786,000,000	97,510,000	83,000,000	180,510,000	41—1963
2,703,000,000	94,605,000	85,000,000	179,605,000	42—1964
2,618,000,000	91,630,000	89,000,000	180,630,000	43—1965
2,529,000,000	88,515,000	94,000,000	182,515,000	44—1966
2,435,000,000	85,225,000	96,000,000	181,225,000	45—1967
2,339,000,000	81,865,000	100,000,000	181,865,000	46—1968
2,239,000,000	78,365,000	105,000,000	183,365,000	47—1969
2,134,000,000	74,690,000	110,000,000	184,690,000	48—1970
2,024,000,000	70,840,000	114,000,000	184,840,000	49—1971
1,910,000,000	66,850,000	119,000,000	185,850,000	50—1972
1,791,000,000	62,685,000	123,000,000	185,685,000	51—1973
1,668,000,000	58,380,000	127,000,000	185,380,000	52—1974
1,541,000,000	53,935,000	132,000,000	185,935,000	53—1975
1,409,000,000	49,315,000	136,000,000	185,315,000	54—1976
1,273,000,000	44,555,000	141,000,000	185,555,000	55—1977
1,132,000,000	39,620,000	146,000,000	185,620,000	56—1978
986,000,000	34,510,000	151,000,000	185,510,000	57—1979
835,000,000	29,225,000	156,000,000	185,225,000	58—1980
679,000,000	23,765,000	162,000,000	185,765,000	59—1981
517,000,000	18,095,000	167,000,000	185,095,000	60—1982
350,000,000	12,250,000	175,000,000	187,350,000	61—1983
175,000,000	6,125,000	175,000,000	181,125,000	62—1984
	$6,505,965,000	$4,600,000,000	$11,105,965,000	

IV. DEBT SETTLEMENT WITH FINLAND *

*Agreement signed May 1, 1923. Approved on the part
of the United States by the Act of Congress of March
12, 1924. Finnish Parliament authorized by law of
April 10, 1923, the negotiation of a funding agreement.*

A. Agreement

Made the First Day of May, 1923, at the City of Washington, District of Columbia, between the GOVERN-
MENT OF THE REPUBLIC OF FINLAND, hereinafter called FINLAND, party of the first part, and
the GOVERNMENT OF THE UNITED STATES
OF AMERICA, hereinafter called the UNITED
STATES, party of the second part.

Whereas Finland is indebted to the United States as of
December 15, 1922, upon obligations maturing June 30,
1921, in the aggregate principal amount of $8,281,926.17,
together with interest accrued and unpaid thereon; and

Whereas Finland desires to fund said indebtedness to
the United States, both principal and interest, through
the issue of bonds to the United States, and the United
States is prepared to accept bonds from Finland upon
the terms and conditions hereinafter set forth;

Now, therefore, in consideration of the premises and
of the mutual covenants herein contained, it is agreed as
follows:

1. *Amount of indebtedness.*—The amount of the indebtedness to be funded, after allowing for cash payments made or to be made by Finland, is $9,000,000,
which has been computed as follows:

* Official text as issued by the Treasury Department.

Principal amount of obligations to be funded		$8,281,926.17
Interest accrued thereon from June 30, 1919, and June 1, 1920, respectively, to December 15, 1922, at the rate of 4¼ per cent per annum..............	$1,027,389.10	
Less—Payment in cash made by Finland March 8, 1923, on account of Interest ....:....................	300,000.00	727,389.10
Total principal and interest, accrued and unpaid, as of December 15, 1922		9,009,315.27
To be paid in cash by Finland, May 1, 1923		9,315.27
Total indebtedness to be funded into bonds		9,000,000.00

2. *Repayment of principal.*—In order to provide for the repayment of the indebtedness thus to be funded, Finland will issue to the United States at par, as of December 15, 1922, bonds of Finland in the aggregate principal amount of $9,000,000, dated December 15, 1922, and maturing serially on each December 15 in the succeeding years for 62 years, in the amounts and on the several dates fixed in the following schedule: (See p. 251).

Provided, however, That Finland may at its option, upon not less than 90 days' advance notice to the United States, postpone any payment falling due as hereinabove provided to any subsequent June 15 or December 15 not more than two years distant from its due date, but only on condition that in case Finland shall at any time exercise this option as to any payment of principal, the payment falling due in the next succeeding year can not be postponed to any date more than one year distant from the date when it becomes due unless and until the payment previously postponed shall actually have been made, and the payment falling due in the second succeeding year can not be postponed at all unless and until the payment of principal due two years previous thereto shall actually have been made.

All bonds issued or to be issued hereunder to the United States shall be payable to the Government of the United States of America, or order, shall be issued in such denominations as may be requested by the Secretary of the Treasury of the United States, and shall be substantially in the form set forth in the exhibit hereto annexed and marked "Exhibit A." The $9,000,000 principal amount of bonds first to be issued hereunder shall be issued in 62 pieces, in denominations and with maturities corresponding to the annual payments of principal hereinabove set forth.

3. *Payment of interest.*—All bonds issued or to be issued hereunder shall bear interest, payable semiannually on June 15 and December 15 in each year, at the rate of 3 per cent per annum from December 15, 1922, to December 15, 1932, and thereafter at the rate of 3½ per cent per annum until the principal thereof shall have been paid.

4. *Method of payment.*—All bonds issued or to be issued hereunder shall be payable, as to both principal and interest, in United States gold coin of the present standard of value, or, at the option of Finland, upon not less than 30 days' advance notice to the United States, in any bonds of the United States issued after April 6, 1917, to be taken at par and accrued interest to the date

of payment hereunder: *Provided, however,* That Finland may at its option, upon not less than 90 days' advance notice to the United States, pay up to one-half of any interest accruing between December 15, 1922, and December 15, 1927, on the $9,000,000 principal amount of bonds first to be issued hereunder, in bonds of Finland dated and bearing interest from the respective dates when the interest to be paid thereby becomes due, with maturities arranged serially to fall on each December 15 in the succeeding years up to December 15, 1984, substantially in the manner provided for the original issue in paragraph 2 of this agreement, and substantially similar in other respects to the original issue of bonds under this agreement.

All payments, whether in cash or in bonds of the United States, to be made by Finland on account of the principal or interest of any bonds issued or to be issued hereunder and held by the United States, shall be made at the Treasury of the United States in Washington, or, at the option of the Secretary of the Treasury of the United States, at the Federal Reserve Bank of New York, and if in cash shall be made in funds immediately available on the date of payment, or if in bonds of the United States shall be in form acceptable to the Secretary of the Treasury of the United States under the general regulations of the Treasury Department governing transactions in United States bonds.

5. *Exemption from taxation.*—The principal and interest of all bonds issued or to be issued hereunder shall be paid without deduction for, and shall be exempt from, any and all taxes or other public dues, present or future, imposed by or under authority of Finland or any politi-

cal or local taxing authority within the Republic of Finland, whenever, so long as, and to the extent that beneficial ownership is in (*a*) the Government of the United States, (*b*) a person, firm, or association neither domiciled nor ordinarily resident in Finland, or (*c*) a corporation not organized under the laws of Finland.

6. *Payments before maturity.*—Finland may at its option, on any interest date or dates, upon not less than 90 days' advance notice to the United States, make advance payments in amounts of $1,000 or multiples thereof, on account of the principal of any bonds issued or to be issued hereunder and held by the United States. Any such advance payments shall first be applied to the principal of any bonds which shall have been issued hereunder on account of interest accruing between December 15, 1922, and December 15, 1927, and then to the principal of any other bonds issued or to be issued hereunder and held by the United States, as may be indicated by Finland at the time of payment.

7. *Exchange for marketable obligations.*—Finland will issue to the United States at any time, or from time to time, at the request of the Secretary of the Treasury of the United States, in exchange for any or all of the bonds issued or to be issued hereunder and held by the United States, definitive engraved bonds in form suitable for sale to the public, in such amounts and denominations as the Secretary of the Treasury of the United States may request, in bearer form, with provision for registration as to principal, and/or in fully registered form, and otherwise on the same terms and conditions, as to dates of issue and maturity, rate or rates of interest, exemption from taxation, payment in bonds of the United States

issued after April 6, 1917, and the like, as the bonds surrendered on such exchange. Finland will deliver definitive engraved bonds to the United States in accordance herewith within six months of receiving notice of any such request from the Secretary of the Treasury of the United States, and pending the delivery of the definitive engraved bonds will, at the request of the Secretary of the Treasury of the United States, deliver temporary bonds or interim receipts in form satisfactory to the Secretary of the Treasury of the United States within 30 days of the receipt of such request, all without expense to the United States. The United States, before offering any such bonds or interim receipts for sale in Finland, will first offer them to Finland for purchase at par and accrued interest, and Finland shall likewise have the option, in lieu of issuing any such bonds or interim receipts, to make advance redemption, at par and accrued interest, of a corresponding principal amount of bonds issued or to be issued hereunder and held by the United States. Finland agrees that the definitive engraved bonds called for by this paragraph shall contain all such provisions, and that it will cause to be promulgated all such rules, regulations, and orders as shall be deemed necessary or desirable by the Secretary of the Treasury of the United States in order to facilitate the sale of the bonds in the United States, in Finland, or elsewhere, and that if requested by the Secretary of the Treasury of the United States it will use its good offices to secure the listing of the bonds on the stock exchange in Helsingfors.

8. *Cancellation and surrender of demand obligations.*— Upon the execution of this agreement, the payment to the United States of cash in the sum of $9,315.27 as pro-

vided in paragraph 1 of this agreement, and the delivery to the United States of the $9,000,000 principal amount of bonds of Finland first to be issued hereunder, together with satisfactory evidence of authority for the execution of the agreement and the bonds on behalf of Finland by its envoy extraordinary and minister plenipotentiary at Washington, the United States will cancel and surrender to Finland, at the Treasury of the United States in Washington, the obligations of Finland in the principal amount of $8,281,926.17, described in the preamble to this agreement.

9. *Notices.*—Any notice, request, or consent under the hand of the Secretary of the Treasury of the United States shall be deemed and taken as the notice, request, or consent of the United States, and shall be sufficient if delivered at the legation of Finland at Washington or at the office of the minister of finance in Helsingfors; and any notice, request, or election from or by Finland shall be sufficient if delivered to the American Legation at Helsingfors or to the Secretary of the Treasury at the Treasury of the United States in Washington. The United States in its discretion may waive any notice required hereunder, but any such waiver shall be in writing and shall not extend to or affect any subsequent notice or impair any right of the United States to require notice hereunder.

10. *Compliance with legal requirements.*—Finland represents and agrees that the execution and delivery of this agreement and of the bonds issued or to be issued hereunder have in all respects been duly authorized and that all acts, conditions, and legal formalities which should have been completed prior to the making of this

agreement and the issuance of bonds hereunder have been completed as required by the laws of Finland and in conformity therewith.

11. *Counterparts.*—This agreement shall be executed in two counterparts, each of which shall have the force and effect of an original.

IN WITNESS WHEREOF, Finland has caused this agreement to be executed on its behalf by its envoy extraordinary and minister plenipotentiary at Washington, thereunto duly authorized, and the United States has likewise caused this agreement to be executed on its behalf by the Secretary of the Treasury, as chairman of the World War Foreign Debt Commission, with the approval of the President, all on the day and year first above written, subject, however, to the approval of Congress, pursuant to the act of Congress approved February 9, 1922, as amended by the act of Congress approved February 28, 1923, notice of which approval, when given by Congress, will be transmitted in due course by the Secretary of the Treasury of the United States to the legation of Finland at Washington.

THE GOVERNMENT OF THE REPUBLIC OF FINLAND,
[SEAL.]   L. ASTROM,
Envoy Extraordinary and Minister Plenipotentiary.

THE GOVERNMENT OF THE UNITED STATES OF AMERICA.
For the commission:
[SEAL.]   By A. W. MELLON,
    Secretary of the Treasury, and Chairman of the
            World War Foreign Debt Commission.
Approved:
    WARREN G. HARDING, *President.*

EXHIBIT A

(Form of bond)

THE GOVERNMENT OF THE REPUBLIC OF FINLAND.

Sixty-two year 3-3½ per cent gold bond, dated December 15, 1922—maturing December 15, $

No.

The Government of the Republic of Finland, hereinafter called Finland, for value received, promises to pay to the Government of the United States of America, hereinafter called the United States, or order, on the 15th day of December,   , the sum of   dollars ($), and to pay interest upon said principal sum semiannually on the fifteenth day of June and December in each year, at the rate of three per cent per annum from December 15, 1922, to December 15, 1932, and at the rate of three and one-half per cent per annum thereafter until the principal hereof shall have been paid. This bond is payable as to both principal and interest in gold coin of the United States of America of the present standard of value, or, at the option of Finland, upon not less than thirty days' advance notice to the United States, in any bonds of the United States issued after April 6, 1917, to be taken at par and accrued interest to the date of payment hereunder. This bond is payable as to both principal and interest without deduction for, and is exempt from, any and all taxes and other public dues, present or future, imposed by or under authority of Finland or any political or local taxing authority within the Republic of Finland, whenever, so long as, and to the extent that, beneficial ownership is in (a) the

Government of the United States, (b) a person, firm, or association neither domiciled nor ordinarily resident in Finland, or (c) a corporation not organized under the laws of Finland. This bond is payable as to both principal and interest at the Treasury of the United States in Washington, D. C., or, at the option of the Secretary of the Treasury of the United States, at the Federal Reserve Bank of New York.

This bond is issued under an agreement, dated May 1, 1923, between Finland and the United States, to which this bond is subject and to which reference is made for a further statement of its terms and conditions.

IN WITNESS WHEREOF, Finland has caused this bond to be executed in its behalf at the city of Washington, District of Columbia, by its envoy extraordinary and minister plenipotentiary at Washington, thereunto duly authorized.

THE GOVERNMENT OF THE REPUBLIC OF FINLAND.

By ——— ———,

Envoy Extraordinary and Minister Plenipotentiary.

Dated, DECEMBER 15, 1922.

(Back)

The following amounts have been paid upon the principal amount of this bond:

Date.   Amount paid.

B. SCHEDULE OF FINNISH PAYMENTS

Principal	Annual Interest Payments	Annual Principal Payments	Total Annual Payments	Year
$9,000,000	$ 270,000	$ 45,000	$ 315,000	1—1923
8,955,000	268,650	45,000	313,650	2—1924
8,910,000	267,300	47,000	314,300	3—1925
8,863,000	265,890	49,000	314,890	4—1926
8,814,000	264,420	50,000	314,420	5—1927
8,764,000	262,920	52,000	314,920	6—1928
8,712,000	261,360	53,000	314,360	7—1929
8,659,000	259,770	55,000	314,770	8—1930
8,604,000	258,120	55,000	313,120	9—1931
8,549,000	256,470	58,000	314,470	10—1932
8,491,000	297,185	62,000	359,185	11—1933
8,429,000	295,015	62,000	357,015	12—1934
8,367,000	292,845	65,000	357,845	13—1935
8,302,000	290,570	67,000	357,570	14—1936
8,235,000	288,225	69,000	357,225	15—1937
8,166,000	285,810	71,000	356,810	16—1938
8,095,000	283,325	74,000	357,325	17—1939
8,021,000	280,735	76,000	356,735	18—1940
7,945,000	278,075	79,000	357,075	19—1941
7,866,000	275,310	82,000	357,310	20—1942
7,784,000	272,440	84,000	356,440	21—1943
7,700,000	269,500	87,000	356,500	22—1944
7,613,000	266,455	90,000	356,455	23—1945
7,523,000	263,305	93,000	356,305	24—1946
7,430,000	260,050	96,000	356,050	25—1947
7,334,000	256,690	100,000	356,690	26—1948
7,234,000	253,190	103,000	356,190	27—1949
7,131,000	249,585	107,000	356,585	28—1950
7,024,000	245,840	110,000	355,840	29—1951
6,914,000	241,990	114,000	355,990	30—1952
6,800,000	238,000	118,000	356,000	31—1953
6,682,000	233,870	122,000	355,870	32—1954
6,560,000	229,600	126,000	355,600	33—1955
6,434,000	225,190	131,000	356,190	34—1956
6,303,000	220,605	136,000	356,605	35—1957
6,167,000	215,845	141,000	356,845	36—1958
6,026,000	210,910	146,000	356,910	37—1959
5,880,000	205,800	151,000	356,800	38—1960
5,729,000	200,515	156,000	356,515	39—1961
5,573,000	195,055	162,000	357,055	40—1962
5,411,000	189,385	167,000	356,385	41—1963
5,244,000	183,540	173,000	356,540	42—1964

B. Schedule of Finnish Payments—*Continued*

Principal	Annual Interest Payments	Annual Principal Payments	Total Annual Payments	Year
$5,071,000	$ 177,485	$ 179,000	$ 356,485	43—1965
4,892,000	171,220	185,000	356,220	44—1966
4,707,000	164,745	192,000	356,745	45—1967
4,515,000	158,025	199,000	357,025	46—1968
4,316,000	151,060	206,000	357,060	47—1969
4,110,000	143,850	213,000	356,850	48—1970
3,897,000	136,395	220,000	356,395	49—1971
3,677,000	128,695	228,000	356,695	50—1972
3,449,000	120,715	236,000	356,715	51—1973
3,213,000	112,455	244,000	356,455	52—1974
2,969,000	103,915	253,000	356,915	53—1975
2,716,000	95,060	262,000	357,060	54—1976
2,454,000	85,890	271,000	356,890	55—1977
2,183,000	76,405	280,000	356,405	56—1978
1,903,000	66,605	290,000	356,605	57—1979
1,613,000	56,455	301,000	357,455	58—1980
1,312,000	45,920	312,000	357,920	59—1981
1,000,000	35,000	322,000	357,000	60—1982
678,000	23,730	333,000	356,730	61—1983
345,000	12,075	345,000	357,075	62—1984
	$12,695,055	$9,000,000	$21,695,055	

V. DEBT SETTLEMENT WITH HUNGARY *

Agreement signed April 25, 1924. Approved on the part of the United States by Act of Congress of May 23, 1924. The Minister's authority was sufficient without ratification.

A. Agreement,

Made the 25th day of April, 1924, at the City of Washington, District of Columbia, between the GOVERNMENT OF THE KINGDOM OF HUNGARY, here-

* Official text as issued by the Treasury Department.

inafter called HUNGARY, party of the first part, and the GOVERNMENT OF THE UNITED STATES OF AMERICA, hereinafter called the UNITED STATES, party of the second part.

Whereas, Hungary is indebted to the United States as of December 15, 1923, upon an obligation maturing January 1, 1925, in the principal amount of $1,685,835.61, described as "Relief Series C of 1920," together with interest accrued and unpaid thereon; and

Whereas, Hungary desires to fund said indebtedness to the United States, both principal and interest, through the issue of bonds to the United States, and the United States is prepared to accept bonds from Hungary upon the terms and conditions hereinafter set forth:

Now, therefore, in consideration of the premises and of the mutual covenants herein contained, it is agreed as follows:

1. *Amount of Indebtedness.*—The amount of the indebtedness to be funded, after allowing for cash payments made or to be made by Hungary, is $1,939,000, which has been computed as follows:

Principal amount of the obligation to be funded..	$1,685,835.61
Interest accrued thereon from May 29, 1920, to December 15, 1923, at the rate of 4¼ per cent per annum	253,917.43
Total principal and interest, accrued and unpaid as of December 15, 1923...................	1,939,753.04
To be paid in cash by Hungary April 25, 1924..	753.04
Total indebtedness to be funded into bonds.......	1,939,000.00

2. *Repayment of Principal.*—In order to provide for the repayment of the indebtedness thus to be funded,

Hungary will issue to the United States at par, as of December 15, 1923, bonds of Hungary in the aggregate principal amount of $1,939,000, dated December 15, 1923, and maturing serially on each December 15 in the succeeding years for 62 years, in the amounts and on the several dates fixed in the following schedule: (see page 264).

Provided, however, that Hungary may at its option, upon not less than ninety days'. advance notice to the United States, postpone any payment falling due as hereinabove provided to any subsequent June 15 or December 15 not more than two years distant from its due date, but only on condition that in case Hungary shall at any time exercise this option as to any payment of principal, the payment falling due in the next succeeding year can not be postponed to any date more than one year distant from the date when it becomes due unless and until the payment previously postponed shall actually have been made, and the payment falling due in the second succeeding year can not be postponed at all unless and until the payment of principal due two years previous thereto shall actually have been made.

All bonds issued or to be issued hereunder to the United States shall be payable to the Government of the United States of America, or order, shall be issued in such denominations as may be requested by the Secretary of the Treasury of the United States, and shall be substantially in the form set forth in the exhibit hereto annexed and marked "Exhibit A." The $1,939,000 principal amount of bonds first to be issued hereunder shall be issued in 62 pieces, in denominations and with maturities corresponding to the annual payments of principal hereinabove set forth.

3. *Payment of Interest.*—All bonds issued or to be issued hereunder shall bear interest, payable semi-annually on June 15 and December 15 in each year, at the rate of 3 per cent per annum from December 15, 1923, to December 15, 1933, and thereafter at the rate of 3½ per cent per annum until the principal thereof shall have been paid.

4. *Method of Payment.*—All bonds issued or to be issued hereunder shall be payable, as to both principal and interest, in United States gold coin of the present standard value, or, at the option of Hungary, upon not less than thirty days' advance notice to the United States, in any obligations of the United States issued after April 6, 1917, to be taken at par and accrued interest to the date of payment hereunder: *Provided, however,* That Hungary may at its option, upon not less than ninety days' advance notice to the United States, pay up to one-half of any interest accruing between December 15, 1923, and December 15, 1928, on the $1,939,000 principal amount of bonds first to be issued hereunder, in bonds of Hungary dated and bearing interest from the respective dates when the interest to be paid thereby becomes due with maturities arranged serially to fall on each December 15 in the succeeding years up to December 15, 1985, substantially in the manner provided for the original issue in section 2 of this Agreement, and substantially similar in other respects to the original issue of bonds under this Agreement.

All payments, whether in cash or in obligations of the United States, to be made by Hungary on account of the principal or interest of any bonds issued or to be issued hereunder and held by the United States, shall be made at the Treasury of the United States in Washington, or, at the option of the Secretary of the Treasury of the United States, at the Federal Reserve Bank of New York, and if in cash shall be made in funds immediately available on the date of payment, or if in obligations of the United States shall be in form acceptable to the Secretary of the Treasury of the United States under the general regulations of the Treasury Department governing transactions in United States obligations.

5. *Exemption from Taxation.*—The principal and interest of all bonds issued or to be issued hereunder shall be paid without deduction for, and shall be exempt from, any and all taxes or other public dues, present or future, imposed by or under authority of Hungary or any political or local taxing authority within the Kingdom of Hungary, whenever, so long as, and to the extent that beneficial ownership is in (a) the Government of the United States, (b) a person, firm, or association neither domiciled nor ordinarily resident in Hungary, or (c) a corporation not organized under the laws of Hungary.

6. *Payments Before Maturity.*—Hungary may at its option, on any interest date or dates, upon not less than ninety days' advance notice to the United States, make advance payments in amounts of $1,000 or multiples thereof, on account of the principal of any bonds issued or to be issued hereunder and held by the United States. Any such advance payments shall first be applied to the principal of any bonds which shall have been issued hereunder on account of interest accruing between December 15, 1923, and December 15, 1928, and then to the

principal of any other bonds issued or to be issued hereunder and held by the United States, as may be indicated by Hungary at the time of the payment.

7. *Security.*—The payment of the principal and interest of all bonds issued or to be issued hereunder shall be secured in the same manner and to the same extent as the obligation of Hungary in the principal amount of $1,685,835.61, described in the preamble to this Agreement; that is to say, shall be "a first charge upon all the assets and revenues of Hungary and shall have a priority over costs of reparation under the Treaty of Trianon or under any treaty or agreement supplementary thereto, or under arrangements concluded between Hungary and the Allied and Associated Powers during the armistice signed on November 3, 1918"; *Provided, however,* That all or any part of such security may be released by the Secretary of the Treasury of the United States on such terms and conditions as he may deem necessary or appropriate in order that the United States may co-operate in any program whereby Hungary may be able to finance its immediate needs by the flotation of a loan for reconstruction purposes, if and when substantially all other creditor nations holding obligations of Hungary similar to that held by the United States and described in the preamble to this Agreement, to wit, Denmark, France, Great Britain, Holland, Norway, Sweden and Switzerland, shall release to a similar extent the security enjoyed by such obligations. The Secretary of the Treasury of the United States shall be authorized to decide when such action has been substantially taken.

8. *Exchange for Marketable Obligations.*—Hungary

will issue to the United States at any time, or from time to time, at the request of the Secretary of the Treasury of the United States, in exchange for any or all of the bonds issued or to be issued hereunder and held by the United States, definitive engraved bonds in form suitable for sale to the public, in such amounts and denominations as the Secretary of the Treasury of the United States may request, in bearer form, with provision for registration as to principal, and/or in fully registered form, and otherwise on the same terms and conditions as to dates of issue and maturity, rate or rates of interest, security, exemption from taxation, payment in obligations of the United States issued after April 6, 1917, and the like, as the bonds surrendered on such exchange. Hungary will deliver definitive engraved bonds to the United States in accordance herewith within six months of receiving notice of any such request from the Secretary of the Treasury of the United States, and pending the delivery of the definitive engraved bonds will, at the request of the Secretary of the Treasury of the United States, deliver temporary bonds or interim receipts in form satisfactory to the Secretary of the Treasury of the United States, within thirty days of the receipt of such request, all without expense to the United States.

The United States, before offering any such bonds or interim receipts for sale in Hungary, will first offer them to Hungary for purchase at par and accrued interest, and Hungary shall likewise have the option, in lieu of issuing any such bonds or interim receipts, to make advance redemption, at par and accrued interest, of a corresponding principal amount of bonds issued or to be issued hereunder and held by the United States. Hungary agrees that the definitive engraved bonds called for by this paragraph shall contain all such provisions, and that it will cause to be promulgated all such rules, regulations, and orders, as shall be deemed necessary or desirable by the Secretary of the Treasury of the United States in order to facilitate the sale of the bonds in the United States, in Hungary or elsewhere, and that if requested by the Secretary of the Treasury of the United States it will use its good offices to secure the listing of the bonds on the stock exchange in Budapest.

9. *Cancellation and Surrender of Relief Obligation.*— Upon the execution of this Agreement, the payment to the United States of cash in the sum of $753.04 as provided in paragraph 1 of this Agreement and the delivery to the United States of the $1,939,000 principal amount of bonds of Hungary first to be issued hereunder, together with satisfactory evidence of authority for the execution of the Agreement and the bonds on behalf of Hungary by its Envoy Extraordinary and Minister Plenipotentiary at Washington, and of appropriate action by the Reparation Commission so as to assure by its approval to the bonds of Hungary to be issued hereunder the same priority over reparations as that now enjoyed by the obligation of Hungary in the principal amount of $1,685,835.61 described in the preamble to this Agreement, the United States will cancel and surrender to Hungary, at the Treasury of the United States in Washington, the obligation of Hungary last described.

10. *Notices.*—Any notice, request, or consent under the hand of the Secretary of the Treasury of the United States shall be deemed and taken as the notice, request, or consent of the United States, and shall be sufficient if

delivered at the Legation of Hungary at Washington or at the office of the Minister of Finance in Budapest; and any notice, request, or election from or by Hungary shall be sufficient if delivered to the American Legation at Budapest or to the Secretary of the Treasury at the Treasury of the United States in Washington. The United States in its discretion may waive any notice required hereunder, but any such waiver shall be in writing and shall not extend to or affect any subsequent notice or impair any right of the United States to require notice hereunder.

11. *Compliance with Legal Requirements.*—Hungary represents and agrees that the execution and delivery of this Agreement and of the bonds issued or to be issued hereunder have in all respects been duly authorized and that all acts, conditions, and legal formalities which should have been completed prior to the making of this Agreement and the issuance of bonds hereunder have been completed as required by the laws of Hungary, and/or applicable treaties and in conformity therewith.

12. *Counterparts.*—This Agreement shall be executed in two counterparts, each of which shall have the force and effect of an original.

IN WITNESS WHEREOF, Hungary has caused this Agreement to be executed on its behalf by its Envoy Extraordinary and Minister Plenipotentiary at Washington, thereunto duly authorized, and the United States has likewise caused this Agreement to be executed on its behalf by the Secretary of the Treasury, as Chairman of the World War Foreign Debt Commission, with the approval of the President, all on the day and year first above written, subject, however, to the approval of Con-

gress, pursuant to the Act of Congress approved February
9, 1922, as amended by the Act of Congress approved
February 28, 1923, notice of which approval, when given
by Congress, will be transmitted in due course by the
Secretary of the Treasury of the United States to the
Legation of Hungary at Washington.

THE GOVERNMENT OF THE
KINGDOM OF HUNGARY,
By
(Sgd.) LASZLO SZECHENYI,
Envoy Extraordinary and Minister Plenipotentiary.

THE GOVERNMENT OF THE
UNITED STATES OF AMERICA,
For the Commission:
By
(Sgd.) A. W. MELLON
Secretary of the Treasury, and
Chairman of the World War Foreign Debt Commission.

Approved:
(Sgd.) CALVIN COOLIDGE,
President.

EXHIBIT A

(Form of Bond)

THE GOVERNMENT OF THE KINGDOM OF HUNGARY

Sixty-two year 3-3½ per cent Gold Bond
Dated December 15, 1923—maturing December 15,
$ No.

The Government of the Kingdom of Hungary, hereinafter called Hungary, for value received, promises to

pay to the Government of the United States of America, hereinafter called the United States, or order, on the 15th day of December,   , the sum of   Dollars ($), and to pay interest upon said principal sum semi-annually on the fifteenth day of June and December in each year, at the rate of three per cent per annum from December 15, 1923, to December 15, 1933, and at the rate of three and one-half per cent per annum thereafter until the principal hereof shall have been paid. This bond is payable as to both principal and interest in gold coin of the United States of America of the present standard of value, or, at the option of Hungary, upon not less than thirty days' advance notice to the United States, in any obligations of the United States issued after April 6, 1917, to be taken at par and accrued interest to the date of payment hereunder. This bond is payable as to both principal and interest without deduction for, and is exempt from, any and all taxes and other public dues present or future, imposed by or under authority of Hungary or any political or local taxing authority within the Kingdom of Hungary, whenever, so long as, and to the extent that, beneficial ownership is in (a) the Government of the United States, (b) a person, firm, or association neither domiciled nor ordinarily resident in Hungary, or (c) a corporation not organized under the laws of Hungary. This bond is payable as to both principal and interest at the Treasury of the United States in Washington, D. C., or, at the option of the Secretary of the Treasury of the United States, at the Federal Reserve Bank of New York.

This bond is issued under an Agreement, dated April 25, 1924, between Hungary and the United States, to which this bond is subject and to which reference is made for a further statement of its terms and conditions.

The payment of the principal and interest on this bond is secured in the same manner and to the same extent as the obligation of Hungary in the principal amount of $1,685,835.61 described in the preamble to said Agreement, subject to release in whole or in part by the Secretary of the Treasury of the United States under authority conferred by Section 7 of said Agreement.

IN WITNESS WHEREOF, Hungary has caused this bond to be executed in its behalf at the City of Washington, District of Columbia, by its Envoy Extraordinary and Minister Plenipotentiary at Washington, thereunto duly authorized.

THE GOVERNMENT OF THE KINGDOM OF HUNGARY:

By ——— ———

Envoy Extraordinary and Minister Plenipotentiary.

Dated, December 15, 1923.

(Back)

The following amounts have been paid upon the principal amount of this bond:

Date.   Amount paid.

B. Schedule of Hungarian Payments

Principal	Annual Interest Payments	Annual Principal Payments	Total Annual Payments	Year
$1,939,000	$ 58,170	$ 9,600	$ 67,770	1—1924
1,929,400	57,882	9,800	67,682	2—1925
1,919,600	57,588	10,000	67,588	3—1926
1,909,600	57,288	10,200	67,488	4—1927
1,899,400	56,982	10,400	67,382	5—1928
1,889,000	56,670	11,000	67,670	6—1929
1,878,000	56,340	11,500	67,840	7—1930
1,866,500	55,995	12,000	67,995	8—1931
1,854,500	55,635	12,000	67,635	9—1932
1,842,500	55,275	12,500	67,775	10—1933
1,830,000	64,050	12,500	76,550	11—1934
1,817,500	63,612.50	13,000	76,612.50	12—1935
1,804,500	63,157.50	13,500	76,657.50	13—1936
1,791,000	62,685	13,500	76,185	14—1937
1,777,500	62,212.50	14,000	76,212.50	15—1938
1,763,500	61,722.50	14,500	76,222.50	16—1939
1,749,000	61,215	15,000	76,215	17—1940
1,734,000	60,690	15,500	76,190	18—1941
1,718,500	60,147.50	16,000	76,147.50	19—1942
1,702,500	59,587.50	17,000	76,587.50	20—1943
1,685,500	58,992.50	17,500	76,492.50	21—1944
1,668,000	58,380	18,000	76,380	22—1945
1,650,000	57,750	19,000	76,750	23—1946
1,631,000	57,085	19,500	76,585	24—1947
1,611,500	56,402.50	20,500	76,902.50	25—1948
1,591,000	55,685	21,000	76,685	26—1949
1,570,000	54,950	22,000	76,950	27—1950
1,548,000	54,180	22,500	76,680	28—1951
1,525,500	53,392.50	23,500	76,892.50	29—1952
1,502,000	52,570	24,000	76,570	30—1953
1,478,000	51,730	25,000	76,730	31—1954
1,453,000	50,855	26,000	76,855	32—1955
1,427,000	49,945	27,000	76,945	33—1956
1,400,000	49,000	27,500	76,500	34—1957
1,372,500	48,037.50	28,500	76,537.50	35—1958
1,344,000	47,040	29,000	76,040	36—1959
1,315,000	46,025	30,000	76,025	37—1960
1,285,000	44,975	32,000	76,975	38—1961
1,253,000	43,855	33,000	76,855	39—1962
1,220,000	42,700	35,000	77,700	40—1963
1,185,000	41,475	36,000	77,475	41—1964
1,149,000	40,215	38,000	78,215	42—1965

B. Schedule of Hungarian Payments—*Continued*

Principal	Annual Interest Payments	Annual Principal Payments	Total Annual Payments	Year
$1,111,000	$ 38,885	$ 40,000	$ 78,885	43—1966
1,071,000	37,485	41,000	78,485	44—1967
1,030,000	36,050	42,000	78,050	45—1968
988,000	34,580	44,000	78,580	46—1969
944,000	33,040	45,000	78,040	47—1970
899,000	31,465	47,000	78,465	48—1971
852,000	29,820	48,000	77,820	49—1972
804,000	28,140	50,000	78,140	50—1973
754,000	26,390	51,000	77,390	51—1974
703,000	24,605	53,000	77,605	52—1975
650,000	22,750	55,000	77,750	53—1976
595,000	20,825	57,000	77,825	54—1977
538,000	18,830	59,000	77,830	55—1978
479,000	16,765	62,000	78,765	56—1979
417,000	14.595	64,000	78,595	57—1980
353,000	12,355	66,000	78,355	58—1981
287,000	10,045	68,000	78,045	59—1982
219,000	7,665	71,000	78,665	60—1983
148,000	5,180	73,000	78,180	61—1984
75,000	2,625	75,000	77,625	62—1985
	$2,754,240	$1,939,000	$4,693,240	

VI. DEBT SETTLEMENT WITH LITHUANIA *

Agreement signed September 22, 1924. Approved on the part of the United States by the Act of Congress of December 22, 1924. Approved by Lithuanian Cabinet of Ministers September 26, 1925.

A. AGREEMENT,

Made the twenty-second day of September, 1924, at the City of Washington, District of Columbia, between the GOVERNMENT OF THE REPUBLIC OF

* Official text as issued by the Treasury Department.

LITHUANIA, hereinafter called LITHUANIA, party of the first part, and the GOVERNMENT OF THE UNITED STATES OF AMERICA, hereinafter called the UNITED STATES, party of the second part.

Whereas, Lithuania is indebted to the United States as of June 15, 1924, upon obligations maturing June 30, 1921 and 1922, in the aggregate principal amount of $4,981,628.03, together with interest accrued and unpaid thereon; and

Whereas, Lithuania desires to fund said indebtedness to the United States, both principal and interest, through the issue of bonds to the United States, and the United States is prepared to accept bonds from Lithuania upon the terms and conditions hereinafter set forth:

Now, therefore, in consideration of the premises and of the mutual covenants herein contained, it is agreed as follows:

1. *Amount of Indebtedness.*—The amount of the indebtedness to be funded, after allowing for cash payments made or to be made by Lithuania, is $6,030,000, which has been computed as follows:

Principal amount of obligations to be funded.....	$4,981,628.03
Interest accrued thereon from June 30, 1919 to June 15, 1924, at the rate of 4¼ per cent per annum	1,049,918.94
Total principal and interest accrued and unpaid as of June 15, 1924......................	6,031,546.97
To be paid in cash by Lithuania, September 22, 1924	1,546.97
Total indebtedness to be funded into bonds.......	6,030,000.00

2. *Repayment of Principal.*—In order to provide for the repayment of the indebtedness thus to be funded,

Lithuania will issue to the United States at par, as of June 15, 1924, bonds of Lithuania in the aggregate principal amount of $6,030,000, dated June 15, 1924, and maturing serially on each June 15 in the succeeding years for 62 years, in the amounts and on the several dates fixed in the following schedules: (see p. 276).

Provided, however, That Lithuania may at its option, upon not less than ninety days' advance notice to the United States, postpone any payment falling due as hereinabove provided to any subsequent June 15 or December 15 not more than two years distant from its due date, but only on condition that in case Lithuania shall at any time exercise this option as to any payment of principal, the payment falling due in the next succeeding year can not be postponed to any date more than one year distant from the date when it becomes due unless and until the payment previously postponed shall actually have been made, and the payment falling due in the second succeeding year can not be postponed at all unless and until the payment of principal due two years previous thereto shall actually have been made.

All bonds issued or to be issued hereunder to the United States shall be payable to the Government of the United States of America, or order, shall be issued in such denominations as may be requested by the Secretary of the Treasury of the United States, and shall be substantially in the form set forth in the exhibit hereto annexed and marked "Exhibit A." The $6,030,000 principal amount of bonds first to be issued hereunder shall be issued in 62 pieces, in denominations and with maturities corresponding to the annual payments of principal hereinabove set forth.

3. *Payment of Interest.*—All bonds issued or to be issued hereunder shall bear interest, payable semi-annually on June 15 and December 15 in each year, at the rate of 3 per cent per annum from June 15, 1924, to June 15, 1934, and thereafter at the rate of 3½ per cent per annum until the principal thereof shall have been paid.

4. *Method of Payment.*—All bonds issued or to be issued hereunder shall be payable, as to both principal and interest, in United States gold coin of the present standard of value, or, at the option of Lithuania, upon not less than thirty days' advance notice to the United States, in any obligations of the United States issued after April 6, 1917, to be taken at par and accrued interest to the date of payment hereunder: *Provided, however,* That Lithuania may at its option, upon not less than ninety days' advance notice to the United States, pay up to one-half of any interest accruing between June 15, 1924, and June 15, 1929, on the $6,030,000 principal amount of bonds first to be issued hereunder, in bonds of Lithuania dated and bearing interest from the respective dates when the interest to be paid thereby becomes due, with maturities arranged serially to fall on each June 15 in the succeeding years up to June 15, 1986, substantially in the manner provided for the original issue in paragraph 2 of this Agreement, and substantially similar in other respects to the original issue of bonds under this Agreement.

All payments, whether in cash or in obligations of the United States, to be made by Lithuania on account of the principal or interest of any bonds issued or to be issued hereunder and held by the United States, shall be made at the 'Treasury of the United States in Washington, or, at the option of the Secretary of the Treasury of the United States, at the Federal Reserve Bank of New York, and if in cash shall be made in funds immediately available on the date of payment, or if in obligations of the United States shall be in form acceptable to the Secretary of the Treasury of the United States under the general regulations of the Treasury Department governing transactions in United States obligations.

5. *Exemption from Taxation.*—The principal and interest of all bonds issued or to be issued hereunder shall be paid without deduction for, and shall be exempt from, any and all taxes or other public dues, present or future, imposed by or under authority of Lithuania or any political or local taxing authority within the Republic of Lithuania, whenever, so long as, and to the extent that beneficial ownership is in (a) the Government of the United States, (b) a person, firm, or association neither domiciled nor ordinarily resident in Lithuania, or (c) a corporation not organized under the laws of Lithuania.

6. *Payments before Maturity.*—Lithuania may at its option, on any interest date or dates, upon not less than ninety days' advance notice to the United States, make advance payments in amounts of $1,000 or multiples thereof, on account of the principal of any bonds issued or to be issued hereunder and held by the United States. Any such advance payments shall first be applied to the principal of any bonds which shall have been issued hereunder on account of interest accruing between June 15, 1924, and June 15, 1929, and then to the principal of any other bonds issued or to be issued hereunder and

held by the United States, as may be indicated by Lithuania at the time of the payment.

7. *Exchange for Marketable Obligations.*—Lithuania will issue to the United States at any time, or from time to time, at the request of the Secretary of the Treasury of the United States, in exchange for any or all of the bonds issued or to be issued hereunder and held by the United States, definitive engraved bonds in form suitable for sale to the public, in such amounts and denominations as the Secretary of the Treasury of the United States may request in bearer form, with provision for registration as to principal, and/or in fully registered form, and otherwise on the same terms and conditions, as to dates of issue and maturity, rate or rates of interest, exemption from taxation, payment in obligations of the United States issued after April 6, 1917, and the like, as the bonds surrendered on such exchange. Lithuania will deliver definitive engraved bonds to the United States in accordance herewith within six months of receiving notice of any such request from the Secretary of the Treasury of the United States, and pending the delivery of the definitive engraved bonds will, at the request of the Secretary of the Treasury of the United States, deliver temporary bonds or interim receipts in form satisfactory to the Secretary of the Treasury of the United States within thirty days of the receipt of such request, all without expense to the United States. The United States, before offering any such bonds or interim receipts for sale in Lithuania, will first offer them to Lithuania for purchase at par and accrued interest, and Lithuania shall likewise have the option, in lieu of issuing any such bonds or interim receipts, to make advance

redemption, at par and accrued interest, of a corresponding principal amount of bonds issued or to be issued hereunder and held by the United States. Lithuania agrees that the definitive engraved bonds called for by this paragraph shall contain all such provisions, and that it will cause to be promulgated all such rules, regulations, and orders, as shall be deemed necessary or desirable by the Secretary of the Treasury of the United States in order to facilitate the sale of the bonds in the United States, in Lithuania or elsewhere, and that if requested by the Secretary of the Treasury of the United States it will use its good offices to secure the listing of the bonds on the stock exchange in Kaunas.

8. *Cancellation and Surrender of Obligations.*—Upon the execution of this Agreement, the payment to the United States of cash in the sum of $1,546.97 as provided in paragraph 1 of this Agreement and the delivery to the United States of the $6,030,000, principal amount of bonds of Lithuania first to be issued hereunder, together with satisfactory evidence of authority for the execution of the Agreement and the bonds on behalf of Lithuania by its Envoy Extraordinary and Minister Plenipotentiary at Washington, the United States will cancel and surrender to Lithuania, at the Treasury of the United States in Washington, the obligations of Lithuania in the principal amount of $4,981,628.03, described in the preamble to this Agreement.

9. *Notices.*—Any notice, request, or consent under the hand of the Secretary of the Treasury of the United States shall be deemed and taken as the notice, request, or consent of the United States, and shall be sufficient if delivered at the Legation of Lithuania at Washington or

at the office of the Minister of Finance in Kaunas; and any notice, request, or election from or by Lithuania shall be sufficient if delivered to the American Minister accredited to Lithuania or to the Secretary of the Treasury of the United States in Washington. The United States in its discretion may waive any notice required hereunder, but any such waiver shall be in writing and shall not extend to or affect any subsequent notice or impair any right of the United States to require notice hereunder.

10. *Compliance with Legal Requirements.*—Lithuania represents and agrees that subject to the ratification of this Agreement by the Seimas of Lithuania, the execution and delivery of this Agreement and of the bonds issued or to be issued hereunder have in all respects been duly authorized and that subject to such ratification all acts, conditions, and legal formalities which should have been completed prior to the making of this Agreement and the issuance of bonds hereunder have been completed as required by the laws of Lithuania and in conformity therewith.

11. *Counterparts.*—This Agreement shall be executed in two counterparts, each of which shall have the force and effect of an original.

IN WITNESS WHEREOF, Lithuania has caused this Agreement to be executed on its behalf by its Envoy Extraordinary and Minister Plenipotentiary at Washington, thereunto duly authorized, and the United States has likewise caused this Agreement to be executed on its behalf by the Secretary of the Treasury, as Chairman of the World War Foreign Debt Commission, with the approval of the President, all on the day and year first above written, subject, however, to the approval, respectively, of the Seimas of Lithuania and of the Congress of the United States, pursuant to the Act of Congress approved February 9, 1922, as amended by the Act of Congress approved February 28, 1923, notice of which approval, when given, will be transmitted, respectively, to the United States and to Lithuania in the manner provided in paragraph 9 of this Agreement.

THE GOVERNMENT OF THE
REPUBLIC OF LITHUANIA,

[SEAL]   By K. BIZAUSKAS,
Envoy Extraordinary and Minister Plenipotentiary.

THE GOVERNMENT OF THE
UNITED STATES OF AMERICA,

For the Commission:

[SEAL]   By A. W. MELLON,
Secretary of the Treasury, and
Chairman of the World War Foreign Debt Commission.

Approved:

CALVIN COOLIDGE,
President.

————

EXHIBIT A

(Form of Bond)

THE GOVERNMENT OF THE REPUBLIC OF LITHUANIA

Sixty-two year 3-3½ per cent Gold Bond .
Dated June 15, 1924—Maturing June 15,

$ No.

The Government of the Republic of Lithuania, hereinafter called Lithuania, for value received, promises to pay to the Government of the United States of America, hereinafter called the United States, or order, on the 15th day of June,   , the sum of ·   Dollars ($), and to pay interest upon said principal sum semiannually on the fifteenth day of June and December in each year, at the rate of three per cent per annum from June 15, 1924, to June 15, 1934, and at the rate of three and one-half per cent per annum thereafter until the principal hereof shall have been paid.   This bond is payable as to both principal and interest in gold coin of the United States of America of the present standard of value, or, at the option of Lithuania, upon not less than thirty days' advance notice to the United States, in any obligations of the United States issued after April 6, 1917, to be taken at par and accrued interest to the date of payment hereunder.   This bond is payable as to both principal and interest without deduction for, and is exempt from, any and all taxes and other public dues, present or future, imposed by or under authority of Lithuania or any political or local taxing authority within the Republic of Lithuania, whenever, so long as, and to the extent that, beneficial ownership is in (a) the Government of the United States, (b) a person, firm, or association neither domiciled nor ordinarily resident in Lithuania, or (c) a corporation not organized under the laws of Lithuania.   This bond is payable as to both principal and interest at the Treasury of the United States in Washington, D. C., or, at the option of the Secretary of the Treasury of the United States, at the Federal Reserve Bank of New York.

This bond is issued under an Agreement, dated September 22, 1924, between Lithuania and the United States, to which this bond is subject and to which reference is made for a further statement of its terms and conditions.

IN WITNESS WHEREOF, Lithuania has caused this bond to be executed in its behalf at the City of Washington, District of Columbia, by its Envoy Extraordinary and Minister Plenipotentiary at Washington, thereunto duly authorized.

The Government of the Republic of Lithuania:

By

Envoy Extraordinary and Minister Plenipotentiary.

Dated, June 15, 1924.

(Back)

The following amounts have been paid upon the principal amount of this bond:

Date.   Amount paid.

THE WHITE HOUSE,
Washington, September 22, 1924.

MY DEAR MR. SECRETARY: I have signed the two copies of the debt funding agreement between Lithuania and the Government of the United States, which accompanied your letter of September 22d, and am returning them to you, herewith.

Very truly yours,

CALVIN COOLIDGE.

Hon. ANDREW W. MELLON,
Secretary of the Treasury,
Washington, D. C.

B. SCHEDULE OF LITHUANIAN PAYMENTS

Principal	Annual Interest Payments	Annual Principal Payments	Total Annual Payments	Year
$6,030,000	$ 180,900	$ 30,000	$ 210,900	1—1925
6,000,000	180,000	30,000	210,000	2—1926
5,970,000	179,100	31,000	210,100	3—1927
5,939,000	178,170	32,000	210,170	4—1928
5,907,000	177,210	33,000	210,210	5—1929
5,874,000	176,220	34,000	210,220	6—1930
5,840,000	175,200	35,000	210,200	7—1931
5,805,000	174,150	36,000	210,150	8—1932
5,769,000	173,070	37,000	210,070	9—1933
5,732,000	171,960	39,000	210,960	10—1934
5,693,000	199,255	40,000	239,255	11—1935
5,653,000	197,855	42,000	239,855	12—1936
5,611,000	196,385	43,000	239,385	13—1937
5,568,000	194,880	45,000	239,880	14—1938
5,523,000	193,305	46,000	239,305	15—1939
5,477,000	191,695	48,000	239,695	16—1940
5,429,000	190,015	49,000	239,015	17—1941
5,380,000	188,300	51,000	239,300	18—1942
5,329,000	186,515	53,000	239,515	19—1943
5,276,000	184,660	55,000	239,660	20—1944
5,221,000	182,735	57,000	239,735	21—1945
5,164,000	180,740	59,000	239,740	22—1946
5,105,000	178,675	61,000	239,675	23—1947
5,044,000	176,540	63,000	239,540	24—1948
4,981,000	174,335	65,000	239,335	25—1949
4,916,000	172,060	67,000	239,060	26—1950
4,849,000	169,715	69,000	238,715	27—1951
4,780,000	167,300	72,000	239,300	28—1952
4,708,000	164,780	75,000	239,780	29—1953
4,633,000	162,155	77,000	239,155	30—1954
4,556,000	159,460	80,000	239,460	31—1955
4,476,000	156,660	83,000	239,660	32—1956
4,393,000	153,755	86,000	239,755	33—1957
4,307,000	150,745	89,000	239,745	34—1958
4,218,000	147,630	92,000	239,630	35—1959
4,126,000	144,410	95,000	239,410	36—1960
4,031,000	141,085	98,000	239,085	37—1961
3,933,000	137,655	102,000	239,655	38—1962
3,831,000	134,085	105,000	239,085	39—1963
3,726,000	130,410	109,000	239,410	40—1964
3,617,000	126,595	112,000	238,595	41—1965
3,505,000	122,675	116,000	238,675	42—1966

B. Schedule of Lithuanian Payments—*Continued*

Principal	Annual Interest Payments	Annual Principal Payments	Total Annual Payments	Year
$3,389,000	$ 118,615	$ 120,000	$ 238,615	43—1967
3,269,000	114,415	124,000	238,415	44—1968
3,145,000	110,075	128,000	238,075	45—1969
3,017,000	105,595	133,000	238,595	46—1970
2,884,000	100,940	138,000	238,940	47—1971
2,746,000	96,110	143,000	239,110	48—1972
2,603,000	91,105	148,000	239,105	49—1973
2,455,000	85,925	153,000	238,925	50—1974
2,302,000	80,570	158,000	238,570	51—1975
2,144,000	75,040	163,000	238,040	52—1976
1,981,000	69,335	169,000	238,335	53—1977
1,812,000	63,420	175,000	238,420	54—1978
1,637,000	57,295	181,000	238,295	55—1979
1,456,000	50,960	188,000	238,960	56—1980
1,268,000	44,380	194,000	238,380	57—1981
1,074,000	37,590	201,000	238,590	58—1982
873,000	30,555	208,000	238,555	59—1983
665,000	23,275	215,000	238,275	60—1984
450,000	15,750	223,000	238,750	61—1985
227,000	7,945	227,000	234,945	62—1986
	$8,501,940	$6,030,000	$14,531,940	

VII.   DEBT SETTLEMENT WITH POLAND *

Agreement signed November 14, 1924. Approved on the part of the United States by the Act of Congress of December 22, 1924. Approved by the Polish Diet January 17, 1925.

A.   Agreement,

Made the fourteenth day of November, 1924, at the City of Washington, District of Columbia, between the GOVERNMENT OF THE REPUBLIC OF

* Official text as issued by the Treasury Department.

POLAND, hereinafter called POLAND, party of the first part, and the GOVERNMENT OF THE UNITED STATES OF AMERICA, hereinafter called the UNITED STATES, party of the second part.

Whereas Poland is indebted to the United States as of December 15, 1922, upon obligations in the aggregate principal amount of $159,666,972.39, together with interest accrued and unpaid thereon; and

Whereas, Poland desires to fund said indebtedness to the United States, both principal and interest, through the issue of bonds to the United States, and the United States is prepared to accept bonds from Poland upon the terms and conditions hereinafter set forth:

Now, therefore, in consideration of the premises and of the mutual covenants herein contained, it is agreed as follows:

1. *Amount of Indebtedness.*—The amount of the indebtedness to be funded, after allowing for cash payments made or to be made by Poland, is $178,560,000, which has been computed as follows:

Principal amount of obligations to be funded....	$159,666,972.39
Interest accrued and unpaid thereon to December 15, 1922, at the rate of 4¼ per cent per annum	18,898,053.60
Total principal and interest accrued and unpaid as of December 15, 1922..............	178,565,025.99
To be paid in cash by Poland November 14, 1924	5,025.99
Total indebtedness to be funded into bonds......	178,560,000.00

2. *Repayment of Principal.*—In order to provide for the repayment of the indebtedness thus to be funded, Poland will issue to the United States at par, as of De-

cember 15, 1922, bonds of Poland in the aggregate principal amount of $178,560,000, dated December 15, 1922, and maturing serially on each December 15 in the succeeding years for 62 years, in the amounts and on the several dates fixed in the following schedule: (see p. 288).

Provided, however, That Poland, at its option, upon not less than ninety days' advance notice to the United States, may postpone any payment falling due as hereinabove provided, except those falling due on or before December 15, 1929, hereinafter referred to in paragraph 4 of this Agreement, to any subsequent June 15 or December 15 not more than two years distant from its due date, but only on condition that in case Poland shall at any time exercise this option as to any payment of principal, the payment falling due in the next succeeding year can not be postponed to any date more than one year distant from the date when it becomes due unless and until the payment previously postponed shall actually have been made, and the payment falling due in the second succeeding year can not be postponed at all unless and until the payment of principal due two years previous thereto shall actually have been made.

All bonds issued or to be issued hereunder to the United States shall be payable to the Government of the United States of America, or order, shall be issued in such denominations as may be requested by the Secretary of the Treasury of the United States, and shall be substantially in the form set forth in the exhibit hereto annexed and marked "Exhibit A." The $178,560,000 principal amount of bonds first to be issued hereunder shall be issued in 62 pieces, in denominations and with maturities corresponding to the annual payments of principal hereinabove set forth.

3. *Payment of Interest.*—All bonds issued or to be issued hereunder shall bear interest, payable semi-annually on June 15 and December 15 in. each year, at the rate of 3 per cent per annum from December 15, 1922, to December 15, 1932, and thereafter at the rate of 3½ per cent per annum until the principal thereof shall have been paid.

4. *Method of Payment.*—All bonds issued or to be issued hereunder shall be payable, as to both principal and interest, in United States gold coin of the present standard of value, or, at the option of Poland, upon not less than thirty days' advance notice to the United States, in any obligations of the United States issued after April 6, 1917, to be taken at par and accrued interest to the date of payments hereunder: *Provided, however*, that with reference to the payments on account of principal and/or interest falling due hereunder on or before December 15, 1929, Poland, at its option, may pay the following amounts on the dates specified:

June 15, 1925........	$ 500,000	June 15, 1928	$ 1,250,000
December 15, 1925 ..	500,000	December 15, 1928 ..	1,250,000
June 15, 1926	750,000	June 15, 1929	1,500,000
December 15, 1926 ..	750,000	December 15, 1929 ..	1,500,000
June 15, 1927	1,000,000		
December 15, 1927..	1,000,000	Total	$10,000,000

and the balance, including interest on all overdue payments at the rate of 3 per cent per annum from their respective due dates, in bonds of Poland dated December 15, 1929, bearing interest at the rate of 3 per cent per annum from December 15, 1929, to December 15, 1932, and thereafter at the rate of 3½ per cent per annum until the principal thereof shall have been paid, such bonds to mature serially on December 15 of each year up to and including December 15, 1984, substantially in the manner provided in paragraph 2 of this Agreement, and to be substantially similar in other respects to the bonds first to be issued hereunder.

All payments, whether in cash or in obligations of the United States, to be made by Poland on account of the principal or interest of any bonds issued or to be issued hereunder and held by the United States, shall be made at the Treasury of the United States in Washington, or, at the option of the Secretary of the Treasury of the United States, at the Federal Reserve Bank of New York, and if in cash shall be made in funds immediately available on the date of payment, or if in obligations of the United States shall be in form acceptable to the Secretary of the Treasury of the United States under the general regulations of the Treasury Department governing transactions in United States obligations.

5. *Exemption from Taxation.*—The principal and interest of all bonds issued or to be issued hereunder shall be paid without deduction for, and shall be exempt from, any and all taxes or other public dues, present or future, imposed by or under authority of Poland or any political or local taxing authority within the Republic of Poland, whenever, so long as, and to the extent that beneficial ownership is in (*a*) the Government of the United States,. (*b*) a person, firm, or association neither domiciled nor ordinarily resident in Poland, or (*c*) a corporation not organized under the laws of Poland.

6. *Payments before Maturity.*—Poland, at its option,

on any interest date or dates, upon not less than ninety days' advance notice to the United States, may make advance payments in amounts of $1,000 or multiples thereof, on account of the principal of any bonds issued or to be issued hereunder and held by the United States. Any such advance payments shall first be applied to the principal of any bonds which shall have been issued hereunder on account of principal and/or interest accruing between December 15, 1922, and December 15, 1929, and then to the principal of any other bonds issued hereunder and held by the United States, as may be indicated by Poland at the time of the payment.

7. *Exchange for Marketable Obligations.*—Poland will issue to the United States at any time, or from time to time, at the request of the Secretary of the Treasury of the United States, in exchange for any or all of the bonds issued or to be issued hereunder and held by the United States, definitive engraved bonds in form suitable for sale to the public, in such amounts and denominations as the Secretary of the Treasury of the United States may request, in bearer form, with provision for registration as to principal, and/or in fully registered form, and otherwise on the same terms and conditions, as to dates of issue and maturity, rate or rates of interest, exemption from taxation, payment in obligations of the United States issued after April 6, 1917, and the like, as the bonds surrendered on such exchange. Poland will deliver definitive engraved bonds to the United States in accordance herewith within six months of receiving notice of any such request from the Secretary of the Treasury of the United States, and pending the delivery of the definitive engraved bonds will deliver, at the re-

quest of the Secretary of the Treasury of the United States, temporary bonds or interim receipts in form satisfactory to the Secretary of the Treasury of the United States within thirty days of the receipt of such request, all without expense to the United States. The United States, before offering any such bonds or interim receipts for sale in Poland, will first offer them to Poland for purchase at par and accrued interest, and Poland shall likewise have the option, in lieu of issuing any such bonds or interim receipts, to make advance redemption, at par and accrued interest, of a corresponding principal amount of bonds issued or to be issued hereunder and held by the United States. Poland agrees that the definitive engraved bonds called for by this paragraph shall contain all such provisions, and that it will cause to be promulgated all such rules, regulations, and orders, as shall be deemed necessary or desirable by the Secretary of the Treasury of the United States in order to facilitate the sale of the bonds in the United States, in Poland or elsewhere, and that if requested by the Secretary of the Treasury of the United States, it will use its good offices to secure the listing of the bonds on the stock exchange in Warsaw.

8. *Cancellation and Surrender of Obligations.*—Upon the execution of this Agreement, the payment to the United States of cash in the sum of $5,025.99 as provided in paragraph 1 of this Agreement and the delivery to the United States of the $178,560 principal amount of bonds of Poland first to be issued hereunder, together with satisfactory evidence of authority for the execution of the Agreement and the bonds on behalf of Poland by its Envoy Extraordinary and Minister Plenipotentiary

at Washington, the United States will cancel and surrender to Poland, at the Treasury of the United States in Washington, the obligations of Poland in the principal amount of $159,666,972.39, described in the preamble to this Agreement.

9. *Notices.*—Any notice, request, or consent under the hand of the Secretary of the Treasury of the United States, shall be deemed and taken as the notice, request, or consent of the United States, and shall be sufficient if delivered at the Legation of Poland at Washington or at the office of the Minister of Finance in Warsaw; and any notice, request, or election from or by Poland shall be sufficient if delivered to the American Legation at Warsaw or to the Secretary of the Treasury at the Treasury of the United States in Washington. The United States in its discretion may waive any notice required hereunder, but any such waiver shall be in writing and shall not extend to or affect any subsequent notice or impair any right of the United States to require notice hereunder.

10. *Compliance with Legal Requirements.*—Poland represents and agrees that the execution and delivery of this Agreement and of the bonds issued or to be issued hereunder have in all respects been duly authorized and that all acts, conditions, and legal formalities which should have been completed prior to the making of this Agreement and the issuance of bonds hereunder have been completed as required by the laws of Poland and in conformity therewith.

11. *Counterparts.*—This Agreement shall be executed in two counterparts, each of which shall have the force and effect of an original.

IN WITNESS WHEREOF, Poland has caused this Agreement to be executed on its behalf by its Envoy Extraordinary and Minister Plenipotentiary at Washington, thereunto duly authorized, and the United States has likewise caused this Agreement to be executed on its behalf by the Secretary of the Treasury, as Chairman of the World War Foreign Debt Commission, with the approval of the President, all on the day and year first above written, subject, however, to the approval of Congress, pursuant to the Act of Congress approved February 9, 1922, as amended by the Act of Congress approved February 28, 1923, notice of which approval, when given by Congress, will be transmitted in due course by the Secretary of the Treasury of the United States to the Legation of Poland at Washington.

THE GOVERNMENT OF THE
REPUBLIC OF POLAND,

By WLADYSLAW WRÓBLEWSKI,
Envoy Extraordinary and
Minister Plenipotentiary.

[SEAL.]   THE GOVERNMENT OF THE
UNITED STATES OF AMERICA,

For the Commission:

[SEAL.]   By A. W. MELLON,
Secretary of the Treasury, and
Chairman of the World War
Foreign Debt Commission.

Approved:

CALVIN COOLIDGE,
President.

EXHIBIT A

(Form of bond)

THE GOVERNMENT OF THE REPUBLIC OF POLAND

Sixty-two year 3-3½ per cent Gold Bond

Dated December 15, 1922—maturing December 15,

$ No.

The Government of the Republic of Poland, hereinafter called Poland, for value received, promises to pay to the Government of the United States of America, hereinafter called the United States, or order, on the 15th day of December,   , the sum of   Dollars ($), and to pay interest upon said principal sum semiannually on the fifteenth day of June and December in each year, at the rate of three per cent per annum from December 15, 1922, to December 15, 1932, and at the rate of three and one-half per cent per annum thereafter until the principal hereof shall have been paid. This bond is payable as to both principal and interest in gold coin of the United States of America of the present standard of value, or, at the option of Poland, upon not less than thirty days' advance notice to the United States, in any obligations of the United States issued after April 6, 1917, to be taken at par and accrued interest to the date of payment hereunder. This bond is payable as to both principal and interest without deduction for, and is exempt from, any and all taxes and other public dues, present or future, imposed by or under authority of Poland or any political or local taxing authority within the Republic of Poland, whenever, so long as, and to the extent that, beneficial ownership is in (a) the Government of the United States, (b) a person, firm, or association neither domiciled nor ordinarily resident in Poland, or (c) a corporation not organized under the laws of Poland. This bond is payable as to both principal and interest at the Treasury of the United States in Washington, D. C., or at the option of the Secretary of the Treasury of the United States, at the Federal Reserve Bank of New York.

This bond is issued under an Agreement, dated November 14, 1924, between Poland and the United States, to which this bond is subject and to which reference is made for a further statement of its terms and conditions.

IN WITNESS WHEREOF, Poland has caused this bond to be executed in its behalf at the City of Washington, District of Columbia, by its Envoy Extraordinary and Minister Plenipotentiary at Washington, thereunto duly authorized.

The Government of the Republic of Poland:

By

Envoy Extraordinary and
Minister Plenipotentiary.

Dated, December 15, 1922.

(Back)

The following amounts have been paid upon the principal amount of this bond:

Date.   Amount paid.

B. Schedule of Polish Payments

Principal	Annual Interest Payments	Annual Principal Payments	Total Annual Payments	Year
$178,560,000	$ 5,356,800	$ 560,000	$ 5,916,800	1—1923
178,000,000	5,340,000	925,000	6,265,000	2—1924
177,075,000	5,312,250	950,000	6,262,250	3—1925
176,125,000	5,283,750	975,000	6,258,750	4—1926
175,150,000	5,254,500	1,000,000	6,254,500	5—1927
174,150,000	5,224,500	1,025,000	6,249,500	6—1928
173,125,000	5,193,750	1,050,000	6,243,750	7—1929
172,075,000	5,162,250	1,075,000	6,237,250	8—1930
171,000,000	5,130,000	1,100,000	6,230,000	9—1931
169,900,000	5,097,000	1,125,000	6,222,000	10—1932
168,775,000	5,907,125	1,150,000	7,057,125	11—1933
167,625,000	5,866,875	1,200,000	7,066,875	12—1934
166,425,000	5,824,875	1,225,000	7,049,875	13—1935
165,200,000	5,782,000	1,250,000	7,032,000	14—1936
163,950,000	5,738,250	1,275,000	7,013,250	15—1937
162,675,000	5,693,625	1,300,000	6,993,625	16—1938
161,375,000	5,648,125	1,325,000	6,973,125	17—1939
160,050,000	5,601,750	1,350,000	6,951,750	18—1940
158,700,000	5,554,500	1,400,000	6,954,500	19—1941
157,300,000	5,505,500	1,450,000	6,955,500	20—1942
155,850,000	5,454,750	1,500,000	6,954,750	21—1943
154,350,000	5,402,250	1,550,000	6,952,250	22—1944
152,800,000	5,348,000	1,600,000	6,948,000	23—1945
151,200,000	5,292,000	1,675,000	6,967,000	24—1946
149,525,000	5,233,375	1,750,000	6,983,375	25—1947
147,775,000	5,172,125	1,825,000	6,997,125	26—1948
145,950,000	5,108,250	1,900,000	7,008,250	27—1949
144,050,000	5,041,750	1,975,000	7,016,750	28—1950
142,075,000	4,972,625	2,075,000	7,047,625	29—1951
140,000,000	4,900,000	2,200,000	7,100,000	30—1952
137,800,000	4,823,000	2,300,000	7,123,000	31—1953
135,500,000	4,742,500	2,400,000	7,142,500	32—1954
133,100,000	4,658,500	2,500,000	7,158,500	33—1955
130,600,000	4,571,000	2,600,000	7,171,000	34—1956
128,000,000	4,480,000	2,700,000	7,180,000	35—1957
125,300,000	4,385,500	2,800,000	7,185,500	36—1958
122,500,000	4,287,500	2,900,000	7,187,500	37—1959
119,600,000	4,186,000	3,000,000	7,186,000	38—1960
116,600,000	4,081,000	3,100,000	7,181,000	39—1961
113,500,000	3,972,500	3,200,000	7,172,500	40—1962
110,300,000	3,860,500	3,300,000	7,160,500	41—1963
107,000,000	3,745,000	3,400,000	7,145,000	42—1964

B. Schedule of Polish Payments—*Continued*

Principal	Annual Interest Payments	Annual Principal Payments	Total Annual Payments	Year
$103,600,000	$ 3,626,000	$ 3,500,000	$ 7,126,000	43—1965
100,100,000	3,503,500	3,600,000	7,103,500	44—1966
96,500,000	3,377,500	3,700,000	7,077,500	45—1967
92,800,000	3,248,000	3,800,000	7,048,000	46—1968
89,000,000	3,115,000	3,900,000	7,015,000	47—1969
85,100,000	2,978,500	4,000,000	6,978,500	48—1970
81,100,000	2,838,500	4,100,000	6,938,500	49—1971
77,000,000	2,695,000	4,200,000	6,895,000	50—1972
72,800,000	2,548,000	4,400,000	6,948,000	51—1973
68,400,000	2,394,000	4,600,000	6,994,000	52—1974
63,800,000	2,233,000	4,800,000	7,033,000	53—1975
59,000,000	2,065,000	5,000,000	7,065,000	54—1976
54,000,000	1,890,000	5,200,000	7,090,000	55—1977
48,800,000	1,708,000	5,400,000	7,108,000	56—1978
43,400,000	1,519,000	5,800,000	7,319,000	57—1979
37,600,000	1,316,000	6,200,000	7,516,000	58—1980
31,400,000	1,099,000	6,800,000	7,899,000	59—1981
24,600,000	861,000	7,400,000	8,261,000	60—1982
17,200,000	602,000	8,200,000	8,802,000	61—1983
9,000,000	315,000	9,000,000	9,315,000	62—1984
	$257,127,550	$178,560,000	$435,687,530	

VIII. DEBT SETTLEMENT WITH BELGIUM *

Agreement signed August 18, 1925. Approved on the part of the United States by Act of Congress of April 30, 1926. Approved in Belgium by the law of March 2, 1926.

A. Agreement,

Made the eighteenth day of August, 1925, at the City of Washington, District of Columbia, between the GOVERNMENT OF THE KINGDOM OF BEL-

* Official text as issued by the Treasury Department.

GIUM, hereinafter called BELGIUM, party of the first part, and the GOVERNMENT OF THE UNITED STATES OF AMERICA, hereinafter called the UNITED STATES, party of the second part.

Whereas, Belgium is indebted to the United States as of June 15, 1925, upon obligations in the aggregate principal amount of $377,029,570.06, together with interest accrued and unpaid thereon; and

Whereas, Belgium desires to fund said indebtedness to the United States, both principal and interest, through the issue of bonds to the United States, and the United States is prepared to accept bonds from Belgium upon the terms and conditions hereinafter set forth;

Now, therefore, in consideration of the premises and of the mutual covenants herein contained, it is agreed as follows:

1. *Amount of Indebtedness.*—The indebtedness is divided into two classes—that incurred prior to November 11, 1918, hereinafter called Pre-Armistice indebtedness, and that incurred subsequent to November 11, 1918, hereinafter called Post-Armistice indebtedness.

(a) The amount of the Pre-Armistice indebtedness to be funded is $171,780,000, which is the principal amount of the obligations of Belgium received by the United States for cash advances made prior to November 11, 1918.

(b) The amount of the Post-Armistice indebtedness to be funded after allowing for certain cash payments made or to be made by Belgium is $246,000,000, which has been computed as follows:

Principal of obligations for cash advanced	$175,430,808.68	
Accrued and unpaid interest at 4¼ per cent per annum to December 15, 1922	26,314,491.66	
		$201,745,300.34
Principal of obligations for war material sold on credit.............	29,818,933.39	
Accrued and unpaid interest at 4¼ per cent per annum to December 15, 1922	491,359.24	
		30,310,292.63
Total indebtedness as of December 15, 1922		$232,055,592.97
Accrued interest thereon at 3 per cent per annum from December 15, 1922, to June 15, 1925........		17,404,169.47
Total indebtedness as of June 15, 1925		$249,459,762.44
Deduct:		
Payments on account of interest received between December 15, 1922, and June 15, 1925, on obligations for war material.................	$ 3,442,346.20	
Principal payment of $172.01 made August 7, 1923, together with interest thereon at 3 per cent per annum to June 15, 1925.........	181.58	
		3,442,527.78
Net indebtedness as of June 15, 1925		$246,017,234.66
To be paid in cash upon execution of agreement		17,234.66
Total indebtedness to be funded into bonds		$246,000,000.00

2. *Repayment of Principal.*—(a) In order to provide for the repayment of the Pre-Armistice indebtedness thus to be funded, Belgium will issue to the United States at par bonds of Belgium bearing no interest in the aggregate principal amount of $171,780,000, dated June 15,

1925, and maturing serially on each June 15 in the succeeding years for 62 years, on the several dates and in the amounts fixed in the following schedule: (see p. 304).

(b) In order to provide for the repayment of the Post-Armistice indebtedness thus to be funded Belgium will issue to the United States at par bonds of Belgium in the aggregate principal amount of $246,000,000, dated June 15, 1925, and maturing serially on each June 15, in the succeeding years for 6 years, on the several dates and in the amounts fixed in the following schedule: (see pp. 302-3).

PROVIDED HOWEVER, That Belgium at its option, upon not less than ninety days' advance notice to the United States, may postpone any payment on account of principal falling due as hereinabove provided after June 15, 1935, to any subsequent June 15 or December 15 not more than two years distant from its due date, but only on condition that in case Belgium shall at any time exercise this option as to any payment of principal, the payment falling due in the next succeeding year can not be postponed to any date more than one year distant from the date when it becomes due unless and until the payment previously postponed shall actually have been made, and the payment falling due in the second succeeding year can not be postponed at all unless and until the payment of principal due two years previous thereto shall actually have been made.

3. *Form of Bonds.*—All bonds issued or to be issued hereunder to the United States shall be payable to the Government of the United States of America, or order, and shall be signed for Belgium by its Ambassador Extraordinary and Plenipotentiary at Washington, or by

its other duly authorized representative. The bonds issued for the Pre-Armistice indebtedness shall be substantially in the form set forth in the exhibit hereto annexed and marked "Exhibit A," and shall be issued in 62 pieces with maturities and in denominations corresponding to the annual payments hereinabove set forth. The bonds issued for the Post-Armistice indebtedness shall be substantially in the form set forth in the exhibit hereto annexed and marked "Exhibit B," and shall be issued in 62 pieces with maturities and in denominations corresponding to the annual payments of principal hereinabove set forth.

4. *Payments of Interest.*—All bonds issued for the Post-Armistice indebtedness shall bear interest from June 15, 1925, payable in the amounts and on the dates set forth in the following schedule:

December 15, 1925 ..	$ 870,000	December 15, 1930 ..	$1,625,000
June 15, 1926	870,000	June 15, 1931	1,625,000
December 15, 1926 ..	1,000,000	December 15, 1931 ...	1,875,000
June 15, 1927	1,000,000	June 15, 1932	1,875,000
December 15, 1927 ..	1,125,000	December 15, 1932..	2,125,000
June 15, 1928	1,125,000	June 15, 1933	2,125,000
December 15, 1928 ..	1,250,000	December 15, 1933 ..	2,375,000
June 15, 1929	1,250,000	June 15, 1934	2,375,000
December 15, 1929 ..	1,375,000	December 15, 1934 ..	2,625,000
June 15, 1930	1,375,000	June 15, 1935	2,625,000

until and including June 15, 1935, and thereafter at the rate of 3½ per cent per annum payable semiannually on June 15 and December 15 of each year until the principal of said bonds shall have been paid.

5. *Method of Payment.*—All bonds issued or to be issued hereunder shall be payable, as to both principal and interest, in United States gold coin of the present

standard of value, or, at the option of Belgium, upon not less than thirty days' advance notice to the United States, in any obligations of the United States issued after April 6, 1917, to be taken at par and accrued interest to the date of payment hereunder.

All payments, whether in cash or in obligations of the United States, to be made by Belgium on account of the principal of or interest on any bonds issued or to be issued hereunder and held by the United States, shall be made at the Treasury of the United States in Washington, or, at the option of the Secretary of the Treasury of the United States, at the Federal Reserve Bank of New York, and if in cash shall be made in funds immediately available on the date of payment, or if in obligations of the United States shall be in form acceptable to the Secretary of the Treasury of the United States under the general regulations of the Treasury Department governing transactions in United States obligations.

6. *Exemption from Taxation.*—The principal and interest of all bonds issued or to be issued hereunder shall be paid without deduction for, and shall be exempt from, any and all taxes or other public dues, present or future, imposed by or under authority of Belgium or any political or local taxing authority within the Kingdom of Belgium, whenever, so long as, and to the extent that beneficial ownership is in (a) the Government of the United States, (b) a person, firm, or association neither domiciled nor ordinarily resident in Belgium, or (c) a corporation not organized under the laws of Belgium.

7. *Payments before Maturity.*—Belgium at its option, on June 15 or December 15 of any year, upon not less

than ninety days' advance notice to the United States, may make advance payments in amounts of $1,000 or multiples thereof, on account of the principal of any bonds issued or to be issued hereunder and held by the United States. Any such advance payments shall be applied to the principal of such bonds as may be indicated by Belgium at the time of the payment.

8. *Exchange for Marketable Obligations.*—Belgium will issue to the United States at any time, or from time to time, at the request of the Secretary of the Treasury of the United States, in exchange for any or all of the bonds issued hereunder and held by the United States, definitive engraved bonds in form suitable for sale to the public, in such amounts and denominations as the Secretary of the Treasury of the United States may request, in bearer form with provision for registration as to principal, and/or in fully registered form, and otherwise on the same terms and conditions as to dates of issue and maturity, rate or rates of interest, if any, exemption from taxation, payment in obligations of the United States issued after April 6, 1917, and the like, as the bonds surrendered on such exchange. Belgium will deliver definitive engraved bonds to the United States in accordance herewith within six months of receiving notice of any such request from the Secretary of the Treasury of the United States, and pending the delivery of the definitive engraved bonds will deliver, at the request of the Secretary of the Treasury of the United States, temporary bonds or interim receipts in form satisfactory to the Secretary of the Treasury of the United States within thirty days of the receipt of such request, all without expense to the United States. The United States, be-

fore offering any such bonds or interim receipts for sale in Belgium, will first offer them to Belgium for purchase at par and accrued interest, if any, and Belgium shall likewise have the option, in lieu of issuing any such bonds or interim receipts, to make advance redemption, at par and accrued interest, if any, of a corresponding principal amount of bonds issued hereunder and held by the United States. Belgium agrees that the definitive engraved bonds called for by this paragraph shall contain all such provisions, and that it will cause to be promulgated all such rules, regulations, and orders, as shall be deemed necessary or desirable by the Secretary of the Treasury of the United States in order to facilitate the sale of the bonds in the United States, in Belgium or elsewhere, and that if requested by the Secretary of the Treasury of the United States, it will use its good offices to secure the listing of the bonds on such stock exchanges as the Secretary of the Treasury of the United States may specify.

9. *Cancellation and Surrender of Obligations.*—Upon the execution of this agreement, the payment to the United States of cash in the sum of $17,234.66, as provided in subdivision (b) of paragraph 1 of this Agreement and the delivery to the United States of the $417,780,000 principal amount of bonds of Belgium to be issued hereunder, together with satisfactory evidence of authority for the execution of this Agreement by the representatives of Belgium and for the execution of the bonds to be issued hereunder on behalf of Belgium by its Ambassador Extraordinary and Plenipotentiary at Washington, or by its other duly authorized representative, the United States will cancel and surrender to Belgium, at the

Treasury of the United States in Washington, the obligations of Belgium in the principal amount of $377,029,-570.06, described in the preamble of this Agreement.

10. *Notices.*—Any notice, request, or consent under the hand of the Secretary of the Treasury of the United States, shall be deemed and taken as the notice, request, or consent of the United States, and shall be sufficient if delivered at the Embassy of Belgium at Washington or at the office of the Ministry of Finance in Brussels; and any notice, request, or election from or by Belgium shall be sufficient if delivered to the American Embassy at Brussels or to the Secretary of the Treasury at the Treasury of the United States in Washington. The United States in its discretion may waive any notice required hereunder, but any such waiver shall be in writing and shall not extend to or affect any subsequent notice or impair any right of the United States to require notice hereunder.

11. *Compliance with Legal Requirements.*—Belgium represents and agrees that the execution and delivery of this Agreement have in all respects been duly authorized and that all acts, conditions, and legal formalities which should have been completed prior to the making of this Agreement have been completed as required by the laws of Belgium and in conformity therewith.

12. *Counterparts.*—This agreement shall be executed in two counterparts, each of which shall have the force and effect of an original. .

IN WITNESS WHEREOF, Belgium has caused this Agreement to be executed on its behalf by Bon de Cartier de Marchienne, F. Cattier, E. Francqui, G. Theunis, its Special Commissioners at Washington, thereunto duly authorized, subject, however, to the approval of the competent authorities of the Kingdom of Belgium, and the United States has likewise caused this Agreement to be executed on its behalf by the Secretary of the Treasury, as Chairman of the World War Foreign Debt Commission, with the approval of the President, subject, however, to the approval of Congress, pursuant to the Act of Congress approved February 9, 1922, as amended by the Act of Congress approved February 28, 1923, and as further amended by the Act of Congress approved January 21, 1925, all on the day and year first above written.

THE GOVERNMENT OF THE KINGDOM OF BELGIUM,
By BON DE CARTIER DE MARCHIENNE
    F. CATTIER
    E. FRANCQUI
    G. THEUNIS

THE GOVERNMENT OF THE UNITED STATES OF AMERICA,
    For the World War Foreign Debt Commission:
By A. W. MELLON
             Secretary of the Treasury and
              Chairman of the Commission.

Approved:
                CALVIN COOLIDGE,
                      President.

EXHIBIT A.

(Form of Bond)

THE GOVERNMENT OF THE KINGDOM OF BELGIUM

$ No.

The Government of the Kingdom of Belgium, hereinafter called Belgium, for value received promises to
pay to the Government of the United States of America,
hereinafter called the United States, or order, on June
15, 19 , the sum of   Dollars ($).
This bond is payable in gold coin of the United States of
America of the present standard of value, or, at the option
of Belgium, upon not less than thirty days' advance
notice to the United States, in any obligations of the
United States issued after April 6, 1917, to be taken at
par and accrued interest to the date of payment
hereunder.

This bond is payable without deduction for, and is
exempt from, any and all taxes and other public dues,
present or future, imposed by or under authority of
Belgium or any political or local taxing authority within
the Kingdom of Belgium, whenever, so long as, and to
the extent that, beneficial ownership is in (a) the Government of the United States, (b) a person, firm, or
association neither domiciled nor ordinarily resident
in Belgium, or (c) a corporation not organized under
the laws of Belgium. This bond is payable at the
Treasury of the United States in Washington, D. C., or
at the option of the Secretary of the Treasury of the
United States at the Federal Reserve Bank of New York.

This bond is issued pursuant to the provisions of sub-
division (a) of paragraph 2 of an Agreement, dated
August 18, 1925, between Belgium and the United States,
to which Agreement this bond is subject and to which
reference is hereby made.

IN WITNESS WHEREOF, Belgium has caused this
bond to be executed in its behalf at the City of Washing-

ton, District of Columbia, by its   at Washington, thereunto duly authorized, as of June 15, 1925.

THE GOVERNMENT OF THE KINGDOM OF BELGIUM.

By

(Back)

The following amounts have been paid upon the principal amount of this bond.

Date   Amount paid.

EXHIBIT B.

(Form of Bond)

THE GOVERNMENT OF THE KINGDOM OF BELGIUM

$ No.

The Government of the Kingdom of Belgium hereinafter called Belgium, for value received, promises to pay to the Government of the United States of America, hereinafter called the United States, or order, on June 15,   , the sum of   Dollars ($), and to pay as interest upon said principal sum from June 15, 1925, to and including June 15, 1935, so long as the principal of this bond shall be unpaid, on the dates specified in paragraph 4 of the Agreement hereinafter referred to, such proportion of the amount of interest specified in said paragraph 4 for the dates therein stated as the principal amount of this bond bears to all bonds on such dates outstanding issued for Post-Armistice indebtedness under said Agreement, and after June 15, 1935, Belgium promises to pay interest hereon at the rate of 3½% per annum, payable semi-annually on June 15 and December 15 each year until the principal hereof has been paid. This bond is payable as to both principal and interest in gold coin of the United States of America of the present standard of value, or, at the option of Belgium upon not less than thirty days' advance notice to the United States, in any obligations of the United States issued after April 6, 1917, to be taken at par and accrued interest to the date of payment hereunder.

This bond is payable as to both principal and interest without deduction for, and is exempt from, any and all taxes and other public dues, present or future, imposed by or under authority of Belgium or any political or local taxing authority within the Kingdom of Belgium whenever, so long as, and to the extent that, beneficial ownership is in (a) the Government of the United States, (b) a person, firm, or association neither domiciled nor ordinarily resident in Belgium, or (c) a corporation not organized under the laws of Belgium. This bond is payable as to both principal and interest at the Treasury of the United States in Washington, D. C., or at the option of the Secretary of the Treasury of the United States at the Federal Reserve Bank of New York.

This bond is issued pursuant to the provisions of sub-division (b) of paragraph 2 of an Agreement, dated August 18, 1925, between Belgium and the United States, to which Agreement this bond is subject and to which reference is hereby made.

IN WITNESS WHEREOF, Belgium has caused this

bond to be executed in its behalf at the City of Washington, District of Columbia, by

at Washington,

thereunto duly authorized, as of June 15, 1925.

THE GOVERNMENT OF THE KINGDOM OF BELGIUM,

By

(Back)

The following amounts have been paid upon the principal amount of this bond.

Date.   Amount paid.

B. SCHEDULE OF BELGIAN PAYMENTS

1. Post-Armistice Debt

Principal	Annual Interest Payments	Annual Principal Payments	Total Annual Payments	Year
$246,000,000	$ 1,740,000	$ 1,100,000	$ 2,840,000	1—1926
244,900,000	2,000,000	1,100,000	3,100,000	2—1927
243,800,000	2,250,000	1,200,000	3,450,000	3—1928
242,600,000	2,500,000	1,200,000	3,700,000	4—1929
241,400,000	2,750,000	1,200,000	3,950,000	5—1930
240,200,000	3,250,000	1,300,000	4,550,000	6—1931
238,900,000	3,750,000	1,300,000	5,050,000	7—1932
237,600,000	4,250,000	1,300,000	5,550,000	8—1933
236,300,000	4,750,000	1,400,000	6,150,000	9—1934
234,900,000	5,250,000	1,400,000	6,650,000	10—1935
233,500,000	8,172,500	1,600,000	9,772,500	11—1936
231,900,000	8,116,500	1,700,000	9,816,500	12—1937
230,200,000	8,057,000	1,800,000	9,857,000	13—1938
228,400,000	7,994,000	1,800,000	9,794,000	14—1939
226,600,000	7,931,000	1,900,000	9,831,000	15—1940
224,700,000	7,864,500	1,900,000	9,764,500	16—1941
222,800,000	7,798,000	2,000,000	9,798,000	17—1942
220,800,000	7,728,000	2,100,000	9,828,000	18—1943
218,700,000	7,654,500	2,100,000	9,754,500	19—1944
216,600,000	7,581,000	2,200,000	9,781,000	20—1945
214,400,000	7,504,000	2,300,000	9,804,000	21—1946
212,100,000	7,423,500	2,400,000	9,823,500	22—1947

B. Schedule of Belgian Payments—*Continued*

Principal	Annual Interest Payments	Annual Principal Payments	Total Annual Payments	Year
$209,700,000	$7,339,500	$2,500,000	$9,839,500	23—1948
207,200,000	7,252,000	2,500,000	9,752,000	24—1949
204,700,000	7,164,500	2,600,000	9,764,500	25—1950
202,100,000	7,073,500	2,700,000	9,773,500	26—1951
199,400,000	6,979,000	2,800,000	9,779,000	27—1952
196,600,000	6,881,000	2,900,000	9,781,000	28—1953
193,700,000	6,779,500	3,000,000	9,779,500	29—1954
190,700,000	6,674,500	3,100,000	9,774,500	30—1955
187,600,000	6,566,000	3,300,000	9,866,000	31—1956
184,300,000	6,450,500	3,400,000	9,850,500	32—1957
180,900,000	6,331,500	3,500,000	9,831,500	33—1958
177,400,000	6,209,000	3,600,000	9,809,000	34—1959
173,800,000	6,083,000	3,700,000	9,783,000	35—1960
170,100,000	5,953,500	3,800,000	9,753,500	36—1961
166,300,000	5,820,500	4,000,000	9,820,500	37—1962
162,300,000	5,680,500	4,100,000	9,780,500	38—1963
158,200,000	5,537,000	4,300,000	9,837,000	39—1964
153,900,000	5,386,500	4,400,000	9,786,500	40—1965
149,500,000	5,232,500	4,600,000	9,832,500	41—1966
144,900,000	5,071,500	4,700,000	9,771,500	42—1967
140,200,000	4,907,000	4,900,000	9,807,000	43—1968
135,300,000	4,735,500	5,100,000	9,835,500	44—1969
130,200,000	4,557,000	5,300,000	9,857,000	45—1970
124,900,000	4,371,500	5,400,000	9,771,500	46—1971
119,500,000	4,182,500	5,600,000	9,782,500	47—1972
113,900,000	3,986,500	5,800,000	9,786,500	48—1973
108,100,000	3,783,500	6,000,000	9,783,500	49—1974
102,100,000	3,573,500	6,300,000	9,873,500	50—1975
95,800,000	3,353,000	6,600,000	9,953,000	51—1976
89,200,000	3,122,000	6,800,000	9,922,000	52—1977
82,400,000	2,884,000	7,000,000	9,884,000	53—1978
75,400,000	2,639,000	7,200,000	9,839,000	54—1979
68,200,000	2,387,000	7,500,000	9,887,000	55—1980
60,700,000	2,124,500	7,800,000	9,924,500	56—1981
52,900,000	1,851,500	8,100,000	9,951,500	57—1982
44,800,000	1,568,000	8,400,000	9,968,000	58—**1983**
36,400,000	1,274,000	8,600,000	9,874,000	59—1984
27,800,000	973,000	8,900,000	9,873,000	60—1985
18,900,000	661,500	9,300,000	9,961,500	61—1986
9,600,000	336,000	9,600,000	9,936,000	62—1987
	$310,050,500	$246,000,000	$556,050,500	

2. Pre-Armistice Debt

Annual Principal Payments	Year	Annual Principal Payments	Year
$ 1,000,000	1926	$ 2,900,000	1958
1,000,000	1927	2,900,000	1959
1,250,000	1928	2,900,000	1960
1,750,000	1929	2,900,000	1961
2,250,000	1930	2,900,000	1962
2,750,000	1931	2,900,000	1963
2,900,000	1932	2,900,000	1964
2,900,000	1933	2,900,000	1965
2,900,000	1934	2,900,000	1966
2,900,000	1935	2,900,000	1967
2,900,000	1936	2,900,000	1968
2,900,000	1937	2,900,000	1969
2,900,000	1938	2,900,000	1970
2,900,000	1939	2,900,000	1971
2,900,000	1940	2,900,000	1972
2,900,000	1941	2,900,000	1973
2,900,000	1942	2,900,000	1974
2,900,000	1943	2,900,000	1975
2,900,000	1944	2,900,000	1976
2,900,000	1945	2,900,000	1977
2,900,000	1946	2,900,000	1978
2,900,000	1947	2,900,000	1979
2,900,000	1948	2,900,000	1980
2,900,000	1949	2,900,000	1981
2,900,000	1950	2,900,000	1982
2,900,000	1951	2,900,000	1983
2,900,000	1952	2,900,000	1984
2,900,000	1953	2,900,000	1985
2,900,000	1954	2,900,000	1986
2,900,000	1955	2,280,000	1987
2,900,000	1956		
2,900,000	1957	$171,780,000	

IX. DEBT SETTLEMENT WITH LATVIA*

Agreement signed September 24, 1925. Approved on the part of the United States by the Act of Congress of April 30, 1926. Passed by Latvian Saeima on March 26, 1926.

* Official text as issued by the Treasury Department.

A. Agreement,

Made the twenty-fourth day of September, 1925, at the City of Washington, District of Columbia, between the GOVERNMENT OF THE REPUBLIC OF LATVIA, hereinafter called LATVIA, party of the first part, and the GOVERNMENT OF THE UNITED STATES OF AMERICA, hereinafter called the UNITED STATES, party of the second part.

Whereas, Latvia is indebted to the United States as of December 15, 1922, upon obligations in the aggregate principal amount of $5,132,287.14, together with interest accrued and unpaid thereon; and

Whereas, Latvia desires to fund said indebtedness to the United States, both principal and interest, through the issue of bonds to the United States, and the United States is prepared to accept bonds from Latvia upon the terms and conditions hereinafter set forth:

Now, therefore, in consideration of the premises and of the mutual covenants herein contained, it is agreed as follows:

1. *Amount of Indebtedness.*—The amount of the indebtedness to be funded, after allowing for cash payments made or to be made by Latvia, is $5,775,000, which has been computed as follows:

Principal amount of obligations to be funded........	$5,132,287.14
Interest accrued and unpaid thereon to December 15, 1922, at the rate of 4¼ per cent per annum....	647,275.62
Total principal and interest accrued and unpaid as of December 15, 1922.....................	5,779,562.76
To be paid in cash by Latvia upon execution of Agreement	4,562.76
Total indebtedness to be funded into bonds....	$5,775,000.00

2. *Repayment of Principal.*—In order to provide for the repayment of the indebtedness thus to be funded, Latvia will issue to the United States at par, as of December 15, 1922, bonds of Latvia in the aggregate principal amount of $5,775,000, dated December 15, 1922, and maturing serially on each December 15 in the succeeding years for 62 years, in the amounts and on the several dates fixed in the following schedule: (see p. 315).

PROVIDED, HOWEVER, That Latvia, at its option, upon not less than ninety days' advance notice to the United States, may postpone any payment falling due as hereinabove provided, except those falling due on or before December 15, 1930, hereinafter referred to in paragraph 5 of this Agreement, to any subsequent June 15 or .December 15 not more than two years distant from its due date, but only on condition that in case Latvia shall at any time exercise this option as to any payment of principal, the payment falling due in the next succeeding year can not be postponed to any date more than one year distant from the date when it becomes due unless and until the payment previously postponed shall actually have been made, and the payment falling due in the second succeeding year can not be postponed at all unless and until the payment of principal due two years previous thereto shall actually have been made.

3. *Form of Bonds.*—All bonds issued or to be issued hereunder to the United States shall be payable to the Government of the United States of America, or order, shall be issued in such denominations as may be requested by the Secretary of the Treasury of the United States, substantially in the form set forth in the exhibit hereto annexed and marked "Exhibit A," and shall be

signed for Latvia by its Envoy Extraordinary and Minister Plenipotentiary at Washington, or by its other duly authorized representative. The $5,775,000 principal amount of bonds first to be issued hereunder shall be issued in 62 pieces, in denominations and with maturities corresponding to the annual payments of principal hereinabove set forth.

4. *Payment of Interest.*—All bonds issued or to be issued hereunder shall bear interest, payable semiannually on June 15 and December 15 in each year, at the rate of 3 per cent per annum from December 15, 1922, to December 15, 1932, and thereafter at the rate of 3½ per cent per annum until the principal thereof shall have been paid.

5. *Method of Payment.*—All bonds issued or to be issued hereunder shall be payable, as to both principal and interest, in United States gold coin of the present standard of value, or, at the option of Latvia, upon not less than thirty days' advance notice to the United States, in any obligations of the United States issued after April 6, 1917, to be taken at par and accrued interest to the date of payment hereunder: PROVIDED, HOWEVER, that with reference to the payments on account of principal and/or interest falling due hereunder on or before December 15, 1930, Latvia, at its option, may pay the following amounts on the dates specified:

June 15, 1926	$ 30,000	June 15, 1929	$ 45,000
December 15, 1926	30,000	December 15, 1929	45,000
June 15, 1927	35,000	June 15, 1930	50,000
December 15, 1927	35,000	December 15, 1930	50,000
June 15, 1928	40,000		
December 15, 1928	40,000	Total	$400,000

and the balance, including interest on all overdue payments at the rate of 3 per cent per annum from their respective due dates, in bonds of Latvia dated December 15, 1930, bearing interest at the rate of 3 per cent per annum from December 15, 1930, to December 15, 1932, and thereafter at the rate of 3½ per cent per annum until the principal thereof shall have been paid, such bonds to mature serially on December 15 of each year up to and including December 15, 1984, substantially in the manner provided in paragraph 2 of this Agreement, and to be substantially similar in other respects to the bonds first to be issued hereunder.

All payments, whether in cash or in obligations of the United States, to be made by Latvia on account of the principal of or interest on any bonds issued or to be issued hereunder and held by the United States, shall be made at the Treasury of the United States in Washington, or, at the option of the Secretary of the Treasury of the United States, at the Federal Reserve Bank of New York, and if in cash shall be made in funds immediately available on the date of payment, or if in obligations of the United States shall be in form acceptable to the Secretary of the Treasury of the United States under the general regulations of the Treasury Department governing transactions in United States obligations.

6. *Exemption from Taxation.*—The principal and interest of all bonds issued or to be issued hereunder shall be paid without deduction for, and shall be exempt from, any and all taxes or other public dues, present or future, imposed by or under authority of Latvia or any political or local taxing authority within the Republic of Latvia, whenever, so long as, and to the extent that beneficial

ownership is in (a) the Government of the United States, (b) a person, firm, or association neither domiciled nor ordinarily resident in Latvia, or (c) a corporation not organized under the laws of Latvia.

7. *Payments before Maturity.*—Latvia, at its option, on June 15 or December 15 of any year, upon not less than ninety days' advance notice to the United States, may make advance payments in amounts of $1,000 or multiples thereof, on account of the principal of any bonds issued or to be issued hereunder and held by the United States. Any such advance payments shall first be applied to the principal of any bonds which shall have been issued hereunder on account of principal and/or interest accruing between December 15, 1922, and December 15, 1930, and then to the principal of any other bonds issued hereunder and held by the United States, as may be indicated by Latvia at the time of the payment.

8. *Exchange for Marketable Obligations.*—Latvia will issue to the United States at any time, or from time to time, at the request of the Secretary of the Treasury of the United States, in exchange for any or all of the bonds issued or to be issued hereunder and held by the United States, definitive engraved bonds in form suitable for sale to the public, in such amounts and denominations as the Secretary of the Treasury of the United States may request, in bearer form, with provision for registration as to principal, and/or in fully registered form, and otherwise on the same terms and conditions, as to dates of issue and maturity, rate or rates of interest, exemption from taxation, payment in obligations of the United States issued after April 6, 1917, and the like, as the

bonds surrendered on such exchange. Latvia will deliver definitive engraved bonds to the United States in accordance herewith within six months of receiving notice of any such request from the Secretary of the Treasury of the United States, and pending the delivery of the definitive engraved bonds will deliver, at the request of the Secretary of the Treasury of the United States, temporary bonds or interim receipts in form satisfactory to the Secretary of the Treasury of the United States within thirty days of the receipt of such request, all without expense to the United States. The United States, before offering any such bonds or interim receipts for sale in Latvia, will first offer them to Latvia for purchase at par and accrued interest, and Latvia shall likewise have the option, in lieu of issuing any such bonds or interim receipts, to make advance redemption, at par and accrued interest, of a corresponding principal amount of bonds issued or to be issued hereunder and held by the United States. Latvia agrees that the definitive engraved bonds called for by this paragraph shall contain all such provisions, and that it will cause to be promulgated all such rules, regulations, and orders as shall be deemed necessary or desirable by the Secretary of the Treasury of the United States in order to facilitate the sale of the bonds in the United States, in Latvia or elsewhere, and that if requested by the Secretary of the Treasury of the United States, it will use its good offices to secure the listing of the bonds on such stock exchanges as he may request.

9. *Cancellation and Surrender of Obligations.*—Upon the execution of this Agreement, the payment to the United States of cash in the sum of $4,562.76 as provided

in paragraph 1 of this Agreement and the delivery to
the United States of the $5,775,000 principal amount of
bonds of Latvia first to be issued hereunder, together
with satisfactory evidence of authority for the execution
of this Agreement and the bonds on behalf of Latvia by
its Envoy Extraordinary and Minister Plenipotentiary
at Washington, or by its other duly authorized representative, the United States will cancel and surrender
to Latvia, at the Treasury of the United States in Washington, the obligations of Latvia in the principal amount
of $5,132,287.14 described in the preamble to this
Agreement.

10. *Notices*—Any notice, request, or consent under the
hand of the Secretary of the Treasury of the United
States, shall be deemed and taken as the notice, request,
or consent of the United States, and shall be sufficient
if delivered at the Legation of Latvia at Washington
or at the office of the Minister of Finance in Riga; and
any notice, request, or election from or by Latvia shall
be sufficient if delivered to the American Legation at
Riga or to the Secretary of the Treasury at the Treasury
of the United States in Washington. The United States
in its discretion may waive any notice required hereunder, but any such waiver shall be in writing and shall
not extend to or affect any subsequent notice or impair any right of the United States to require notice
hereunder.

11. *Compliance with Legal Requirements.*—Latvia
represents and agrees that the execution and delivery of
this Agreement have in all respects been duly authorized
and that all acts, conditions, and legal formalities which
should have been completed prior to the making of this

Agreement and the issuance of bonds hereunder have been completed as required by the laws of Latvia and in conformity therewith.

12. *Counterparts.*—This Agreement shall be executed in two counterparts, each of which shall have the force and effect of an original.

IN WITNESS WHEREOF, Latvia has caused this Agreement to be executed on its behalf by its Envoy Extraordinary and Minister Plenipotentiary at Washington, thereunto duly authorized, subject, however, to the approval of the Saeima, and the United States has likewise caused this Agreement to be executed on its behalf by the Secretary of the Treasury, as Chairman of the World War Foreign Debt Commission, with the approval of the President, subject, however, to the approval of Congress, pursuant to the Act of Congress approved February 9, 1922, as amended by the Act of Congress approved February 28, 1923, and as further amended by the Act of Congress approved January 21, 1925, all on the day and year first above written.

THE GOVERNMENT OF THE REPUBLIC OF LATVIA,
By LOUIS SEYA,
Envoy Extraordinary and Minister Plenipotentiary.

THE GOVERNMENT OF THE UNITED STATES OF AMERICA,
For the World War Foreign Debt Commission:
By A. W. MELLON,
Secretary of the Treasury and
Chairman of the Commission.

Approved:

CALVIN COOLIDGE,
President.

EXHIBIT A

(Form of Bond)

THE GOVERNMENT OF THE REPUBLIC OF LATVIA

$ No.

The Government of the Republic of Latvia, hereinafter called Latvia, for value received, promises to pay to the Government of the United States of America, hereinafter called the United States, or order, on December 15,   , the sum of   Dollars ($), and to pay interest upon said principal sum semiannually on June 15 and December 15 in each year, at the rate of 3% per annum from December 15, 1922, to December 15, 1932, and at the rate of 3½% per annum thereafter until the principal hereof shall have been paid. This bond is payable as to both principal and interest in gold coin of the United States of America of the present standard of value, or, at the option of Latvia, upon not less than thirty days' advance notice to the United States, in any obligations of the United States issued after April 6, 1917, to be taken at par and accrued interest to the date of payment hereunder.

This bond is payable as to both principal and interest without deduction for, and is exempt from, any and all taxes and other public dues, present or future, imposed by or under authority of Latvia or any political or local taxing authority within the Republic of Latvia whenever, so long as, and to the extent that, beneficial ownership is in (a) the Government of the United States, (b) a person, firm, or association neither domiciled nor ordinarily resident in Latvia, or (c) a corporation not organized under the laws of Latvia. This bond is payable as to both principal and interest at the Treasury of the United States in Washington, D. C., or at the option of the Secretary of the Treasury of the United States at the Federal Reserve Bank of New York.

This bond is issued under an Agreement, dated September 24, 1925, between Latvia and the United States, to which this bond is subject and to which reference is hereby made.

IN WITNESS WHEREOF, Latvia has caused this bond to be executed in its behalf at the City of Washington, District of Columbia, by its
                                              at Washington,
thereunto duly authorized, as of December 15, 1922.

THE GOVERNMENT OF THE REPUBLIC OF LATVIA,

    By

(Back)

The following amounts have been paid upon the principal amount of this bond.

Date.   Amount paid.

B. Schedule of Latvian Payments

Principal	Annual Interest Payments	Annual Principal Payments	Total Annual Payments	Year
$5,775,000	$ 173,250	$ 28,000	$ 201,250	1923
5,747,000	172,410	29,000	201,410	1924
5,718,000	171,540	30,000	201,540	1925
5,688,000	170,640	31,000	201,640	1926
5,657,000	169,710	32,000	201,710	1927
5,625,000	168,750	33,000	201,750	1928
5,592,000	167,760	34,000	201,760	1929
5,558,000	166,740	35,000	201,740	1930
5,523,000	165,690	36,000	201,690	1931
5,487,000	164,610	37,000	201,610	1932
5,450,000	190,750	38,000	228,750	1933
5,412,000	189,420	39,000	228,420	1934
5,373,000	188,055	40,000	228,055	1935
5,333,000	186,655	42,000	228,655	1936
5,291,000	185,185	43,000	228,185	1937
5,248,000	183,680	45,000	228,680	1938
5,203,000	182,105	46,000	228,105	1939
5,157,000	180,495	48,000	228,495	1940
5,109,000	178,815	50,000	228,815	1941
5,059,000	177,065	51,000	228,065	1942
5,008,000	175,280	53,000	228,280	1943
4,955,000	173,425	55,000	228,425	1944
4,900,000	171,500	57,000	228,500	1945
4,843,000	169,505	59,000	228,505	1946
4,784,000	167,440	61,000	228,440	1947
4,723,000	165,305	63,000	228,305	1948
4,660,000	163,100	65,000	228,100	1949
4,595,000	160,825	68,000	228,825	1950
4,527,000	158,445	70,000	228,445	1951
4,457,000	155,995	73,000	228,995	1952
4,384,000	153,440	75,000	228,440	1953
4,309,000	150,815	78,000	228,815	1954
4,231,000	148,085	80,000	228,085	1955
4,151,000	145,285	83,000	228,285	1956
4,068,000	142,380	86,000	228,380	1957
3,982,000	139,370	89,000	228,370	1958
3,893,000	136,255	92,000	228,255	1959
3,801,000	133,035	95,000	228,035	1960
3,706,000	129,710	99,000	228,710	1961
3,607,000	126,245	102,000	228,245	1962
3,505,000	122,675	107,000	229,675	1963
3,398,000	118,930	111,000	229,930	1964

B. Schedule of Latvian Payments—*Continued*

Principal	Annual Interest Payments	Annual Principal Payments	Total Annual Payments	Year
$3,287,000	$115,045	$114,000	$229,045	1965
3,173,000	111,055	118,000	229,055	1966
3,055,000	106,925	123,000	229,925	1967
2,932,000	102,620	128,000	230,620	1968
2,804,000	98,140	132,000	230,140	1969
2,672,000	93,520	138,000	231,520	1970
2,534,000	88,690	143,000	231,690	1971
2,391,000	83,685	148,000	231,685	1972
2,243,000	78,505	153,000	231,505	1973
2,090,000	73,150	158,000	231,150	1974
1,932,000	67,620	164,000	231,620	1975
1,768,000	61,880	170,000	231,880	1976
1,598,000	55,930	176,000	231,930	1977
1,422,000	49,770	182,000	231,770	1978
1,240,000	43,400	188,000	231,400	1979
1,052,000	36,820	195,000	231,820	1980
857,000	29,995	202,000	231,995	1981
655,000	22,925	209,000	231,925	1982
446,000	15,610	218,000	233,610	1983
228,000	7,980	228,000	235,980	1984
	$8,183,635	$5,775,000	$13,958,635	

X. DEBT SETTLEMENT WITH CZECHOSLOVAKIA *

Agreement signed October 13, 1925. Approved on the part of the United States by the Act of Congress of May 3, 1926. We have not been informed of ratification in Czechoslovakia.

A. Agreement,

Made the thirteenth day of October, 1925, at the City of Washington, District of Columbia, between THE CZECHOSLOVAK REPUBLIC, hereinafter called

* Official text as issued by the Treasury Department.

CZECHOSLOVAKIA, party of the first part, and
THE UNITED STATES OF AMERICA, hereinafter
called the UNITED STATES, party of the second
part.

Whereas, the United States now holds certain obligations of Czechoslovakia and there are outstanding open
accounts in favor of the United States and claims against
the United States which are in dispute; and
Whereas, the United States and Czechoslovakia wish to
settle the financial differences between the two governments and/or their agencies and to fix the net amount
of the indebtedness of Czechoslovakia to the United
States, both principal and interest, as of June 15, 1925,
and to fund such indebtedness;
Now, therefore, in consideration of the premises and
of the mutual covenants herein contained, it is agreed as
follows:
1. *Amount of Indebtedness.*—The amount of the indebtedness of Czechoslovakia as of June 15, 1925, is
fixed at $115,000,000.
2. *Payment.*—In order to provide for the payment of
the indebtedness thus to be funded Czechoslovakia will
issue to the United States at par bonds of Czechoslovakia
in the aggregate principal amount of $185,071,023.07,
dated June 15, 1925, and maturing serially on the several
dates and in amounts fixed in the following schedule:
(see p. 327).
PROVIDED HOWEVER, That Czechoslovakia, at its option,
upon not less than ninety days' advance notice to the
United States, may postpone any payment on account of
principal falling due as hereinabove provided after June

15, 1943, to any subsequent June 15 or December 15 not more than two years distant from its due date, but only on condition that in case Czechoslovakia shall at any time exercise this option as to any payment of principal, the payment falling due in the next succeeding year can not be postponed to any date more than one year distant from the date when it becomes due unless and until the payment previously postponed shall actually have been made, and the payment falling due in the second succeeding year can not be postponed at all unless and until the payment of principal due two years previous thereto shall actually have been made.

3. *Form of Bonds.*—All bonds issued or to be issued hereunder to the United States shall be payable to the Government of the United States of America, or order, and shall be signed for Czechoslovakia by its Minister of Finance and countersigned by the President of the Supreme Accounting Control Office in Prague and likewise countersigned by its Envoy Extraordinary and Minister Plenipotentiary at Washington, or by its other duly authorized representative. The bonds issued for the first thirty-six semiannual payments shall be substantially in the form set forth in the exhibit hereto annexed and marked "Exhibit A," and shall be issued in 36 pieces of the principal amount of $1,500,000 each maturing serially on December 15, 1925, and semiannually thereafter up to and including June 15, 1943, and shall not bear interest before maturity. The bonds maturing subsequent to June 15, 1943, shall be substantially in the form set forth in the exhibit hereto annexed and marked "Exhibit B," and shall be issued in 44 pieces with maturities and in denominations as here-

inabove set forth and shall bear interest at the rate of
3½% per annum from June 15, 1943, payable semiannually on June 15 and December 15 of each year
until the principal of such bonds shall be paid.

4. *Method of Payment.*—All bonds issued or to be
issued hereunder shall be payable, as to both principal
and interest, in United States gold coin of the present
standard of value, or, at the option of Czechoslovakia,
upon not less than thirty days' advance notice to the
United States, in any obligations of the United States
issued after April 6, 1917, to be taken at par and accrued
interest to the date of payment hereunder.

All payments, whether in cash or in obligations of the
United States, to be made by Czechoslovakia on account
of the principal of or interest on any bonds issued or to
be issued hereunder and held by the United States, shall
be made at the Treasury of the United States in Washington, or, at the option of the Secretary of the Treasury
of the United States, at the Federal Reserve Bank of
New York, and if in cash shall be made in funds immediately available on the date of payment, or if in
obligations of the United States shall be in form acceptable to the Secretary of the Treasury of the United
States under the general regulations of the Treasury
Department governing transactions in United States
obligations.

5. *Exemption from Taxation.*—The principal and interest of all bonds issued or to be issued hereunder shall
be paid without deduction for, and shall be exempt from,
any and all taxes or other public dues, present or future,
imposed by or under authority of Czechoslovakia or
any political or local taxing authority within the Czecho-

slovak Republic, whenever, so long as, and to the extent that beneficial ownership is in (a) the Government of the United States, (b) a person, firm, or association neither domiciled nor ordinarily resident in Czechoslovakia, or (c) a corporation not organized under the laws of Czechoslovakia.

6. *Payments before Maturity.*—Czechoslovakia, at its option, on June 15 or December 15 of any year, upon not less than ninety days' advance notice to the United States, may make advance payments in amounts of $1,000 or multiples thereof, on account of the principal of any bonds issued or to be issued hereunder and held by the United States. Any such advance payments shall be applied to the principal of such bonds as may be indicated by Czechoslovakia at the time of the payment.

7. *Exchange for Marketable Obligations.*—Czechoslovakia will issue to the United States at any time, or from time to time, at the request of the Secretary of the Treasury of the United States, in exchange for any or all of the bonds issued hereunder and held by the United States, definitive engraved bonds in form suitable for sale to the public, in such amounts and denominations as the Secretary of the Treasury of the United States may request, in bearer form, with provision for registration as to principal, and/or in fully registered form, and otherwise on the same terms and conditions, as to dates of issue and maturity, rate or rates of interest, if any, exemption from taxation, payment in obligations of the United States issued after April 6, 1917, and the like, as the bonds surrendered on such exchange. Czechoslovakia will deliver definitive engraved bonds to the United States in accordance herewith within six months

of receiving notice of any such request from the Secretary of the Treasury of the United States, and pending the delivery of the definitive engraved bonds will deliver, at the request of the Secretary of the Treasury of the United States, temporary bonds or interim receipts in form satisfactory to the Secretary of the Treasury of the United States within thirty days of the receipt of such request, all without expense to the United States. The United States, before offering any such bonds or interim receipts for sale in Czechoslovakia, will first offer them to Czechoslovakia for purchase at par and accrued interest, if any, and Czechoslovakia shall likewise have the option, in lieu of issuing any such bonds or interim receipts, to make advance redemption, at par and accrued interest, if any, of a corresponding principal amount of bonds issued hereunder and held by the United States. Czechoslovakia agrees that the definitive engraved bonds called for by this paragraph shall contain all such provisions, and that it will cause to be promulgated all such rules, regulations, and orders as shall be deemed necessary or desirable by the Secretary of the Treasury of the United States in order to facilitate the sale of the bonds in the United States, in Czechoslovakia or elsewhere, and that if requested by the Secretary of the Treasury of the United States, it will use its good offices to secure the listing of the bonds on such stock exchanges as the Secretary of the Treasury of the United States may specify.

8. *Cancellation and Surrender of Obligations.*—Upon the execution of this Agreement, the delivery to the United States of the $185,071,023.07 principal amount of bonds of Czechoslovakia to be issued hereunder, to-

gether with satisfactory evidence of authority for the execution of this Agreement by the representatives of Czechoslovakia and for the execution of the bonds to be issued hereunder, the United States will cancel and surrender to Czechoslovakia at the Treasury of the United States in Washington, the obligations of Czechoslovakia held by the United States and a satisfaction shall be had of all financial claims existing between the two governments and/or their agencies.

9. *Notices.*—Any notice, request, or consent under the hand of the Secretary of the Treasury of the United States, shall be deemed and taken as the notice, request, or consent of the United States, and shall be sufficient if delivered at the Legation of Czechoslovakia at Washington or at the office of the Ministry of Finance in Czechoslovakia; and any notice, request, or election from or by Czechoslovakia shall be sufficient if delivered to the American Legation at Prague or to the Secretary of the Treasury at the Treasury of the United States in Washington. The United States in its discretion may waive any notice required hereunder, but any such waiver shall be in writing and shall not extend to or affect any subsequent notice or impair any right of the United States to require notice hereunder.

10. *Compliance with Legal Requirements.*—Czechoslovakia represents and agrees that the execution and delivery of this Agreement have in all respects been duly authorized and that all acts, conditions, and legal formalities which should have been completed prior to the making of this Agreement have been completed as required by the laws of Czechoslovakia and in conformity therewith.

11. *Counterparts.*—This Agreement shall be executed in two counterparts, each of which shall have the force and effect of an original.

IN WITNESS WHEREOF, Czechoslovakia has caused this Agreement to be executed on its behalf by Dr. Vilém Pospîšil, Karel Kučera and Dr. Karel Brabenec, its plenipotentiaries at Washington, thereunto duly authorized, subject, however, to constitutional ratification in Czechoslovakia, and the United States has likewise caused this Agreement to be executed on its behalf by the Secretary of the Treasury, as Chairman of the World War Foreign Debt Commission, with the approval of the President, subject, however, to the approval of Congress, pursuant to the Act of Congress approved February 9, 1922, as amended by the Act of Congress approved February 28, 1923, and as further amended by the Act of Congress approved January 21, 1925, all on the day and year first above written.

THE CZECHOSLOVAK REPUBLIC,
By DR. VILÉM POSPÍŠIL,
KAREL KUČERA,
DR. KAREL BRABENEC.

THE UNITED STATES OF AMERICA,
For the World War Foreign Debt Commission:
By A. W. MELLON,
Secretary of the Treasury and Chairman of the Commission.

Approved:

CALVIN COOLIDGE,
President.

·Exhibit A
(Form of Bond)
The Czechoslovak Republic

$1,500,000   No.

The Czechoslovak Republic, hereinafter called Czechoslovakia, for value received, promises to pay to the Government of the United States of America, hereinafter called the United States, or order, on   19 , the sum of One Million Five Hundred Thousand Dollars ($1,500,000). This bond is payable in gold coin of the United States of America of the present standard of value, or, at the option of Czechoslovakia, upon not less than thirty days' advance notice to the United States, in any obligations of the United States issued after April 6, 1917, to be taken at par and accrued interest to the date of payment hereunder.

This bond is payable without deduction for, and is exempt from, any and all taxes and other public dues, present or future, imposed by or under authority of Czechoslovakia or any political or local taxing authority within Czechoslovakia, whenever, so long as, and to the extent that, beneficial ownership is in (a) the Government of the United States, (b) a person, firm, or association neither domiciled nor ordinarily resident in Czechoslovakia, or (c) a corporation not organized under the laws of Czechoslovakia. This bond is payable at the Treasury of the United States in Washington, D. C., or at the option of the Secretary of the Treasury of the United States or at the Federal Reserve Bank of New York.

This bond is issued pursuant to the provisions of paragraph 2 of an Agreement dated October 13, 1925, between

Czechoslovakia and the United States, to which Agreement this bond is subject and to which reference is hereby made.

IN WITNESS WHEREOF, Czechoslovakia has caused this bond to be executed in its behalf by its Minister of Finance and countersigned by the President of the Supreme Accounting Control' Office in Prague and likewise countersigned at the City of Washington, District of Columbia, by its

at Washington, thereunto duly authorized, as of June 15, 1925.

THE CZECHOSLOVAK REPUBLIC,

By

Minister of Finance.

EXHIBIT B
(Form of Bond)
THE CZECHOSLOVAK REPUBLIC

$ No.

The Czechoslovak Republic, hereinafter called Czechoslovakia, for value received, promises to pay to the Government of the United States of America, hereinafter called the United States, or order, on June 15, 19 , the sum of   Dollars ($), and to pay interest upon said principal sum from June 15, 1943, at the rate of 3½% per annum, payable semiannually on the 15th day of December and June in each year, until the principal hereof has been paid. This bond is payable as to both principal and interest in gold coin of the United States of America of the present standard of value, or, at the option of Czechoslovakia, upon not less than thirty days' advance notice to the United States, in any obligations of the United States issued after April 6, 1917, to be taken at par and accrued interest to the date of payment hereunder.

This bond is payable as to both principal and interest without deduction for, and is exempt from, any and all taxes and other public dues, present or future, imposed by or under authority of Czechoslovakia or any political or local taxing authority within the Czechoslovak Republic whenever, so long as, and to the extent that, beneficial ownership is in (a) the Government of the United States, (b) a person, firm or association neither domiciled nor ordinarily resident in Czechoslovakia, or (c) a corporation not organized under the laws of Czechoslovakia. This bond is payable as to both principal and interest at the Treasury of the United States in Washington, D. C., or at the option of the Secretary of the Treasury of the United States at the Federal Reserve Bank of New York.

This bond is issued pursuant to the provisions of paragraph 2 of an Agreement dated October 13, 1925, between Czechoslovakia and the United States, to which Agreement this bond is subject and to which reference is hereby made.

IN WITNESS WHEREOF, Czechoslovakia has caused this bond to be executed in its behalf by its Minister of Finance and countersigned by the President of the Supreme Accounting Control Office in Prague and likewise countersigned at the City of Washington, District of Columbia, by its

at Washington, thereunto duly authorized, as of June 15, 1925.

THE CZECHOSLOVAK REPUBLIC,

By   *Minister of Finance.*

B. Schedule of Czechoslovak Payments

1. *First 18 Years*

Principal	Annual Interest Due	Annual Principal Due	Total Amount Due Annually	Total Amount to Be Paid Annually	Amount Deferred Each Year	Value of Each Deferred Amount on 19th Year	Year
$115,000,000	$ 3,450,000	$ 575,000	$ 4,025,000	$ 3,000,000	$ 1,025,000	$ 1,761,086.23	1926
114,425,000	3,432,750	595,000	4,027,750	3,000,000	1,027,750	1,714,379.79	1927
113,830,000	3,414,900	610,000	4,024,900	3,000,000	1,024,900	1,659,831.06	1928
113,220,000	3,396,600	630,000	4,026,600	3,000,000	1,026,600	1,614,158.82	1929
112,590,000	3,377,700	645,000	4,022,700	3,000,000	1,022,700	1,561,192.58	1930
111,945,000	3,358,350	665,000	4,023,350	3,000,000	1,023,350	1,516,684.65	1931
111,280,000	3,338,400	690,000	4,028,400	3,000,000	1,028,400	1,479,775.62	1932
110,590,000	3,317,700	710,000	4,027,700	3,000,000	1,027,700	1,435,697.46	1933
109,880,000	3,296,400	730,000	4,026,400	3,000,000	1,026,400	1,392,117.83	1934
109,150,000	3,274,500	750,000	4,024,500	3,000,000	1,024,500	1,349,068.77	1935
108,400,000	3,794,000	770,000	4,564,000	3,000,000	1,564,000	1,989,842.79	1936
107,630,000	3,767,050	795,000	4,562,050	3,000,000	1,562,050	1,920,156.21	1937
106,835,000	3,739,225	825,000	4,564,225	3,000,000	1,564,225	1,857,806.57	1938
106,010,000	3,710,350	855,000	4,565,350	3,000,000	1,565,350	1,796,273.56	1939
105,155,000	3,680,425	885,000	4,565,425	3,000,000	1,565,425	1,735,613.31	1940
104,270,000	3,649,450	915,000	4,564,450	3,000,000	1,564,450	1,675,877.95	1941
103,355,000	3,617,425	945,000	4,562,425	3,000,000	1,562,425	1,617,109.87	1942
102,410,000	3,584,350	980,000	4,564,350	3,000,000	1,564,350	1,564,350.00	1943
$101,430,000	$63,199,575	$13,570,000	$76,769,575	$54,000,000	$22,769,575	$29,641,023.07	

2. Remaining 44 Years

Principal	Annual Interest Payments	Annual Principal Payments	Total Annual Payments	Year
$131,071,023.07	$ 4,587,485.81	$ 1,296,023.07	$ 5,883,508.88	1944
129,775,000	4,542,125	1,340,000	5,882,125	1945
128,435,000	4,495,225	1,385,000	5,880,225	1946
127,050,000	4,446,750	1,435,000	5,881,750	1947
125,615,000	4,396,525	1,485,000	5,881,525	1948
124,130,000	4,344,550	1,540,000	5,884,550	1949
122,590,000	4,290,650	1,590,000	5,880,650	1950
121,000,000	4,235,000	1,645,000	5,880,000	1951
119,355,000	4,177,425	1,705,000	5,882,425	1952
117,650,000	4,117,750	1,765,000	5,882,750	1953
115,885,000	4,055,975	1,825,000	5,880,975	1954
114,060,000	3,992,100	1,890,000	5,882,100	1955
112,170,000	3,925,950	1,960,000	5,885,950	1956
110,210,000	3,857,350	2,025,000	5,882,350	1957
108,185,000	3,786,475	2,100,000	5,886,475	1958
106,085,000	3,712,975	2,170,000	5,882,975	1959
103,915,000	3,637,025	2,245,000	5,882,025	1960
101,670,000	3,558,450	2,325,000	5,883,450	1961
99,345,000	3,477,075	2,405,000	5,882,075	1962
96,940,000	3,392,900	2,490,000	5,882,900	1963
94,450,000	3,305,750	2,575,000	5,880,750	1964
91,875,000	3,215,625	2,665,000	5,880,625	1965
89,210,000	3,122,350	2,760,000	5,882,350	1966
86,450,000	3,025,750	2,855,000	5,880,750	1967
83,595,000	2,925,825	2,955,000	5,880,825	1968
80,640,000	2,822,400	3,060,000	5,882,400	1969
77,580,000	2,715,300	3,165,000	5,880,300	1970
74,415,000	2,604,525	3,280,000	5,884,525	1971
71,135,000	2,489,725	3,395,000	5,884,725	1972
67,740,000	2,370,900	3,510,000	5,880,900	1973
64,230,000	2,248,050	3,635,000	5,883,050	1974
60,595,000	2,120,825	3,760,000	5,880,825	1975
56,835,000	1,989,225	3,890,000	5,879,225	1976
52,945,000	1,853,075	4,030,000	5,883,075	1977
48,915,000	1,712,025	4,170,000	5,882,025	1978
44,745,000	1,566,075	4,315,000	5,881,075	1979
40,430,000	1,415,050	4,465,000	5,880,050	1980
35,965,000	1,258,775	4,625,000	5,883,775	1981
31,340,000	1,096,900	4,785,000	5,881,900	1982
26,555,000	929,425	4,950,000	5,879,425	1983
21,605,000	756,175	5,125,000	5,881,175	1984
16,480,000	576,800	5,305,000	5,881,800	1985
11,175,000	391,125	5,490,000	5,881,125	1986
5,685,000	198,975	5,685,000	5,883,975	1987
	$127,740,410.81	$131,071,023.07	$258,811,433.88	

Add total amount received first 18 years..   54,000,000.00

$312,811,433.88

XI. DEBT SETTLEMENT WITH ESTHONIA *

Agreement signed October 28, 1925. Approved on the part of the United States by Act of Congress of April 30, 1926. Approved by Esthonia by the law of March 26, 1926, and published in official gazette No. 36 of April 22, 1926.

A. AGREEMENT,

Made the twenty-eighth day of October, 1925, at the City of Washington, District of Columbia, between THE REPUBLIC OF ESTHONIA, hereinafter called ESTHONIA, party of the first part, and THE UNITED STATES OF AMERICA, hereinafter called THE UNITED STATES, party of the second part.

Whereas, Esthonia is indebted to the United States as of December 15, 1922, upon obligations in the aggregate principal amount of $13,999,145.60, together with interest accrued and unpaid thereon; and

Whereas, Esthonia desires to fund said indebtedness to the United States, both principal and interest, through the issue of bonds to the United States, and the United States is prepared to accept bonds from Esthonia upon the terms and conditions hereinafter set forth;

Now, therefore, in consideration of the premises and of the mutual covenants herein contained, it is agreed as follows:

1. *Amount of Indebtedness.*—The amount of the indebtedness to be funded, after allowing for cash payments made or to be made by Esthonia and the credit

* Official text as issued by the Treasury Department.

set out below, is $13,830,000, which has been computed as follows:

Principal amount of obligations to be funded......	$13,999,145.00
Credit allowed for total loss of cargo on sinking of S.S. *John Russ* sunk by a mine in Baltic Sea.....	1,932,923.45
	$12,066,222.15
Interest accrued and unpaid thereon to December 15, 1922, at the rate of 4¼ per cent a year.......	1,765,219.73
Total principal and interest accrued and unpaid as of December 15, 1922................·......	$13,831,441.88
To be paid in cash by Esthonia upon execution of Agreement	1,441.88
Total indebtedness to be funded into bonds....	$13,830,000.00

2. *Repayment of Principal.*—In order to provide for the repayment of the indebtedness thus to be funded Esthonia will issue to the United States at par as of December 15, 1922, bonds of Esthonia in the aggregate principal amount of $13,830,000, dated December 15, 1922, and maturing serially on each December 15 in the succeeding years for 62 years, in the amounts and on the several dates fixed in the following schedule: (see p. 339).

PROVIDED HOWEVER, That Esthonia, at its option, upon not less than ninety days' advance notice to the United States, may postpone any payment falling due as hereinabove provided, except those falling due on or before December 15, 1930, hereinafter referred to in paragraph 5 of this Agreement, to any subsequent June 15 or December 15 not more than two years distant from its due date, but only on condition that in case Esthonia shall at any time exercise this option as to any payment of principal, the payment falling due in the next succeeding year can not be postponed to any date more than one year distant from the date when it becomes due unless and until the payment previously postponed shall actually have been made, and the payment falling due in the second succeeding year can not be postponed at all unless and until the payment of principal due two years previous thereto shall actually have been made.

3. *Form of Bond.*—All bonds issued or to be issued hereunder to the United States shall be payable to the Government of the United States of America, or order, shall be issued in such denominations as may be requested by the Secretary of the Treasury of the United States, substantially in the form set forth in the exhibit hereto annexed and marked "Exhibit A," and shall be signed for Esthonia by its Envoy Extraordinary and Minister Plenipotentiary at Washington, or by its other duly authorized representative. The $13,830,000 principal amount of bonds first to be issued hereunder shall be issued in 62 pieces, in denominations and with maturities corresponding to the annual payments of principal hereinabove set forth.

4. *Payment of Interest.*—All bonds issued or to be issued hereunder shall bear interest, payable •semi-annually on June 15 and December 15 in each year, at the rate of 3 per cent a year from December 15, 1922, to December 15, 1932, and thereafter at the rate of 3½ per cent a year until the principal thereof shall have been paid.

5. *Method of Payment.*—All bonds issued or to be issued hereunder shall be payable, as to both principal and interest, in United States gold coin of the present standard of value, or, at the option of Esthonia, upon not less than thirty days' advance notice to the United

States, in any obligations of the United States issued
after April 6, 1917, to be taken at par and accrued interest to the date of payment hereunder: PROVIDED,
HOWEVER, that with reference to the payments on account
of principal and/or interest falling due hereunder on or
before December 15, 1930, Esthonia, at its option, may
pay the following amounts on the dates specified:

June 15, 1926	$ 50,000	June 15, 1929	$125,000
December 15, 1926 ..	50,000	December 15, 1929 ..	125,000
June 15, 1927	75,000	June 15, 1930	150,000
December 15, 1927 ..	75,000	December 15, 1930 ..	150,000
June 15, 1928	100,000		
December 15, 1928 ..	100,000	Total..............	$1,000,000

and the balance, including interest on all overdue payments at the rate of 3 per cent a year from their respective due dates, in bonds of Esthonia dated December
15, 1930, bearing interest at the rate of 3 per cent a
year from December 15, 1930, to December 15, 1932,
and thereafter at the rate of 3½ per cent a year until
the principal thereof shall have been paid, such bonds
to mature serially on December 15 of each year up to
and including December 15, 1984, substantially in the
manner provided in paragraph 2 of this Agreement, and
to be substantially similar in other respects to the bonds
first to be issued hereunder.

   All payments, whether in cash or in obligations of the
United States, to be made by Esthonia on account of the
principal of or interest on any bonds issued or to be
issued hereunder and held by the United States, shall
be made at the Treasury of the United States in Washington, or, at the option of the Secretary of the Treasury
of the United States, at the Federal Reserve Bank of

New York, and if in cash shall be made in funds immediately available on the date of payment, or if in obligations of the United States shall be in form acceptable to the Secretary of the Treasury of the United States under the general regulations of the Treasury Department governing transactions in United States obligations.

6. *Exemption from Taxation.*—The principal and interest of all bonds issued or to be issued hereunder shall be paid without deduction for, and shall be exempt from, any and all taxes or other public dues, present or future, imposed by or under authority of Esthonia or any political or local taxing authority within the Republic of Esthonia, whenever, so long as, and to the extent that beneficial ownership is in (a) the Government of the United States, (b) a person, firm, or association neither domiciled nor ordinarily resident in Esthonia, or (c) a corporation not organized under the laws of Esthonia.

7. *Payments before Maturity.*—Esthonia, at its option, on any interest date or dates, upon not less than ninety days' advance notice to the United States, may make advance payments in amounts of $1,000 or multiples thereof, on account of the principal of any bonds issued or to be issued hereunder and held by the United States. Any such advance payments shall first be applied to the principal of any bonds which shall have been issued hereunder on account of principal and/or interest accruing between December 15, 1922, and December 15, 1930, and then to the principal of any other bonds issued hereunder and held by the United States, as may be indicated by Esthonia at the time of the payment.

8. *Exchange for Marketable Obligations.*—Esthonia,

will issue to the United States at any time, or from time to time, at the request of the Secretary of the Treasury of the United States, in exchange for any or all of the bonds issued or to be issued hereunder and held by the United States, definitive engraved bonds in form suitable for sale to the public, in such amounts and denominations as the Secretary of the Treasury of the United States may request, in bearer form, with provision for registration as to principal, and/or in fully registered form, and otherwise on the same terms and conditions, as to dates of issue and maturity, rate or rates of interest, exemption from taxation, payment in obligations of the United States issued after April 6, 1917, and the like, as the bonds surrendered on such exchange. .Esthonia will deliver definitive engraved bonds to the United States in accordance herewith within six months of receiving notice of any such request from the Secretary of the Treasury of the United States, and pending the delivery of the definitive engraved bonds will deliver, at the request of the Secretary of the Treasury of the United States, temporary bonds or interim receipts in form satisfactory to the Secretary of the Treasury of the United States within thirty days of the receipt of such request, all without expense to the United States. The United States, before offering any such bonds or interim receipts for sale in Esthonia, will first offer them to Esthonia for purchase at par and accrued interest, and Esthonia shall likewise have the option, in lieu of issuing any such bonds or interim receipts, to make advance redemption, at par and accrued interest, of a corresponding principal amount of bonds issued or to be issued hereunder and held by the United States. Esthonia agrees that the definitive engraved bonds called for by this paragraph shall contain all such provisions, and that it will cause to be promulgated all such rules, regulations, and orders as shall be deemed necessary or desirable by the Secretary of the Treasury of the United States in order to facilitate the sale of the bonds in the United States, in Esthonia or elsewhere, and that if requested by the Secretary of the Treasury of the United States, it will use its good offices to secure the listing of the bonds on such stock exchanges as he may request.

9. *Cancellation and Surrender of Obligations.*—Upon the execution of this Agreement, the payment to the United States of cash in the sum of $1,441.88 as provided in paragraph 1 of this Agreement and the delivery to the United States of the $13,830,000 principal amount of bonds of Esthonia first to be issued hereunder, together with satisfactory evidence of authority for the execution of this Agreement and the bonds on behalf of Esthonia by its Envoy Extraordinary and Minister Plenipotentiary at Washington, or by its other duly authorized representative, the United States will cancel and surrender to Esthonia, at the Treasury of the United States in Washington, the obligations of Esthonia in the principal amount of $13,999,145.60 described in the preamble to this Agreement.

10. *Notices.*—Any notice, request, or consent under the hand of the Secretary of the Treasury of the United States, shall be deemed and taken as the notice, request, or consent of the United States, and shall be sufficient if delivered at the legation of Esthonia at Washington or at the office of the Minister of Finance in Tallinn; and any notice, request, or election from or by Esthonia shall

336 WORLD WAR DEBT SETTLEMENTS

be sufficient if delivered to the American Legation at Tallinn or to the Secretary of the Treasury at the Treasury of the United States in Washington. The United States in its discretion may waive any notice required hereunder, but any such waiver shall be in writing and shall not extend to or affect any subsequent notice or impair any right of the United States to require notice hereunder.

11. *Compliance with Legal Requirements.*—Esthonia represents and agrees that the execution and delivery of this Agreement have in all respects been duly authorized and that all acts, conditions, and legal formalities which should have been completed prior to the making of this Agreement and the issuance of bonds hereunder have been completed as required by the laws of Esthonia and in conformity therewith.

12. *Counterparts.*—This Agreement shall be executed in two counterparts, each of which shall have the force and effect of an original.

IN WITNESS WHEREOF, Esthonia has caused this Agreement to be executed on its behalf by its Envoy Extraordinary and Minister Plenipotentiary at Washington, thereunto duly authorized, subject however, to the approval of the State Assembly, and the United States has likewise caused this Agreement to be executed on its behalf by the Secretary of the Treasury, as chairman of the World War Foreign Debt Commission, with the approval of the President, subject, however, to the approval of Congress, pursuant to the Act of Congress approved February 9, 1922, as amended by the Act of Congress approved February 28, 1923, and as further amended by the Act of Congress approved

January 21, 1925, all on the day and year above written.

> THE REPUBLIC OF ESTHONIA,
> By A. PIIP,
>> *Envoy Extraordinary and Minister Plenipotentiary.*

> THE UNITED STATES OF AMERICA,
>> For the World War Foreign Debt Commission:
> By A. W. MELLON,
>> *Secretary of the Treasury and Chairman of the Commission.*

Approved:

> CALVIN COOLIDGE,
>> *President.*

EXHIBIT A

(Form of Bond)

THE REPUBLIC OF ESTHONIA

$ No.

The Republic of Esthonia, hereinafter called Esthonia, for value received, promises to pay to the Government of the United States of America, hereinafter called the United States, or order, on December 15,   , the sum of   Dollars ($), and to pay interest upon said principal sum semiannually on June 15 and December 15 in each year, at the rate of three per cent a year from December 15, 1922, to December 15, 1932, and at the rate of three and one-half per cent a year thereafter until the principal hereof shall have been paid. This bond is payable as to both principal and interest in gold coin of the United States of America of the present standard of value, or, at the option of Esthonia, upon not less than thirty days' advance notice to the United States, in any obligations of the United States issued after April 6, 1917, to be taken at par and accrued interest to the date of payment hereunder.

This bond is payable as to both principal and interest without deduction for, and is exempt from, any and all taxes and other public dues, present or future, imposed by or under authority of Esthonia or any political or local taxing authority within the Republic of Esthonia, whenever, so long as, and to the extent that, beneficial ownership is in (a) the Government of the United States, (b) a person, firm, or association neither domiciled nor ordinarily resident in Esthonia, or (c) a corporation not organized under the laws of Esthonia. This bond is payable as to both principal and interest at the Treasury of the United States in Washington, D. C., or at the option of the Secretary of the Treasury of the United States at the Federal Reserve Bank of New York.

This bond is issued under an Agreement dated October 28, 1925, between Esthonia and the United States, to which this bond is subject and to which reference is hereby made.

IN WITNESS WHEREOF, Esthonia has caused this bond to be executed in its behalf at the City of Washington, District of Columbia, by its
              at Washington, thereunto duly authorized, as of December 15, 1922.

THE REPUBLIC OF ESTHONIA:
          By

B. Schedule of Esthonian Payments

Principal	Annual Interest Payments	Annual Principal Payments	Total Annual Payments	Year
$13,830,000	$ 414,900	69,000	$ 483,900	1923
13,761,000	412,830	71,000	483,830	1924
13,690,000	410,700	73,000	483,700	1925
13,617,000	408,510	75,000	483,510	1926
13,542,000	406,260	78,000	484,260	1927
13,464,000	403,920	80,000	483,920	1928
13,384,000	401,520	82,000	483,520	1929
13,302,000	399,060	85,000	484,060	1930
13,217,000	396,510	88,000	484,510	1931
13,129,000	393,870	90,000	483,870	1932
13,039,000	456,365	92,000	548,365	1933
12,947,000	453,145	95,000	548,145	1934
12,852,000	449,820	98,000	547,820	1935
12,754,000	446,390	101,000	547,390	1936
12,653,000	442,855	105,000	547,855	1937
12,548,000	439,180	109,000	548,180	1938
12,439,000	435,365	113,000	548,365	1939
12,326,000	431,410	117,000	548,410	1940
12,209,000	427,315	121,000	548,315	1941
12,088,000	423,080	125,000	548,080	1942
11,963,000	418,705	129,000	547,705	1943
11,834,000	414,190	134,000	548,190	1944
11,700,000	409,500	138,000	547,500	1945
11,562,000	404,670	143,000	547,670	1946
11,419,000	399,665	148,000	547,665	1947
11,271,000	394,485	153,000	547,485	1948
11,118,000	389,130	159,000	548,130	1949
10,959,000	383,565	165,000	548,565	1950
10,794,000	377,790	170,000	547,790	1951
10,624,000	371,840	176,000	547,840	1952
10,448,000	365,680	182,000	547,680	1953
10,266,000	359,310	189,000	548,310	1954
10,077,000	352,695	195,000	547,695	1955
9,882,000	345,870	202,000	547,870	1956
9,680,000	338,800	209,000	547,800	1957
9,471,000	331,485	217,000	548,485	1958
9,254,000	323,890	224,000	547,890	1959
9,030,000	316,050	232,000	548,050	1960
8,798,000	307,930	240,000	547,930	1961
8,558,000	299,530	249,000	548,530	1962
8,309,000	290,815	257,000	547,815	1963
8,052,000	281,820	266,000	547,820	1964

B. Schedule of Esthonian Payments—*Continued*

Principal	Annual Interest Payments	Annual Principal Payments	Total Annual Payments	Year
$7,786,000	$272,510	$275,000	$547,510	1965
7,511,000	262,885	285,000	547,885	1966
7,226,000	252,910	295,000	547,910	1967
6,931,000	242,585	305,000	547,585	1968
6,626,000	231,910	316,000	547,910	1969
6,310,000	220,850	327,000	547,850	1970
5,983,000	209,405	339,000	548,405	1971
5,644,000	197,540	350,000	547,540	1972
5,294,000	185,290	363,000	548,290	1973
4,931,000	172,585	375,000	547,585	1974
4,556,000	159,460	388,000	547,460	1975
4,168,000	145,880	402,000	547,880	1976
3,766,000	131,810	416,000	547,810	1977
3,350,000	117,250	431,000	548,250	1978
2,919,000	102,165	446,000	548,165	1979
2,473,000	86,555	461,000	547,555	1980
2,012,000	70,420	477,000	547,420	1981
1,535,000	53,725	494,000	547,725	1982
1,041,000	36,435	511,000	547,435	1983
530,000	18,550	530,000	548,550	1984
	$19,501,140	$13,830,000	$33,331,140	

XII. DEBT SETTLEMENT WITH RUMANIA *

Agreement signed December 4, 1925. Approved on the part of the United States by Act of Congress of May 3, 1926. Ratified by Rumania by law of March 26, 1926. Published in Moniturul Oficial of March 29, 1926.

A. Agreement,

Made the fourth day of December, 1925, at the City of Washington, District of Columbia, between THE KINGDOM OF RUMANIA, hereinafter called

* Official text as issued by the Treasury Department.

RUMANIA, party of the first part, and THE
UNITED STATES OF AMERICA, hereinafter called
the UNITED STATES, party of the second part.

Whereas, Rumania is indebted to the United States as
of June 15, 1925, upon obligations in the aggregate principal amount of $36,128,494.94, together with interest
accrued and unpaid thereon; and

Whereas, Rumania desires to fund said indebtedness
to the United States, both principal and interest, through
the issue of bonds to the United States, and the United
States is prepared to accept bonds from Rumania upon
the terms and conditions hereinafter set forth;

Now, therefore, in consideration of the premises and
of the mutual covenants herein contained, it is agreed as
follows:

1. *Amount of Indebtedness.*—The amount of the indebtedness to be funded, after allowing for cash payments made or to be made by Rumania and the credit
set out below, is $44,590,000, which has been computed
as follows:

Principal amount of indebtedness to be funded....	$36,128,494.94
Interest accrued and unpaid thereon to December 15, 1922, at the rate of 4¼ per cent a year......	5,365,806.08
Total indebtedness as of December 15, 1922...	$41,494,301.02
Interest accrued and unpaid thereon to June 15, 1925, at the rate of 3 per cent a year...........	3,112,072.59
	$44,606,373.61
Credits allowed by War Department for material, together with interest thereon.................	11,922.07
Total net indebtedness as of June 15, 1925....	$44,594,451.54
To be paid in cash upon execution of agreement..	4,451.54
Total indebtedness to be funded into bonds...	$44,590,000.00

2. *Payment.*—In order to provide for the payment of
the indebtedness thus to be funded Rumania will issue
to the United States at par bonds of Rumania dated
June 15, 1925, in the principal amounts and maturing
serially on the several dates fixed in the following
schedule: (see p. 351).

PROVIDED, HOWEVER, That Rumania, at its option,
upon not less than ninety days' advance notice to the
United States, may postpone any payment on account
of principal falling due as hereinabove provided after
June 15, 1939, to any subsequent June 15 or December
15 not more than two years distant from its due date,
but only on condition that in case Rumania shall at any
time exercise this option as to any payment of principal,
the payment falling due in the next succeeding year can
not be postponed to any date more than one year distant
from the date when it becomes due unless and until the
payment previously postponed shall actually have been
made, and the payment falling due in the second succeeding year can not be postponed at all unless and until
the payment of principal due two years previous thereto
shall actually have been made.

3. *Form of Bond.*—All bonds issued or to be issued
hereunder to the United States shall be payable to the
Government of the United States of America, or order,
and shall be signed for Rumania by its Envoy Extraordinary and Minister Plenipotentiary at Washington, or
by its other duly authorized representative. The bonds
issued for the first fourteen annual payments shall be
substantially in the form set forth in the exhibit hereto
annexed and marked "Exhibit A," shall be issued in
fourteen pieces in the principal amounts fixed in the pre-

ceding schedule, maturing annually on June 15 of each year up to and including June 15, 1939, and shall not bear interest before maturity. The bonds maturing subsequent to June 15, 1939, shall be substantially in the form set forth in the exhibit hereto annexed and marked "Exhibit B," and shall be issued in 48 pieces with maturities and in denominations as hereinabove set forth and shall bear interest at the rate of 3½% per annum from June 15, 1939, payable semiannually on June 15 and December 15 of each year until the principal of such bonds shall be paid.

4. *Method of Payment.*—All bonds issued or to be issued hereunder shall be payable, as to both principal and interest, in United States gold coin of the present standard of value, or, at the option of Rumania, upon not less than thirty days' advance notice to the United States, in any obligations of the United States issued after April 6, 1917, to be taken at par and accrued interest to the date of payment hereunder.

All payments, whether in cash or in obligations of the United States, to be made by Rumania on account of the principal of or interest on any bonds issued or to be issued hereunder and held by the United States, shall be made at the Treasury of the United States in Washington, or, at the option of the Secretary of the Treasury of the United States, at the Federal Reserve Bank of New York, and if in cash shall be made in funds immediately available on the date of payment, or if in obligations of the United States shall be in form acceptable to the Secretary of the Treasury of the United States under the general regulations of the Treasury Department governing transactions in United States obligations.

5. *Exemption from Taxation.*—The principal and interest of all bonds issued or to be issued hereunder shall be paid without deduction for, and shall be exempt from, any and all taxes or other public dues, present or future, imposed by or under authority of Rumania or any political or local taxing authority within the Kingdom of Rumania, whenever, so long as, and to the extent that beneficial ownership is in (a) the Government of the United States, (b) a person, firm, or association neither domiciled nor ordinarily resident in Rumania, or (c) a corporation not organized under the laws of Rumania.

6. *Payments before Maturity.*—Rumania, at its option, on June 15 or December 15 of any year, upon not less than ninety days' advance notice to the United States, may make advance payments in amounts of $1,000 or multiples thereof, on account of the principal of any bonds issued or to be issued hereunder and held by the United States. Any such advance payments shall be applied to the principal of such bonds as may be indicated by Rumania at the time of the payment.

7. *Exchange for Marketable Obligations.*—Rumania will issue to the United States at any time, or from time to time, at the request of the Secretary of the Treasury of the United States, in exchange for any or all of the bonds issued hereunder and held by the United States, definitive engraved bonds in form suitable for sale to the public, in such amounts and denominations as the Secretary of the Treasury of the United States may request, in bearer form, with provision for registration as to principal and/or in fully registered form, and otherwise on the same terms and conditions, as to dates of issue and maturity, rate or rates of interest, if any, exemption from

taxation, payment in obligations of the United States issued after April 6, 1917, and the like, as the bonds surrendered on such exchange. Rumania will deliver definitive engraved bonds to the United States in accordance herewith within six months of receiving notice of any such request from the Secretary of the Treasury of the United States, and pending the delivery of the definitive engraved bonds will deliver, at the request of the Secretary of the Treasury of the United States, temporary bonds or interim receipts in form satisfactory to the Secretary of the Treasury of the United States within thirty days of the receipt of such request, all without expense to the United States. The United States, before offering any such bonds or interim receipts for sale in Rumania will first offer them to Rumania for purchase at par and accrued interest, if any, and Rumania shall likewise have the option, in lieu of issuing any such bonds or interim receipts, to make advance redemption, at par and accrued interest, if any, of a corresponding principal amount of bonds issued hereunder and held by the United States. Rumania agrees that the definitive engraved bonds called for by this paragraph shall contain all such provisions, and that it will cause to be promulgated all such rules, regulations, and orders as shall be deemed necessary or desirable by the Secretary of the Treasury of the United States in order to facilitate the sale of the bonds in the United States, in Rumania or elsewhere, and that if requested by the Secretary of the Treasury of the United States, it will use its good offices to secure the listing of the bonds on such stock exchanges as the Secretary of the Treasury of the United States may specify.

8. *Cancellation and Surrender of Obligations.*—Upon the execution of this Agreement, the delivery to the United States of the $66,560,560.43 principal amount of bonds of Rumania to be issued hereunder, together with satisfactory evidence of authority for the execution of this Agreement by the representatives of Rumania and for the execution of the bonds to be issued hereunder, the United States will cancel and surrender to Rumania at the Treasury of the United States in Washington, the obligations of Rumania held by the United States.

9. *Notices.*—Any notice, request, or consent under the hand of the Secretary of the Treasury of the United States, shall be deemed and taken as the notice, request, or consent of the United States, and shall be sufficient if delivered at the Legation of Rumania at Washington or at the office of the Ministry of Finance in Rumania; and any notice, request, or election from or by Rumania shall be sufficient if delivered to the American Legation at Bucharest or to the Secretary of the Treasury at the Treasury of the United States in Washington. The United States in its discretion may waive any notice required hereunder, but any such waiver shall be in writing and shall not extend to or affect any subsequent notice or impair any right of the United States to require notice hereunder.

10. *Compliance with Legal Requirements.*—Rumania represents and agrees that the execution and delivery of this Agreement have in all respects been duly authorized and that all acts, conditions, and legal formalities which should have been completed prior to the making of this Agreement have been completed as required by the laws of Rumania and in conformity therewith.

11. *Counterparts.*—This Agreement shall be executed in two counterparts, each of which shall have the force and effect of an original.

IN WITNESS WHEREOF, Rumania has caused this Agreement to be executed on its behalf by N. Titulescu, Envoy Extraordinary and Minister Plenipotentiary to his Britannic Majesty and President of the Rumanian Debt Funding Commission at Washington, thereunto duly authorized, subject, however, to ratification by Rumanian Parliament, and the United States has likewise caused this Agreement to be executed on its behalf by the Secretary of the Treasury as Chairman of the World War Foreign Debt Commission, with the approval of the President, subject, however, to the approval of Congress, pursuant to the Act of Congress approved February 9, 1922, as amended by the Act of Congress approved February 28, 1923, and as further amended by the Act of Congress approved January 21, 1925, all on the day and the year first above written.

THE KINGDOM OF RUMANIA,
By N. TITULESCU.

THE UNITED STATES OF AMERICA,
For the World War Foreign Debt Commission:
By A. W. MELLON,
Secretary of the Treasury and Chairman of the Commission.

Approved:

CALVIN COOLIDGE,
President.

Exhibit A

(Form of Bond)

The Kingdom of Rumania

$ No.

The Kingdom of Rumania, hereinafter called Rumania, for value received, promises to pay to the Government of the United States of America, hereinafter called the United States, or order, on June 15, 19 , the sum of Dollars ($). This bond is payable in gold coin of the United States of America of the present standard of value, or, at the option of Rumania, upon not less than thirty days' advance notice to the United States, in any obligations of the United States issued after April 6, 1917, to be taken at par and accrued interest to the date of payment hereunder.

This bond is payable without deduction for, and is exempt from, any and all taxes and other public dues, present or future, imposed by or under authority of Rumania or any political or local taxing authority within Rumania, whenever, so long as, and to the extent that, beneficial ownership is in (a) the Government of the United States, (b) a person, firm, or association neither domiciled nor ordinarily resident in Rumania, or (c) a corporation not organized under the laws of Rumania. This bond is payable at the Treasury of the United States in Washington, D. C., or at the option of the Secretary of the Treasury of the United States at the Federal Reserve Bank of New York.

This bond is issued pursuant to the provisions of paragraph 2 of an Agreement dated December 4, 1925, between Rumania and the United States, to which Agreement this bond is subject and to which reference is hereby made.

In witness whereof, Rumania has caused this bond to be executed in its behalf by its
                    at the City of Washington, District of Columbia, thereunto duly authorized, as of June 15, 1925.

THE KINGDOM OF RUMANIA

      By

EXHIBIT B

(Form of Bond)

THE KINGDOM OF RUMANIA

$ No.

The Kingdom of Rumania, hereinafter called Rumania, for value received, promises to pay to the Government of the United States of America, hereinafter called the United States, or order, on June 15, 19 , the sum of   Dollars ($), and to pay interest upon said principal sum from June 15, 1939, at the rate of 3½% per annum, payable semiannually on the 15th day of December and June in each year, until the principal hereof has been paid. This bond is payable as to both principal and interest in gold coin of the United States of America of the present standard of value, or, at the option of Rumania, upon not less than thirty days' advance notice to the United States, in any obligations of the United States issued after April 6,

1917, to be taken at par and accrued interest to the date of payment hereunder.

This bond is payable as to both principal and interest without deduction for, and is exempt from, any and all taxes and other public dues, present or future, imposed by or under authority of Rumania or any political or local taxing authority within the Kingdom of Rumania, whenever, so long as, and to the extent that, beneficial ownership is in (a) the Government of the United States, (b) a person, firm, or association neither domiciled nor ordinarily resident in Rumania, or (c) a corporation not organized under the laws of Rumania. This bond is payable as to both principal and interest at the Treasury of the United States in Washington, D. C., or at the option of the Secretary of the Treasury of the United States at the Federal Reserve Bank of New York.

This bond is issued pursuant to the provisions of paragraph 2 of an Agreement dated December 4, 1925, between Rumania and the United States, to which Agreement this bond is subject and to which reference is hereby made.

IN WITNESS WHEREOF, Rumania has caused this bond to be executed in its behalf by its

at the City of Washington, District of Columbia, thereunto duly authorized, as of June 15, 1925.

THE KINGDOM OF RUMANIA

By

B. SCHEDULE OF RUMANIAN PAYMENTS

1. *First 14 Years*

Principal	Annual Interest Due	Annual Principal Due	Total Amount Due Annually	Total Amount to Be Paid Annually	Amount Deferred Each Year	Value of Each Deferred Amount on 15th Year	Year
$44,590,000	1,337,700	$ 222,000	$ 1,559,700	$ 200,000	$1,359,700	$ 2,035,817.04	1926
44,368,000	1,331,040	229,000	1,560,040	300,000	1,260,040	1,831,651.22	1927
44,139,300	1,324,170	236,000	1,560,170	400,000	1,160,170	1,637,355.26	1928
43,903,000	1,317,090	243,000	1,560,090	500,000	1,060,090	1,452,535.10	1929
43,660,000	1,309,800	250,000	1,559,800	600,000	959,800	1,276,814.66	1930
43,410,000	1,302,300	258,000	1,560,300	700,000	860,300	1,111,117.32	1931
43,152,000	1,294,560	265,000	1,559,560	800,000	759,560	952,433.76	1932
42,887,000	1,286,610	273,000	1,559,610	1,000,000	559,610	681,272.62	1933
42,614,000	1,278,420	282,000	1,560,420	1,200,000	360,420	425,997.58	1934
42,332,000	1,269,960	290,000	1,559,960	1,400,000	159,960	183,567.62	1935
42,042,000	1,471,470	296,000	1,767,470	1,600,000	167,470	185,676.84	1936
41,746,000	1,461,110	338,890	1,800,000	1,800,000	......	......	1937
41,407,110	1,449,248.85	550,751.15	2,000,000	2,000,000	......	......	1938
40,856,358.85	1,429,972.56	770,027.44	2,200,000	2,200,000	......	......	1939
$40,086,331.41	$18,863,451.41	$4,503,668.59	$23,367,120	$14,700,000	$8,667,120	$11,774,229.02	

2. Remaining 48 Years

Principal	Annual Interest Payments	Annual Principal Payments	Total Annual Payments	Year
$51,860,560.43	$ 1,815,119.62	$ 450,560.43	$ 2,245,680.05	1940
51,430,000	1,800,050	445,000	2,245,050	1941
50,985,000	1,784,475	462,000	2,246,475	1942
50,523,000	1,768,305	478,000	2,246,305	1943
50,045,000	1,751,575	494,000	2,245,575	1944
49,551,000	1,734,285	512,000	2,246,285	1945
49,039,000	1,716,365	529,000	2,245,365	1946
48,510,000	1,697,850	548,000	2,245,850	1947
47,962,000	1,678,670	567,000	2,245,670	1948
47,395,000	1,658,825	587,000	2,245,825	1949
46,808,000	1,638,280	608,000	2,246,280	1950
46,200,000	1,617,000	629,000	2,246,000	1951
45,571,000	1,594,985	651,000	2,245,985	1952
44,920,000	1,572,200	673,000	2,245,200	1953
44,247,000	1,548,645	697,000	2,245,645	1954
43,550,000	1,524,250	722,000	2,246,250	1955
42,828,000	1,498,980	747,000	2,245,980	1956
42,081,000	1,472,835	773,000	2,245,835	1957
41,308,000	1,445,780	800,000	2,245,780	1958
40,508,000	1,417,780	828,000	2,245,780	1959
39,680,000	1,388,800	857,000	2,245,800	1960
38,823,000	1,353,805	887,000	2,245,805	1961
37,936,000	1,327,760	918,000	2,245,760	1962
37,018,000	1,295,630	950,000	2,245,630	1963
36,068,000	1,262,380	984,000	2,246,380	1964
35,084,000	1,227,940	1,018,000	2,245,940	1965
34,066,000	1,192,310	1,053,000	2,245,310	1966
33,013,000	1,155,455	1,090,000	2,245,455	1967
31,923,000	1,117,305	1,129,000	2,246,305	1968
30,794,000	1,077,790	1,168,000	2,245,790	1969
29,626,000	1,036,910	1,209,000	2,245,910	1970
28,417,000	994,595	1,252,000	2,246,595	1971
27,165,000	950,775	1,295,000	2,245,775	1972
25,870,000	905,450	1,341,000	2,246,450	1973
24,529,000	858,515	1,387,000	2,245,515	1974
23,142,000	809,970	1,436,000	2,245,970	1975
21,706,000	759,710	1,486,000	2,245,710	1976
20,220,000	707,700	1,539,000	2,246,700	1977
18,681,000	653,855	1,592,000	2,245,835	1978
17,089,000	598,115	1,648,000	2,246,115	1979
15,441,000	540,435	1,706,000	2,246,435	1980
13,735,000	480,725	1,765,000	2,245,725	1981
11,970,000	418,950	1,827,000	2,245,950	1982
10,143,000	355,005	1,891,000	2,246,005	1983
8,252,000	288,820	1,957,000	2,245,820	1984
6,295,000	220,325	2,026,000	2,246,325	1985
4,269,000	149,415	2,097,000	2,246,415	1986
2,172,000	76,020	2,172,000	2,248,020	1987
	$55,945,699.62	$51,860,560.43	$107,806,260.05	

Add total amount received first 14 years.

14,700,000.00

$122,506,260.05

XIII. DEBT SETTLEMENT WITH ITALY *

Agreement signed November 14, 1925. Approved on the part of the United States by Act of Congress of April 28, 1926. Ratified in Italy by the law of February 14, 1926, and published in the Gazzetta Ufficiale of February 20, 1926.

A. AGREEMENT,

Made the fourteenth day of November, 1925, at the City of Washington, District of Columbia, between the KINGDOM OF ITALY, hereinafter called ITALY, party of the first part, and the UNITED STATES OF AMERICA, hereinafter called the UNITED STATES, party of the second part.

Whereas, Italy is indebted to the United States as of June 15, 1925, upon obligations in the aggregate principal amount of $1,647,869,197.96, together with interest accrued and unpaid thereon; and

Whereas, Italy desires to fund said indebtedness to the United States, both principal and interest, through the issue of bonds to the United States, and the United States is prepared to accept bonds from Italy upon the terms hereinafter set forth;

Now, therefore, in consideration of the premises and of the mutual covenants herein contained, it is agreed as follows:

1. *Amount of Indebtedness.*—The amount of indebtedness to be funded, after allowing for certain cash payments made or to be made by Italy is $2,042,000,000, which has been computed as follows:

* Official text as issued by the Treasury Department.

Obligations taken for cash advanced by Treasury	$1,648,034,050.90	
Accrued and unpaid interest at 4¼ per cent per annum to December 15, 1922..............	251,846,654.79	$1,899,880,705.69
Accrued interest at 3 per cent per annum from December 15, 1922, to June 15, 1925..............		142,491,052.93
		$2,042,371,758.62
Deduct payments made on account of principal since December 15, 1922...................	$ 164,852.94	
Interest on principal payments at 3 per cent per annum to June 15, 1925	7,439.34	$ 172,292.28
Total net indebtedness as of June 15, 1925		$2,042,199,466.34
To be paid in cash upon execution of agreement............		199,466.34
Total indebtedness to be funded into bonds		$2,042,000,000.00

2. *Payment.*—In order to provide for the payment of the indebtedness thus to be funded Italy will issue to the United States at par bonds of Italy in the aggregate principal amount of $2,042,000,000, dated June 15, 1925, and maturing serially on the several dates and in the amounts fixed in the following schedule: (see p. 362).

PROVIDED, HOWEVER, That Italy, at its option, upon not less than ninety days' advance notice to the United States, may postpone any payment on account of principal falling due as hereinabove provided, after June 15, 1930, to any subsequent June 15 or December 15 not more than two years distant from its due date, but only on condition that in case Italy shall at any time exercise this option as to any payment of principal, the payment falling due in the second succeeding year can not be postponed at all unless and until the payments of principal due two years and one year previous thereto shall actually have been made. All such postponed payments of principal shall bear interest at the rate of 4¼% per annum payable semiannually.

3. *Form of Bond.*—All bonds issued or to be issued hereunder to the United States shall be payable to the Government of the United States of America, or order, and shall be signed for Italy by its Ambassador at Washington, or by its other duly authorized representative. The bonds shall be substantially in the form set forth in the exhibit hereto annexed and marked "Exhibit A", and shall be issued in 62 pieces with maturities and in denominations as hereinabove set forth and shall bear no interest until June 15, 1930, and thereafter shall bear interest at the rate of ⅛ of 1% per annum from June 15, 1930, to June 15, 1940; at the rate of ¼ of 1% per annum from June 15, 1940, to June 15, 1950; at the rate of ½ of 1% per annum from June 15, 1950, to June 15, 1960; at the rate of ¾ of 1% per annum from June 15, 1960, to June 15, 1970; at the rate of 1% per annum from June 15, 1970, to June 15, 1980, and at the rate of 2% per annum after June 15, 1980, all payable semiannually on June 15 and December 15 of each year.

4. *Method of Payment.*—All bonds issued or to be issued hereunder shall be payable, as to both principal and interest, in United States gold coin of the present standard of value, or, at the option of Italy, upon not less than thirty days' advance notice to the United States, in any obligations of the United States issued

after April 6, 1917, to be taken at par and accrued interest to the date of payment hereunder.

All payments, whether in cash or in obligations of the United States, to be made by Italy on account of the principal of or interest on any bonds issued or to be issued hereunder and held by the United States, shall be made at the Treasury of the United States in Washington, or, at the option of the Secretary of the Treasury of the United States, at the Federal Reserve Bank of New York, and if in cash shall be made in funds immediately available on the date of payment, or if in obligations of the United States shall be in form acceptable to the Secretary of the Treasury of the United States under the general regulations of the Treasury Department governing transactions in United States obligations.

5. *Exemption from Taxation.*—The principal and interest of all bonds issued or to be issued hereunder shall be paid without deduction for, and shall be exempt from, any and all taxes or other public dues, present or future, imposed by or under authority of Italy or any political or local taxing authority within Italy, whenever, so long as, and to the extent that beneficial ownership is in (a) the Government of the United States, (b) a person, firm, or association neither domiciled nor ordinarily resident in Italy, or (c) a corporation not organized under the laws of Italy.

6. *Payments before Maturity.*—Italy, at its option, on June 15 or December 15 of any year, upon not less than ninety days' advance notice to the United States, may make advance payments in amounts of $1,000 or multiples thereof, on account of the principal of any bonds issued or to be issued hereunder and held by the United

States. Any such advance payments shall be applied to the principal of such bonds as may be indicated by Italy at the time of the payment.

7. *Exchange for Marketable Obligations.*—Italy will issue to the United States at any time, or from time to time, at the request of the Secretary of the Treasury of the United States, in exchange for any or all of the bonds issued hereunder and held by the United States, definitive engraved bonds in form suitable for sale to the public, in such amounts and denominations as the Secretary of the Treasury of the United States may request, in bearer form, with provision for registration as to principal, and/or in fully registered form, and otherwise on the same terms and conditions, as to dates of issue and maturity, rate or rates of interest, if any, exemption from taxation, payment in obligations of the United States issued after April 6, 1917, and the like, as the bonds surrendered on such exchange. Italy will deliver definitive engraved bonds to the United States in accordance herewith within six months of receiving notice of any such request from the Secretary of the Treasury of the United States, and pending the delivery of the definitive engraved bonds will deliver, at the request of the Secretary of the Treasury of the United States, temporary bonds or interim receipts in form satisfactory to the Secretary of the Treasury of the United States within thirty days of the receipt of such request, all without expense to the United States. The United States, before offering any such bonds or interim receipts for sale in Italy, will first offer them to Italy for purchase at par and accrued interest, if any, and Italy shall likewise have the option, in lieu of issuing any such

bonds or interim receipts, to make advance redemption, at par and accrued interest, if any, of a corresponding principal amount of bonds issued hereunder and held by the United States. Italy agrees that the definitive engraved bonds called for by this paragraph shall contain all such provisions, and that it will cause to be promulgated all such rules, regulations, and orders as shall be deemed necessary or desirable by the Secretary of the Treasury of the United States in order to facilitate the sale of the bonds in the United States, in Italy or elsewhere, and that if requested by the Secretary of the Treasury of the United States, it will use its good offices to secure the listing of the bonds on such stock exchanges as the Secretary of the Treasury of the United States may specify.

8. *Cancellation and Surrender of Obligations.*—Upon the execution of this Agreement, the delivery to the United States of the principal amount of bonds of Italy to be issued hereunder, together with satisfactory evidence of authority for the execution of this Agreement by the representative of Italy and for the execution of the bonds to be issued hereunder, the United States will cancel and surrender to Italy at the Treasury of the United States in Washington, the obligations of Italy held by the United States.

9. *Notices.*—Any notice, request, or consent under the hand of the Secretary of the Treasury of the United States, shall be deemed and taken as the notice, request, or consent of the United States, and shall be sufficient if delivered at the Embassy of Italy at Washington or at the office of the Ministry of Finance at Rome; and any notice, request, or election from or by Italy shall be

sufficient if delivered to the American Embassy at Rome or to the Secretary of the Treasury at the Treasury of the United States in Washington. The United States in its discretion may waive any notice required hereunder, but any such waiver shall be in writing and shall not extend to or affect any subsequent notice or impair any right of the United States to require notice hereunder.

10. *Compliance with Legal Requirements.*—Italy represents and agrees that the execution and delivery of this Agreement have in all respects been duly authorized and that all acts, conditions, and legal formalities which should have been completed prior to the making of this Agreement have been completed as required by the laws of Italy and in conformity therewith.

11. *Counterparts.*—This Agreement shall be executed in two counterparts, each of which shall have the force and effect of an original.

IN WITNESS WHEREOF, Italy has caused this Agreement to be executed on its behalf by Giuseppe Volpi di Misurata, its Plenipotentiary at Washington, thereunto duly authorized, subject, however, to ratification in Italy, and the United States has likewise caused this Agreement to be executed on its behalf by the Secretary of the Treasury, as Chairman of the World War Foreign Debt Commission, with the approval of the President, subject, however, to the approval of Congress, pursuant to the Act of Congress approved February 9, 1922, as amended by the Act of Congress approved February 28, 1923, and as further amended by the Act of Congress approved January 21, 1925, all on the day and year first above written.

THE KINGDOM OF ITALY,
By GIUSEPPE VOLPI DI MISURATA,

THE UNITED STATES OF AMERICA,
For the World War Foreign Debt
Commission:

By A. W. MELLON,
*Secretary of the Treasury and Chairman of the
Commission.*

Approved:

CALVIN COOLIDGE,
President.

EXHIBIT A

(Form of Bond)

THE KINGDOM OF ITALY

$ No.

The Kingdom of Italy, hereinafter called Italy, for
value received, promises to pay to the Government of the
United States of America, hereinafter called the United
States, or order, on June 15, 19   , the sum of
Dollars ($), and to pay interest upon said prin-
cipal sum after June 15, 1930, at the rate of ⅛ of 1%
per annum from June 15, 1930, to June 15, 1940, at the
rate of ¼ of 1% per annum from June 15, 1940, to June
15, 1950, at the rate of ½ of 1% per annum from June
15, 1950, to June 15, 1960, at the rate of ¾ of 1% per
annum from June 15, 1960, to June 15, 1970, at the rate
of 1% per annum from June 15, 1970, to June 15, 1980,
and at the rate of 2% per annum after June 15, 1980, all
payable semiannually on the 15th day of December and
June in each year. This bond is payable as to both
principal and interest in gold coin of the United States

of America of the present standard of value, or, at the option of Italy, upon not less than thirty days' advance notice to the United States, in any obligations of the United States issued after April 6, 1917, to be taken at par and accrued interest to the date of payment hereunder.

This bond is payable as to both principal and interest without deduction for, and is exempt from, any and all taxes and other public dues, present or future, imposed by or under authority of Italy or any political or local taxing authority within Italy whenever, so long as, and to the extent that beneficial ownership is in (a) the Government of the United States, (b) a person, firm, or association neither domiciled nor ordinarily resident in Italy, or (c) a corporation not organized under the laws of Italy. This bond is payable as to both principal and interest at the Treasury of the United States in Washington, D. C., or at the option of the Secretary of the Treasury of the United States at the Federal Reserve Bank of New York.

This bond is issued pursuant to the provisions of paragraph 2 of an Agreement dated November 14, 1925, between Italy and the United States, to which Agreement this bond is subject and to which reference is hereby made.

IN WITNESS WHEREOF, Italy has caused this bond to be executed in its behalf by its Ambassador Extraordinary and Plenipotentiary at Washington, thereunto duly authorized, as of June 15, 1925.

THE KINGDOM OF ITALY:

By

Ambassador Extraordinary and Plenipotentiary.

B. Schedule of Italian Payments

Principal	Annual Interest Payments	Annual Principal Payments	Total Annual Payments	Year
$2,042,000,000	.... $	5,000,000 $	. 5,000,000	1926
2,037,000,000	....	5,000,000	5,000,000	1927
2,032,000,000	....	5,000,000	5,000,000	1928
2,027,000,000	....	5,000,000	5,000,000	1929
2,022,000,000	....	5,000,000	5,000,000	1930
2,017,000,000	$ 2,521,250	12,100,000	14,621,250	1931
2,004,900,000	2,506,125	12,200,000	14,706,125	1932
1,992,700,000	2,490,875	12,300,000	14,790,875	1933
1,980,400,000	2,475,500	12,600,000	15,075,500	1934
1,967,800,000 ⅛%	2,459,750	13,000,000	15,459,750	1935
1,954,800,000	2,443,500	13,500,000	15,943,500	1936
1,941,300,000	2,426,625	14,200,000	16,626,625	1937
7,927,100,000	2,408,875	14,600,000	17,008,875	1938
1,912,500,000	2,390,625	15,200,000	17,590,625	1939
1,897,300,000	2,371,625	15,800,000	18,171,625	1940
1,881,500,000	4,703,750	16,400,000	21,103,750	1941
1,865,100,000	4,662,750	17,000,000	21,662,750	1942
1,848,100,000	4,620,250	17,600,000	22,220,250	1943
1,830,500,000	4,576,250	18,300,000	. 22,876,250	1944.
1,812,200,000 ¼%	4,530,500	19,000,000	23,530,500	1945
1,793,200,000	4,483,000	19,600,000	24,083,000	1946
1,773,600,000	4,434,000	20,000,000	24,434,000	1947
1,753,600,000	4,384,000	20,600,000	24,984,000	1948
1,733,000,000	4,332,500	21,200,000	25,532,500	1949
1,711,800,000	4,279,500	22,000,000	26,279,500	1950
1,689,800,000	8,449,000	23,000,000	31,449,000	1951
1,666,800,000	8,334,000	23,800,000	32,134,000	1952
1,643,000,000	8,215,000	24,600,000	32,815,000	1953
1,618,400,000	8,092,000	25,400,000	33,492,000	1954
1,593,000,000 ½%	7,965,000	26,500,000	34,465,000	1955
1,566,500,000	7,832,500	27,500,000	35,332,500	1956
1,539,000,000	7,695,000	28,500,000	. 36,195,000	1957
1,510,500,000	7,552,500	29,600,000	37,152,500	1958
1,480,900,000	7,404,500	30,500,000	37,904,500	1959
1,450,400,000	7,252,000	31,500,000	38,752,000	1960

B. Schedule of Italian Payments—*Continued*

Principal	Annual Interest Payments	Annual Principal Payments	Total Annual Payments	Year
$1,418,900,000	$10,641,750	$32,500,000	$43,141,750	1961
1,386,400,000	10,398,000	33,500,000	43,898,000	1962
1,352,900,000	10,146,750	34,500,000	44,646,750	1963
1,318,400,000	9,888,000	35,500,000	45,388,000	1964
1,282,900,000	9,621,750	36,500,000	46,121,750	1965
1,246,400,000 ¾%	9,348,000	38,000,000	47,348,000	1966
1,208,400,000	9,063,000	39,500,000	48,563,000	1967
1,168,900,000	8,766,750	41,500,000	50,266,750	1968
1,127,400,000	8,455,500	43,500,000	51,955,500	1969
1,083,900,000	8,129,250	44,500,000	52,629,250	1970
1,039,400,000	10,394,000	46,000,000	56,394,000	1971
993,400,000	9,934,000	47,500,000	57,434,000	1972
945,900,000	9,459,000	49,000,000	58,459,000	1973
896,900,000	8,969,000	50,500,000	59,469,000	1974
846,400,000 1%	8,464,000	52,000,000	60,464,000	1975
794,400,000	7,944,000	54,000,000	61,944,000	1976
740,400,000	7,404,000	56,000,000	63,404,000	1977
684,400,000	6,844,000	59,000,000	65,844,000	1978
625,400,000	6,254,000	61,000,000	67,254,000	1979
564,400,000	5,644,000	62,000,000	67,644,000	1980
502,400,000	10,048,000	64,000,000	74,048,000	1981
438,400,000	8,768,000	67,000,000	75,768,000	1982
371,400,000	7,428,000	69,000,000	76,428,000	1983
302,400,000 2%	6,048,000	72,000,000	78,048,000	1984
230,400,000	4,608,000	74,000,000	78,608,000	1985
156,400,000	3,128,000	77,000,000	80,128,000	1986
79,400,000	1,588,000	79,400,000	80,988,000	1987
	$365,677,500	$2,042,000,000	$2,407,677,500	

XIV. DEBT SETTLEMENT WITH FRANCE *
Agreement signed April 29, 1926. Approved by U. S. House of Representatives June 2, 1926.

A. Agreement,

Made the 29th day of April, 1926, at the City of Washington, District of Columbia, between the FRENCH

* Official text as issued by the Treasury Department.

REPUBLIC, hereinafter called FRANCE, party of the first part, and the UNITED STATES OF AMERICA, hereinafter called the UNITED STATES, party of the second part.

Whereas, France is indebted to the United States as of June 15, 1925, upon obligations in the aggregate principal amount of $3,340,516,043.72, together with interest accrued and unpaid thereon; and

Whereas, France desires to fund said indebtedness to the United States, both principal and interest, through the issue of bonds to the United States, and the United States is prepared to accept bonds from France upon the terms hereinafter set forth;

Now, therefore, in consideration of the premises and of the mutual covenants herein contained, it is agreed as follows:

1. *Amount of Indebtedness.*—The amount of indebtedness to be funded, after allowing for certain cash payments made or to be made by France is $4,025,000,000, which has been computed as follows: (see p. 365).

2. *Payment.*—In order to provide for the payment of the indebtedness thus to be funded France will issue to the United States at par bonds of France in the aggregate principal amount of $4,025,000,000, dated June 15, 1925, and maturing serially on the several dates and in the amounts fixed in the following schedule: (see p. 373).

PROVIDED, HOWEVER, That France, at its option, upon not less than ninety days' advance notice to the United States, may postpone so much of any payment on account of principal and/or interest falling due in any one year as hereinabove provided after June 15, 1926,

Principal of obligations held for cash advanced under Liberty Bond Acts	$2,933,405,070.15	
Accrued and unpaid interest at 4¼ per cent to December 15, 1922	445,066,027.49	
		$3,378,471,097.64
Principal of obligations given for surplus war supplies purchased on credit	407,341,145.01	
Interest at 4¼ per cent from the last interest-payment date prior to December 15, 1922, to December 15, 1922..............	6,324,940.79	
		413,666,085.80
Total indebtedness as of December 15, 1922..........		3,792,137,183.44
Accrued and unpaid interest at 3 per cent per annum on this amount from December 15, 1922, to June 15, 1925........		284,410,288.75
Total indebtedness as of June 15, 1925		4,076,547,472.19
Credits: Payments received on account of interest between December 15, 1922, and June 15, 1925........	$. 50,917,643.13	
Payments on account of principal since December 15, 1922.......	230,171.44	
Interest on principal payments at 3 per cent per annum from date of payment to June 15, 1925	12,970.73	
		51,160,785.30
Net indebtedness as of June 15, 1925		4,025,386,686.89
To be paid in cash upon execution of agreement		386,686.89
Total indebtedness to be funded into bonds........		4,025,000,000.00

and prior to June 16, 1932, as shall be in excess of $20,000,000 in any one year, to any subsequent June 15 or December 15 not more than three years distant from its due date, and upon like notice France, at its option, may postpone any payment on account of principal falling due as hereinafter provided after June 15, 1932, to any subsequent June 15 or December 15 not more than three years distant from its due date, but any such postponement shall be only on condition that in case France shall at any time exercise this option as to any payment of principal and/or interest, the payment falling due in the third succeeding year can not be postponed at all unless and until the payment of principal and/or interest due three years, two years and one year previous thereto shall actually have been made. All such postponed payments shall bear interest at the rate of 4¼% per annum payable semiannually.

3. *Form of Bond.*—All bonds issued or to be issued hereunder to the United States shall be payable to the Government of the United States of America, or order, and shall be signed for France by its Ambassador at Washington, or by its other duly authorized representative. The bonds shall be substantially in the form set forth in the exhibit hereto annexed and marked "Exhibit A," and shall be issued in 62 pieces with maturities and in denominations as hereinabove set forth and shall bear no interest until June 15, 1930, and thereafter shall bear interest at the rate of 1% per annum from June 15, 1930, to June 15, 1940; at the rate of 2% per annum from June 15, 1940, to June 15, 1950; at the rate of 2½% per annum from June 15, 1950, to June 15, 1958; at the rate of 3% per annum from June 15, 1958, to June 15, 1965; and at the rate of 3½% per

annum after June 15, 1965, all payable semiannually on June 15 and December 15 of each year.

4. *Method of Payment.*—All bonds issued or to be issued hereunder shall be payable, as to both principal and interest, in United States gold coin of the present standard of value, or, at the option of France, upon not less than thirty days' advance notice to the United States, in any obligations of the United States issued after April 6, 1917, to be taken at par and accrued interest to the date of payment hereunder.

All payments, whether in cash or in obligations of the United States, to be made by France on account of the principal of or interest on any bonds issued or to be issued hereunder and held by the United States, shall be made at the Treasury of the United States in Washington, or, at the option of the Secretary of the Treasury of the United States, at the Federal Reserve Bank of New York, and if in cash shall be made in funds immediately available on the date of payment, or if in obligations of the United States shall be in form acceptable to the Secretary of the Treasury of the United States under the general regulations of the Treasury Department governing transactions in United States obligations.

5. *Exemption from Taxation.*—The principal and interest of all bonds issued or to be issued hereunder shall be paid without deduction for, and shall be exempt from, any and all taxes or other public dues, present or future, imposed by or under authority of France or any political or local taxing authority within France, whenever, so long as, and to the extent that beneficial ownership is in (a) the Government of the United States, (b) a person,

firm, or association neither domiciled nor ordinarily resident in France, or (c) a corporation not organized under the laws of France.

6. *Payments before Maturity.*—France, at its option on June 15 or December 15 of any year, upon not less than ninety days' advance notice to the United States, may make advance payments in amounts of $1,000 or multiples thereof, on account of the principal of any bonds issued or to be issued hereunder and held by the United States. Any such advance payments shall be applied to the principal of such bonds as may be indicated by France at the time of the payment.

7. *Exchange for Marketable Obligations.*—France will issue to the United States at any time, or from time to time, at the request of the Secretary of the Treasury of the United States, in exchange for any or all of the bonds issued hereunder and held by the United States, definitive engraved bonds in form suitable for sale to the public, in such amounts and denominations as the Secretary of the Treasury of the United States may request, in bearer form, with provision for registration as to principal and/or in fully registered form, and otherwise on the same terms and conditions, as to dates of issue and maturity, rate or rates of interest, if any, exemption from taxation, payment in obligations of the United States issued after April 6, 1917, and the like, as the bonds, surrendered on such exchange. France will deliver definitive engraved bonds to the United States in accordance herewith within six months of receiving notice of any such request from the Secretary of the Treasury of the United States, and pending the delivery of the definitive engraved bonds will deliver, at the request of

the Secretary of the Treasury of the United States, temporary bonds or interim receipts in form satisfactory to the Secretary of the Treasury of the United States within thirty days of the receipt of such request, all without expense to the United States. The United States, before offering any such bonds or interim receipts for sale in France, will first offer them to France for purchase at par and accrued interest, if any, and France shall likewise have the option, in lieu of issuing any such bonds or interim receipts, to make advance redemption, at par and accrued interest, if any, of a corresponding principal amount of bonds issued hereunder and held by the United States. France agrees that the definitive engraved bonds called for by this paragraph shall contain all such provisions, and that it will cause to be promulgated all such rules, regulations, and orders as shall be deemed necessary or desirable by the Secretary of the Treasury of the United States in order to facilitate the sale of the bonds in the United States, in France, or elsewhere, and that if requested by the Secretary of the Treasury of the United States, it will use its good offices to secure the listing of the bonds on such stock exchanges as the Secretary of the Treasury of the United States may specify.

8. *Cancellation and Surrender of Obligations.*—Upon the execution of this Agreement, the delivery to the United States of the principal amount of bonds of France to be issued hereunder, together with satisfactory evidence of authority for the execution of this Agreement by the representative of France and for the execution of the bonds to be issued hereunder, the United States will cancel and surrender to France at the Treasury of the

United States in Washington, the obligations of France held by the United States.

9. *Notices.*—Any notice, request, or consent under the hand of the Secretary of the Treasury of the United States, shall be deemed and taken as the notice, request, or consent of the United States, and shall be sufficient if delivered at the Embassy of France at Washington or at the office of the Ministry of Finance at Paris; and any notice, request, or election from or by France shall be sufficient if delivered to the American Embassy at Paris or to the Secretary of the Treasury at the Treasury of the United States in Washington. The United States in its discretion may waive any notice required hereunder, but any such waiver shall be in writing and shall not extend to or affect any subsequent notice or impair any right of the United States to require notice hereunder.

10. *Compliance with Legal Requirements.*—France represents and agrees that the execution and delivery of this Agreement have in all respects been duly authorized and that all acts, conditions, and legal formalities which should have been completed prior to the making of this Agreement have been completed as required by the laws of France and in conformity therewith.

11. *Counterparts.*—This Agreement shall be executed in two counterparts, each of which shall have the force and effect of an original.

IN WITNESS WHEREOF, France has caused this Agreement to be executed on its behalf by Hon. Henry Bérenger, its Ambassador Extraordinary and Plenipotentiary at Washington, thereunto duly authorized, subject, however, to ratification in France, and the United

States has likewise caused this Agreement to be executed on its behalf by the Secretary of the Treasury as Chairman of the World War Foreign Debt Commission, with the approval of the President, subject, however, to the approval of Congress, pursuant to the Act of Congress approved February 9, 1922, as amended by the Act of Congress approved February 28, 1923, and as further amended by the Act of Congress approved January 21, 1925, all on the day and the year first above written.

THE FRENCH REPUBLIC,
By HENRY BÉRENGER

THE UNITED STATES OF AMERICA,
(For the World War Foreign Debt Commission):
By ANDREW W. MELLON,
Secretary of the Treasury and Chairman of the Commission.
Approved:

CALVIN COOLIDGE,
President.

———

EXHIBIT A

(Form of Bond)

THE REPUBLIC OF FRANCE

$ No.

The Republic of France, hereinafter called France, for value received, promises to pay to the Government of the United States of America, hereinafter called the United States, or order, on June 15, 19   , the sum of

Dollars ($), and to pay interest upon said prin_ cipal sum after June 15, 1930, at the rate of 1% per annum from June 15, 1930, to June 15, 1940, at the rate of 2% per annum from June 15, 1940, to June 15, 1950, at the rate of 2½% per annum from June 15, 1950, to June 15, 1958, at the rate of 3% per annum from June 15, 1958, to June 15, 1965, and at the rate of 3½% per annum after June 15, 1965, all payable semiannually on the 15th day of December and June in each year. This bond is payable as to both principal and interest in gold coin of the United States of America of the present standard of value, or, at the option of France, upon not less than thirty days' advance notice to the United States, in any obligations of the United States issued after April 6, 1917, to be taken at par and accrued interest to the date of payment hereunder.

This bond is payable as to both principal and interest without deduction for, and is exempt from, any and all taxes and other public dues, present or future, imposed by or under authority of France or any political or local taxing authority within France, whenever, so long as, and to the extent that, beneficial ownership is in (a) the Government of the United States, (b) a person, firm, or association neither domiciled nor ordinarily resident in France, or (c) a corporation not organized under the laws of France. This bond is payable as to both principal and interest at the Treasury of the United States in Washington, D. C., or at the option of the Secretary of the Treasury of the United States at the Federal Reserve Bank of New York.

This bond is issued pursuant to the provisions of paragraph 2 of an Agreement dated April 29, 1926, between

B. Schedule of French Payments

Principal	Annual Interest Payments		Annual Principal Payments	Total Annual Payments	Year
$4,025,000,000.00		....	$ 30,000,000.00	$ 30,000,000.00	1926
3,995,000,000.00		....	30,000,000.00	30,000,000.00	1927
3,965,000,000.00		....	32,500,000.00	32,500,000.00	1928
3,932,500,000.00		....	32,500,000.00	32,500,000.00	1929
3,900,000,000.00		....	35,000,000.00	35,000,000.00	1930
3,865,000,000.00		$ 38,650,000.00	1,350,000.00	40,000,000.00	1931
3,863,650,000.00		38,636,500.00	11,363,500.00	50,000,000.00	1932
3,852,286,500.00		38,522,865.00	21,477,135.00	60,000,000.00	1933
3,830,809,365.00		38,308,093.65	36,691,906.35	75,000,000.00	1934
3,794,117,458.65	1%	37,941,174.59	42,058,825.41	80,000,000.00	1935
3,752,058,633.24		37,520,586.33	52,479,413.67	90,000,000.00	1936
3,699,579,219.57		36,995,792.20	63,004,207.80	100,000,000.00	1937
3,636,575,011.77		36,365,750.12	68,634,249.88	105,000,000.00	1938
3,567,940,761.89		35,679,407.62	74,320,592.38	110,000,000.00	1939
3,493,620,169.51		34,936,201.70	80,063,798.30	115,000,000.00	1940
3,413,556,371.21		68,271,127.42	51,728,872.58	120,000,000.00	1941
3,361,827,498.63		67,236,549.98	57,763,450.02	125,000,000.00	1942
3,304,064,048.61		66,081,280.97	58,918,719.03	125,000,000.00	1943
3,245,145,329.58		64,902,906.59	60,097,093.41	125,000,000.00	1944
3,185,048,236.17	2%	63,700,964.72	61,299,035.28	125,000,000.00	1945
3,123,749,200.89		62,474,984.02	62,525,015.98	125,000,000.00	1946
3,061,224,184.91		61,224,483.70	63,775,516.30	125,000,000.00	1947
2,997,448,668.61		59,948,973.37	65,051,026.63	125,000,000.00	1948
2,932,397,641.98		58,647,952.84	66,352,047.16	125,000,000.00	1949
2,866,045,594.82		57,320,911.90	67,679,088.10	125,000,000.00	1950
2,798,366,506.72		69,959,162.67	55,040,837.33	125,000,000.00	1951
2,743,325,669.39		68,583,141.73	56,416,858.27	125,000,000.00	1952
2,686,908,811.12		67,172,720.29	57,827,279.71	125,000,000.00	1953
2,629,081,531.41	2½%	65,727,088.29	59,272,961.71	125,000,000.00	1954
2,569,808,569.70		64,245,214.24	60,754,785.76	125,000,000.00	1955
2,509,053,783.94		62,726,344.60	62,278,655.40	125,000,000.00	1956
2,446,780,128.54		61,169,503.21	63,830,496.79	125,000,000.00	1957
2,382,949,631.75		59,573,740.79	65,426,259.21	125,000,000.00	1958
2,317,523,372.54		69,525,701.18	55,474,298.87	125,000,000.00	1959
2,262,049,073.72		67,861,472.21	57,138,527.79	125,000,000.00	1960
2,204,910,545.93		66,147,316.38	58,852,683.62	125,000,000.00	1961
2,146,057,862.31	3%	64,381,735.87	60,618,264.13	125,000,000.00	1962
2,085,439,598.18		62,563,187.95	62,436,812.05	125,000,000.00	1963
2,023,002,786.13		60,690,083.58	64,309,916.42	125,000,000.00	1964
1,958,692,869.71		58,760,786.09	66,239,213.91	125,000,000.00	1965
1,892,453,655.80		66,235,877.95	58,764,122.05	125,000,000.00	1966
1,833,689,533.75		64,179,133.68	60,820,866.32	125,000,000.00	1967
1,772,868,667.43		62,050,403.36	62,949,596.64	125,000,000.00	1968
1,709,919,070.79		59,847,167.48	65,152,832.52	125,000,000.00	1969
1,644,766,238.27		57,566,818.34	67,433,181.66	125,000,000.00	1970
1,577,333,056.61		55,206,656.98	69,793,343.02	125,000,000.00	1971
1,507,539,713.59		52,763,889.98	72,236,110.02	125,000,000.00	1972
1,435,303,603.57		50,285,626.12	74,764,373.88	125,000,000.00	1973
1,360,539,229.69		47,618,873.04	77,381,126.96	125,000,000.00	1974
1,283,158,102.73		44,910,533.60	80,089,466.40	125,000,000.00	1975
1,203,068,636.33		42,107,402.27	82,892,597.73	125,000,000.00	1976
1,120,176,038.60	3½%	39,206,161.35	85,793,838.65	125,000,000.00	1977
1,034,382,199.95		36,203,377.00	88,796,623.00	125,000,000.00	1978
945,585,576.95		33,095,495.19	91,904,504.81	125,000,000.00	1979
853,681,072.14		29,878,837.52	95,121,162.48	125,000,000.00	1980
758,559,909.66		26,549,596.84	98,450,403.16	125,000,000.00	1981
660,109,506.50		23,103,832.73	101,896,167.27	125,000,000.00	1982
558,213,339.23		19,537,466.87	105,462,533.13	125,000,000.00	1983
452,750,806.10		15,846,278.21	109,153,721.79	125,000,000.00	1984
343,597,084.31		12,025,897.95	112,974,102.05	125,000,000.00	1985
230,622,982.26		8,071,804.38	116,928,195.62	125,000,000.00	1986
113,694,786.64		3,979,317.53	113,694,786.64	117,674,104.17	1987
		$2,822,674,104.17	$4,025,000,000	$6,847,674,104.17	

373

France and the United States, to which Agreement this bond is subject and to which reference is hereby made.

IN WITNESS WHEREOF, France has caused this bond to be executed in its behalf by its Ambassador Extraordinary and Plenipotentiary at Washington, thereunto duly authorized, as of June 15, 1925.

THE FRENCH REPUBLIC:

By

Ambassador Extraordinary and Plenipotentiary.

XV. DEBT SETTLEMENT WITH YUGOSLAVIA *

Agreement signed May 3, 1926. Approved on the part of the Yugoslav Government under date of June 19, 1926. Approved by U. S. House of Representatives, June 4, 1926.

A. AGREEMENT,

Made the 3rd day of May, 1926, at the City of Washington, District of Columbia, between the KINGDOM OF THE SERBS, CROATS AND SLOVENES, party of the first part, and the UNITED STATES OF AMERICA, hereinafter called the UNITED STATES, party of the second part.

Whereas, the Kingdom of the Serbs, Croats and Slovenes is indebted to the United States as of June 15, 1925, upon obligations in the aggregate principal amount of $51,037,886.39, together with interest accrued and unpaid thereon; and

Whereas, the Kingdom of the Serbs, Croats and
* Official text as issued by the Treasury Department.

Slovenes desires to fund said indebtedness to the United States, both principal and interest, through the issue of bonds to the United States, and the United States is prepared to accept bonds from the Kingdom of the Serbs, Croats and Slovenes upon the terms hereinafter set forth;

Now, therefore, in consideration of the premises and of the mutual covenants herein contained, it is agreed as follows:

1. *Amount of Indebtedness.*—The amount of indebtedness to be funded after allowing for certain cash payments made or to be made by the Kingdom of the Serbs, Croats and Slovenes is $62,850,000, which has been computed as follows: (see p. 376).

2. *Payment.*—In order to provide for the payment of the indebtedness thus to be funded the Kingdom of the Serbs, Croats and Slovenes will issue to the United States at par bonds of the Kingdom of the Serbs, Croats and Slovenes in the aggregate principal amount of $62,-850,000, dated June 15, 1925, and maturing serially on the several dates and in the amounts fixed in the following schedule: (see p. 385).

PROVIDED, HOWEVER, That the Kingdom of the Serbs, Croats and Slovenes, at its option, upon not less than ninety days' advance notice to the United States, may postpone any payment on account of principal falling due as hereinabove provided, after June 15, 1937, to any subsequent June 15 or December 15 not more than two years distant from its due date, but only on condition that in case the Kingdom of the Serbs, Croats and Slovenes shall at any time exercise this option as to any payment of principal, the payment falling due in the

Principal of obligations acquired for cash advanced under Liberty Bond Acts	$26,126,574.59	
Accrued and unpaid interest at 4¼ per cent per annum to December 15, 1922	4,073,423.14	$30,199,997.73
Principal of obligations acquired by Secretary of War for surplus war supplies sold on credit...........	24,978,020.99	
Accrued and unpaid interest at 4¼ per cent per annum to December 15, 1922	3,358,790.45	28,336,811.44
		58,536,809.17
Accrued interest at 3 per cent per annum from December 15, 1922, to June 15, 1925....................		4,390,260.69
		62,927,069.86
Credits: Payments on account of principal since December 15, 1922...........	$ 66,709.19	
Interest thereon at 3 per cent to June 15, 1925	3,248.28	69,957.47
Total net indebtedness as of June 15, 1925		62,857,112.39
To be paid in cash upon execution of agreement		7,112.39
Total indebtedness to be funded into bonds		62,850,000.00

second succeeding year can not be postponed at all unless and until the payments of principal due two years and one year previous thereto shall actually have been made. All such postponed payments of principal shall bear interest at the rate of 4¼% per annum payable semiannually.

3. *Form of Bond.*—All bonds issued or to be issued hereunder to the United States shall be payable to the

Government of the United States of America, or order, and shall be signed for the Kingdom of the Serbs, Croats and Slovenes by its Minister at Washington, or by its other duly authorized representative. The bonds shall be substantially in the form set forth in the exhibit hereto annexed and marked "Exhibit A", and shall be issued in 62 pieces with maturities and in denominations as hereinabove set forth and shall bear no interest until June 15, 1937, and thereafter shall bear interest at the rate of ⅛ of 1% per annum from June 15, 1937, to June 15, 1940; at the rate of ½ of 1% per annum from June 15, 1940, to June 15, 1954; at the rate of 1% per annum from June 15, 1954, to June 15, 1957; at the rate of 2% per annum from June 15, 1957, to June 15, 1960, and at the rate of 3½% per annum after June 15, 1960, all payable semiannually on June 15 and December 15 of each year, until the principal thereof shall have been paid.

4. *Method of Payment.*—All bonds issued or to be issued hereunder shall be payable, as to both principal and interest, in United States gold coin of the present standard of value, or, at the option of the Kingdom of the Serbs, Croats and Slovenes, upon not less than thirty days' advance notice to the United States, in any obligations of the United States issued after April 6, 1917, to be taken at par and accrued interest to the date of payment hereunder.

All payments, whether in cash or in obligations of the United States, to be made by the Kingdom of the Serbs, Croats and Slovenes on account of the principal of or interest on any bonds issued or to be issued hereunder and held by the United States, shall be made at the

Treasury of the United States in Washington, or, at the option of the Secretary of the Treasury of the United States, at the Federal Reserve Bank of New York, and if in cash shall be made in funds immediately available on the date of payment, or if in obligations of the United States shall be in form acceptable to the Secretary of the Treasury of the United States under the general regulations of the Treasury Department governing transactions in United States obligations.

5. *Exemption from Taxation.*—The principal and interest of all bonds issued or to be issued hereunder shall be paid without deduction for, and shall be exempt from, any and all taxes or other public dues, present or future, imposed by or under authority of the Kingdom of the Serbs, Croats and Slovenes or any political or local taxing authority within the Kingdom of the Serbs, Croats and Slovenes, whenever, so long as, and to the extent that beneficial ownership is in (a) the Government of the United States, (b) a person, firm or association neither domiciled nor ordinarily resident in the Kingdom of the Serbs, Croats and Slovenes, or (c) a corporation not organized under the laws of the Kingdom of the Serbs, Croats and Slovenes.

6. *Payments before Maturity.*—The Kingdom of the Serbs, Croats and Slovenes, at its option, on June 15 or December 15 of any year, upon not less than ninety days' advance notice to the United States, may make advance payments in amounts of $1,000 or multiples thereof, on account of the principal of any bonds issued or to be issued hereunder and held by the United States. Any such advance payments shall be applied to the principal of such bonds as may be indicated by the Kingdom

of the Serbs, Croats and Slovenes at the time of the payment.

7. *Exchange for Marketable Obligations.*—The· Kingdom of the Serbs, Croats and Slovenes will issue to the United States at any time, or from time to time, at the request of the Secretary of the Treasury of the United States, in exchange for any or all of the bonds issued hereunder and held by the United States, definitive engraved bonds in form suitable for sale to the public, in such amounts and denominations as the Secretary of the Treasury of the United States may request, in bearer form, with provision for registration as to principal, and/or in fully registered form, and otherwise on the same terms and conditions, as to dates of issue and maturity, rate or rates of interest, if any, exemption from. taxation, payment in obligations of the United States issued after April 6, 1917, and the like, as the bonds surrendered on such exchange. The Kingdom of the Serbs, Croats and Slovenes will deliver definitive engraved bonds to the United States in accordance herewith within six months of receiving notice of any such request from the Secretary of the Treasury of the United States, and pending the delivery of the definitive engraved bonds will deliver, at the request of the Secretary of the Treasury of the United States, temporary bonds or interim receipts in form satisfactory to the Secretary of the Treasury of the United States within thirty days of the receipt of such request, all without expense to the United States. The United States, before offering any such bonds or interim receipts for sale in the Kingdom of the Serbs, Croats and Slovenes, will first offer them to the Kingdom of the Serbs, Croats and Slovenes for

purchase at par and accrued interest, if any, and the Kingdom of the Serbs, Croats and Slovenes shall likewise have the option, in lieu of issuing any such bonds or interim receipts, to make advance redemption, at par and accrued interest, if any, of a corresponding principal amount of bonds issued hereunder and held by the United States. The Kingdom of the Serbs, Croats and Slovenes agrees that the definitive engraved bonds called for by this paragraph shall contain all such provisions, and that it will cause to be promulgated all such rules, regulations, and orders as shall be deemed necessary or desirable by the Secretary of the Treasury of the United States in order to facilitate the sale of the bonds in the United States, in the Kingdom of the Serbs, Croats and Slovenes or elsewhere, and that if requested by the Secretary of the Treasury of the United States, it will use its good offices to secure the listing of the bonds on such stock exchanges as the Secretary of the Treasury of the United States may specify.

8. *Cancellation and Surrender of Obligations.*—Upon the execution of this Agreement, the delivery to the United States of the principal amount of bonds of the Kingdom of the Serbs, Croats and Slovenes to be issued hereunder, together with satisfactory evidence of authority for the execution of this Agreement by the representative of the Kingdom of the Serbs, Croats and Slovenes and for the execution of the bonds to be issued hereunder, the United States will cancel and surrender to the Kingdom of the Serbs, Croats and Slovenes at the Treasury of the United States in Washington, the obligations of the Kingdom of the Serbs, Croats and Slovenes held by the United States.

9. *Notices.*—Any notice, request, or consent under the hand of the Secretary of the Treasury of the United States, shall be deemed and taken as the notice, request, or consent of the United States, and shall be sufficient if delivered at the Legation of the Kingdom of the Serbs, Croats and Slovenes at Washington or at the office of the Ministry of Finance at Belgrade; and any notice, request or election from or by the Kingdom of the Serbs, Croats and Slovenes shall be sufficient if delivered to the American Legation at Belgrade or to the Secretary of the Treasury at the Treasury of the United States in Washington. The United States in its discretion may waive any notice required hereunder, but any such waiver shall be in writing and shall not extend to or affect any subsequent notice or impair any right of the United States to require notice hereunder.

10. *Compliance with Legal Requirements.*—The Kingdom of the Serbs, Croats and Slovenes represents and agrees that the execution and delivery of this Agreement have in all respects been duly authorized and that all acts, conditions, and legal formalities which should have been completed prior to the making of this Agreement have been completed as required by the laws of the Kingdom of the Serbs, Croats and Slovenes and in conformity therewith.

11. *Counterparts.*—This Agreement shall be executed in two counterparts, each of which shall have the force and effect of an original.

IN WITNESS WHEREOF, the Kingdom of the Serbs, Croats and Slovenes has caused this Agreement to be executed on its behalf by Dr. George Diouritch, its Envoy Extraordinary and Minister Plenipotentiary to the

Court of St. James and Commissioner for the funding of the debt at Washington, thereunto duly authorized, subject, however, to ratification in the Kingdom of the Serbs, Croats and Slovenes, and the United States has likewise caused this Agreement to be executed on its behalf by the Secretary of the Treasury, as Chairman of the World War Foreign Debt Commission, with the approval of the President, subject, however, to the approval of Congress, pursuant to the Act of Congress approved February 9, 1922, as amended by the Act of Congress approved February 28, 1923, and as further amended by the Act of Congress approved January 21, 1925, all on the day and year first above written.

THE KINGDOM OF THE SERBS, CROATS AND SLOVENES, By GEORGE DIOURITCH

THE UNITED STATES OF AMERICA,
(For the World War Foreign Debt Commission):
By ANDREW W. MELLON,
Secretary of the Treasury and Chairman of the Commission.
Approved:

CALVIN COOLIDGE,
President.

EXHIBIT A

(Form of Bond)

THE KINGDOM OF THE SERBS, CROATS AND SLOVENES

$ No.

The Kingdom of the Serbs, Croats and Slovenes, for value received, promises to pay to the Government of the

United States of America, hereinafter called the United States, or order, on June 15, 19 , the sum of ·
Dollars ($. ·), and pay interest upon said principal sum after June 15, 1937, at the rate of ⅛ of 1% per annum from June 15, 1937, to June 15, 1940, at the rate of ½ of 1% per annum from June 15, 1940, to June 15, 1954, at the rate of 1% per annum from June 15, 1954, to June 15, 1957, at the rate of 2% per annum from June 15, 1957, to June 15, 1960, and at the rate of 3½% per annum after June 15, 1960, all payable semi-annually on the 15th day of December and June in each year, until the principal hereof shall have been paid. This bond is payable as to both principal and interest in gold coin of the United States of America of the present standard of value, or, at the option of the Kingdom of the Serbs, Croats and Slovenes, upon not less than thirty days' advance notice to the United States, in any obligations of the United States issued after April 6, 1917, to be taken at par and accrued interest to the date of payment hereunder.

This bond is payable as to both principal and interest without deduction for, and is exempt from, any and all taxes and other public dues, present or future, imposed by or under authority of the Kingdom of the Serbs, Croats and Slovenes or any political or local taxing authority within the Kingdom of the Serbs, Croats and Slovenes whenever, so long as, and to the extent that, beneficial ownership is in (a) the Government of the United States, (b) a person, firm, or association neither domiciled nor ordinarily resident in the Kingdom of the Serbs, Croats and Slovenes, or (c) a corporation not organized under the laws of the Kingdom of the Serbs,

Croats and Slovenes. This bond is payable as to both principal and interest at the Treasury of the United States in Washington, D. C., or at the option of the Secretary of the Treasury of the United States at the Federal Reserve Bank of New York.

This bond is issued pursuant to the provisions of paragraph 2 of an Agreement dated May 3, 1926, between the Kingdom of the Serbs, Croats and Slovenes and the United States, to which Agreement this bond is subject and to which reference is hereby made.

IN WITNESS WHEREOF, the Kingdom of the Serbs, Croats and Slovenes has caused this bond to be executed in its behalf by its Envoy Extraordinary and Minister Plenipotentiary at Washington, thereunto duly authorized, as of June 15, 1925.

THE KINGDOM OF THE SERBS, CROATS AND SLOVENES
By

Envoy Extraordinary and Minister Plenipotentiary.

B. Schedule of Yugoslav Payments

Principal	Annual Interest Payments		Annual Principal Payments	Total Annual Payments	Year
$62,850,000	....	$	$ 200,000	$ 200,000	1926
62,650,000	....		.200,000	200,000	1927
62,450,000	....		200,000	200,000	1928
62,250,000	....		200,000	200,000	1929
62,050,000	....		200,000	200,000	1930
61,850,000	....		225,000	225,000	1931
61,625,000	....		250,000	250,000	1932
61,375,000	....		275,000	275,000	1933
61,100,000	....		300,000	300,000	1934
60,800,000	....		325,000	325,000	1935
60,475,000	....		350,000	350,000	1936
60,125,000	....		375,000	375,000	1937
59,750,000	⅛% {	$ 74,687.50	400,000	474,687.50	1938
59,350,000		74,187.50	450,000	524,187.50	1939
58,900,000		73,625	488,000	561,625	1940
58,412,000		292,060	.524,000	816,060	1941
57,888,000		289,440	562,000	851,440	1942
57,326,000		286,630	604,000	890,630	1943
56,722,000		283,610	648,000	931,610	1944
56,074,000		280,370	697,000	977,370	1945
55,377,000		276,885	707,000	983,885	1946
54,670,000	½% {	273,350	718,000	991,350	1947
53,952,000		269,760	729,000	998,760	1948
53,223,000		266,115	746,000	1,012,115	1949
52,477,000		262,385	764,000	1,026,385	1950
51,713,000		258,565	782,000	1,040,565	1951
50,931,000		254,655	801,000	1,055,655	1952
50,130,000		250,650	820,000	1,070,650	1953
49,310,000		246,550	638,000	1,084,550	1954
48,472,000	1% {	484,720	855,000	1,339,720	1955
47,617,000		476,170	873,000	1,349,170	1956
46,744,000		467,440	892,000	1,359,440	1957
45,852,000	2% {	917,040	912,000	1,829,040	1958
44,940,000		898,800	938,000	1,836,800	1959
44,002,000		880,040	961,000	1,841,040	1960

B. Schedule of Yugoslav Payments—*Continued*

Principal	Annual Interest Payments	Annual Principal Payments	Total Annual Payments	Year
$43,041,000	$1,506,435	$ 984,000	$2,490,435	1961
42,057,000	1,471,995	1,018,000	2,489,995	1962
41,039,000	1,436,365	1,054,000	2,490,365	1963
39,985,000	1,399,475	1,090,000	2,489,475	1964
38,895,000	1,361,325	1,129,000	2,490,325	1965
37,766,000	1,321,810	1,168,000	2,489,810	1966
36,598,000	1,280,930	1,209,000	2,489,930	1967
35,389,000	1,238,615	1,251,000	2,489,615	1968
34,138,000	1,194,830	1,295,000	2,489,830	1969
32,843,000	1,149,505	1,340,000	2,489,505	1970
31,503,000	1,102,605	1,388,000	2,490,605	1971
30,115,000	1,054,025	1,436,000	2,490,025	1972
28,679,000	1,003,765	1,486,000	2,489,765	1973
27,193,000 3½%	951,755	1,538,000	2,489,755	1974
25,655,000	897,925	1,592,000	2,489,925	1975
24,063,000	842,205	1,648,000	2,490,205	1976
22,415,000	784,525	1,706,000	2,490,525	1977
20,709,000	724,815	1,765,000	2,489,815	1978
18,944,000	663,040	1,827,000	2,490,040	1979
17,117,000	599,095	1,891,000	2,490,095	1980
15,226,000	532,910	1,957,000	2,489,910	1981
13,269,000	464,415	2,026,000	2,490,415	1982
11,243,000	393,505	2,097,000	2,490,505	1983
9,146,000	320,110	2,170,000	2,490,110	1984
6,976,000	244,160	2,246,000	2,490,160	1985
4,730,000	165,550	2,324,000	2,489,550	1986
2,406,000	84,210	2,406,000	2,490,210	1987
	$32,327,635	$62,850,000	$95,177,635	

XVI. CONGRESSIONAL JOINT RESOLUTION RELATIVE TO THE AUSTRIAN DEBT *

(Approved April 6, 1922)

Joint Resolution Authorizing the extension, for a period of not to exceed twenty-five years, of the time for the payment of the principal and interest of the debt in-

* Official text (Public Resolution—No. 46—67th Congress, S. J. Res. 160, 42 Stat. L., 491).

curred by Austria for the purchase of flour from the United States Grain Corporation, and for other purposes.

Whereas the economic structure of Austria is approaching collapse and great numbers of the people of Austria are, in consequence, in imminent danger of starvation and threatened by diseases growing out of extreme privation and starvation; and

Whereas this Government wishes to cooperate in relieving Austria from the immediate burden created by her outstanding debts:

Therefore be it

Resolved by the Senate and House of Representatives of the United States of America in Congress assembled, That the Secretary of the Treasury is hereby authorized to extend, for a period not to exceed twenty-five years, the time of payment of the principal and interest of the debt incurred by Austria for the purchase of flour from the United States Grain Corporation, and to release Austrian assets pledged for the payment of such loan, in whole or in part, as may in the judgment of the Secretary of the Treasury be necessary for the accomplishment of the purposes of this resolution: *Provided, however,* That substantially all the other creditor nations, to wit: Czechoslovakia, Denmark, France, Great Britain, Greece, Holland, Italy, Norway, Rumania, Sweden, Switzerland, and Yugoslavia shall take action with regard to their respective claims against Austria similar to that herein set forth. The Secretary of the Treasury shall be authorized to decide when this proviso has been substantially complied with.

XVII. SECRETARY MELLON ON DEBT SETTLEMENTS *

A. STATEMENT TO THE WAYS AND MEANS COMMITTEE OF
THE HOUSE OF REPRESENTATIVES, JANUARY 4, 1926..

During the war the United States made loans to the
Allies largely to assist them in purchases of supplies in the
United States. The original loans bore interest at 3½%,
being the interest rate carried on the First Liberty Loan
issue. The rate was subsequently made 5%. After the
Armistice the United States continued to make advances
to the Allies to complete their contracts in the United
States and to purchase food and surplus war supplies
from the United States. Relief was also extended to a
number of the smaller nations largely born of the war.
At the conclusion of the war period, the Treasury held
the obligations of some twenty nations, in general payable on demand with interest at 5% per annum.

The world was in a state of financial disorder. No
nation could have paid its debt had we demanded it.
Most could not even pay the interest rate of 5% called
for by their obligations. Only with time and more settled
conditions did possibility of adjustment arise.

Recognizing the fact that our debtors could not pay
on demand, Congress originally authorized debt funding
on not longer than a 25-year basis and at not less than
4¼% interest. Subsequently, when it was apparent that
this basis of settlement was beyond the capacity of most
of the debtors, the American Debt Commission was given
general authority to recommend settlements to Congress.
It is as the expert body created by Congress that we

* Text as issued by the Treasury Department.

have presented our recommendations in the six cases
now pending.

Since foreign debt settlements do not seem to be clearly
understood, I wish to mention some rather elemental
facts. The obligations held by the Treasury generally
call for payment on demand and such payment cannot
be made. We must find practical terms. Now if we are
owed $62 and payment is made to-day, we receive the
full value of our loan. If payment is made at the rate
of $1 a year for 62 years without interest, we would be
conceding a part of the debt. What this concession
amounts to can be variously estimated depending on the
rate of discount arbitrarily taken. If we use $4\frac{1}{4}\%$, the
present value of a $1 annuity for 62 years is a little over
$21; if we use 3%, its present value is $28. If, however,
instead of $1 a year for 62 years without interest we
should charge interest at the cost of money to us, we
get the full value of the loan, since we could borrow the
$62 to-day, pay interest on the borrowing, and repay the
principal as annuities are received. From the United
States standpoint, therefore, the question of whether a
particular settlement represents a reduction in the debt
depends on whether the interest charged over the entire
period of the agreement is less than the average cost
to us of money during that period. The flexibility in debt
settlements is found in the interest rate to be charged.

The situation of each debtor nation is particular, that
is, its capacity to pay is not the same as the capacity of
some other nation. It has been felt by the Debt Commission, however, that repayment of principal is essential in order that the debtor might feel that it had paid
its debt in full and that we might know that we had our

capital returned to us. The Commission felt, therefore, that no funding should be made which did not repay the principal, and thus we have maintained the integrity of international obligations. Adjustment. to the capacity of each case is made in the interest to be paid over the period of the agreement.

Great Britain was the first nation to recognize the desirability of putting its house in order. Great Britain owed some $4,600,000,000 of principal and interest on its demand obligations. The American Debt Commission recommended a settlement on the basis of principal payments over a 62-year period, with interest at the rate of 3% per annum for the first 10 years and 3½% thereafter. Congress has approved the settlement. Taking into account the current interest rate when the settlement was made, the British agreement does not represent payment in full. If we figure the present value of the settlement at 4¼%, we cancelled 20% of the debt. The settlement was, however, entirely based on our estimation of Great Britain's capacity to pay. It is a precedent for the recognition of the principle of capacity to pay and is not a set formula to control other cases of substantially less capacity.

It is the rule that a debtor cannot prefer one creditor over another. The debtor must treat all creditors alike. On the other hand, the creditor has the option of treating each of its debtors separately. It may insist on payment in full from one, give time to another, and cancel the indebtedness of a third, and no one of the three debtors has a right to complain of the treatment accorded the other. There follows from the foregoing that England, which is also a creditor of many nations who are debtors to us, has the right to insist that no debtor of it pay us more in proportion than England receives. The debtor nation may not discriminate between its two creditors. It has been frequently stated in Parliament that England has no just cause of complaint if the United States settles with one of its debtors on terms easier than those accorded England. As a matter of fact, England itself in dealing with its European debtors has made settlements more favorable to one than to another. I want to be clear that the British-American settlement is one based on capacity to pay, and not a fixed formula to which all others, irrespective of capacity, must conform, and that a creditor is free to settle with its debtors as it may choose.

As other nations have approached the American Debt Commission for a funding of their debts, it has been the position of the American Commission that since England represents the strongest of its debtors, America would not ask heavier terms than those offered by England. The Commission would consider the British-American basis as prima facie a fair basis of settlement. If such a settlement was beyond the capacity of the particular nation, then the Commission would recognize this capacity by way of a reduction in the interest rate, but in no event cancel any of the principal. As we settled with England on her capacity, so consistently we must consider capacity in every other case.

Generally speaking, our foreign indebtedness may be divided into two general classes—advances to carry on the war, and advances after the war for relief and for the stablization of Europe. Among the nations in the first class are included England, France, Italy, Belgium,

Russia, and Serbia, although loans were made after the Armistice. In the second class are the countries on the Baltic Sea, Finland, Lithuania, Latvia, Esthonia, and Poland: the former enemy countries of Austria and Hungary: and the Balkan countries of Czechoslovakia, Rumania, and Greece.

The general plan applied to the settlement of the second class has been the British-American basis, with easier treatments in the earlier years depending upon the particular circumstances of the nation involved. Hungary, Finland, and Lithuania have been settled on the straight British-American basis. Poland, Latvia and Esthonia have been given the option to fund 75% of the payments which would have been due for principal and interest for the first 5 years over the remaining 57 years of the agreement. Czechoslovakia for the first 18 years pays about ¾ of what it would have paid under the straight British-American basis and the balance is funded over the remaining years of the 62-year period. Rumania pays a graduated scale to reach the British-American basis at the end of the twelfth year and the balance is funded. In every case the balance funded is at the interest rates of 3% and 3½%. The variations in the earlier years of these agreements have been occasioned by the present fiscal situation of the nation involved and represent a determination of the capacity of payment for these earlier years. In each case the American Debt Commission was of the opinion that over the whole period, subject to the earlier modifications, the British-American basis was within the capacity of the particular nation.

The debt-funding agreements of the nations in this

second class have been approved by Congress in the cases of Finland, Lithuania, Poland, and Hungary. In the case of Latvia, Esthonia, Czechoslovakia, and Rumania, the debt-funding agreements are now pending. In the case of Austria, Congress has voted a 20-year moratorium recognizing Austria's present want of capacity.

Yugoslavia and Greece have not yet negotiated a settlement.

Coming now to the large debtors, no agreement has been reached with France, but the Commission has negotiated funding agreements with Belgium and Italy.

In the Belgian agreement the indebtedness of Belgium has been separated between pre-armistice debt and post-armistice debt, that is, indebtedness created before or after the 11th of November, 1918. The post-armistice indebtedness has been settled on the British-American basis, with the exception that during the first ten years interest rates are scaled up on an arbitrary basis to reach $3\frac{1}{2}\%$ at the beginning of the eleventh year. As to the pre-armistice indebtedness, the principal is to be repaid in substantially equal installments over the period of 62 years. Accrued and accruing interest is waived. The circumstances which influenced the American Debt Commission in recommending this concession on the pre-armistice debt were these: Almost all of Belgium was occupied by Germany since the early days of the war. Germany had taken from Belgium and moved into Germany most of the industrial machinery and equipment which it had found in Belgium. The value of the war damage done to Belgium was estimated at roughly $1,000,000,000. During the period of occupation, Germany had caused to be printed and circulated in Belgium paper money which the Belgian people, in the occupied territory, were forced to receive. At the conclusion of the war Belgium had to redeem this worthless currency, issuing its own money in exchange therefor. The loss to Belgium on this account was about $1,200,-000,000. Belgium had received prior to the Armistice about $1,300,000,000 in advance from France, Great Britain, and the United States, France advancing over $600,000,000, Great Britain more than $500,000,000, and the United States less than $200,000,000. At the time of the negotiation of the Versailles treaty Belgium demanded that she be given a preferred claim on reparations to the extent of her war damage, that Germany be compelled to redeem in gold the worthless paper marks taken up by Belgium, and that the three principal allies forgive their pre-armistice loans, and Belgium stated that unless such preferences were given she would withdraw from the Peace Conference. In order to prevent a break in the negotiations, representatives of the United States, England and France proposed that Belgium be given a prior charge on reparations of $500,000,000, that each representative recommend to his respective government the adoption of an arrangement under which the pre-armistice debt of Belgium would be assumed by Germany, and Belgium released, and that Belgium withdraw her other demands for the remainder of war damage, and for reimbursement for the German currency. Accepting this compromise, Belgium continued in the conference. Subsequently the United States, entirely within its rights, declined to accept Germany as a substitute for Belgium on the pre-armistice debt. The argument of Belgium was that it had waived its demand for $2,200,-

000,000 of preferred reparations relying on a promise which was unfulfilled, and that it was now too late to restore Belgium to the position it had formerly occupied. The American Commission felt that the equities were with Belgium. We would not agree to substitute Germany as our debtor, although England and France with larger debts than ours have done so. We did not think it just, however, to ask Belgium to repay more than the principal of the pre-armistice advances. Belgium continues solely liable to us.

Taking the Belgium settlement as a whole, both the pre-armistice and post-armistice, the American Commission felt that the payments required from Belgium substantially represent its capacity to pay. Belgium is a small nation, densely populated, with few natural resources, and obliged to import a large proportion of its food supply. Its foreign investments have been exhausted by the war, the balance of trade has for a great many years been adverse, and Belgium will require in the near future large borrowings abroad in order to stabilize its currency and to reduce the inflation caused by the paper money issued by Germany during the occupation.

Another settlement now before Congress is that with Italy. To the original principal of the Italian debt of $1,648,000,000 was added interest at 4¼% per annum to December 15, 1922, the date of the British settlement, and at 3% per annum to the date of the new settlement, making a total to be funded of $2,042,000,000. Repayment of the new principal is made on the same scale as on the British-American basis, with the exception that in the first five years there is a slight modification. To meet Italy's capacity to pay, interest rates during the period of the funding agreement after the first 5 years have been fixed during successive 10-year periods at ⅛ of 1%, ¼ of 1%, ½ of 1%, ¾ of 1%, 1%, and 2% for the last seven years. The interest rates recognize the quite material difference between Italy and other debtor countries with whom negotiations for settlement have been made. Italy has no natural resources and no productive colonies. Its balance of trade has always been adverse; a large part of the country is mountainous and it must import food for its rapidly increasing population. Coal, iron, copper, cotton, oil, and other raw materials have to be imported. The standard of living and the taxable capacity of its people are extremely low. The assets of Italy are but the labor of its people and its water-power.

No better example of the equitable principle of capacity to pay which must apply to a debt settlement can be given than in the case of Italy. Italy owes the United States over $2,000,000,000. It owes England about 25% more than this. Any payment to the United States must be contemporaneously met by proportionately greater payments to England. To pay a dollar to the United States in debt settlement means that Italy must pay $1.25 to England. The settlement of the Italian-American debt on the British-American basis would have meant that Italy must pay at once $71,000,000 per year, and a similar settlement of the British-Italian debt would require the payment of $89,000,000 per year, a total to be added to the tax burden of the Italian people of $160,000,000. The present total of all Italian taxes is about $850,000,000. The present total of all American taxes is about $7,500,000,000. Adding $160,000,000 to the Italian taxes would be the same as adding $1,400,-000,000 to taxation in America. This would be a terrific burden to America but we might stand it because our average income is high and the American people would not be forced below the level of subsistence, that is, we would still have enough to live on. The Italian people, however, are now so heavily taxed in proportion to the national income that this additional tax would have forced them below the level at which life can be supported. Such payments to-day are impossible. We should have made a China of Italy. You will appreciate what I mean by the present close approach of the Italian to the level of subsistence when it is understood that the adoption in the Italian income tax law of the same exemptions carried in our 1924 law (not the increased exemptions under the proposed law) would reduce the Italian Government's revenue from income tax by 99%. All insistence of a settlement of the Italian-American debt on the British-American basis would have been entirely futile. Italy could not have paid, and such an insistence would have meant only that the United States would receive nothing.

The comparative burdens of the war debt settlements of England, Belgium, and Italy are a fair test of the adequacy from an American standpoint of the Italian settlement. It must be remembered that Italy owes Great Britain 25% more than it owes the United States and any American settlement will probably have to be followed by an English settlement on substantially a proportionate basis. There are three principal factors in the finances of any country which furnish indices by which a comparison of the weight of a new fiscal burden can be measured. These are the total budget, representing what all instrumentalities of government collect from the people; the total foreign trade, which has a bearing on the capacity to transfer payments abroad; and the total national income, which is the ultimate source of a country's capacity to pay. If we apply these indices to the three settlements we obtain the following comparison:. The British-American settlement calls for an annual average payment equivalent to 4.6% of the total British budget expenditures; the Belgian settlement 3.5%, and the Italian settlement to America alone 5.17%, and to America and Great Britain 11.47% of Italy's total budget expenditures. The British settlement calls for an annual average charge corresponding to 1.9% of the total British foreign trade. This figure is .88% with Belgium. Italy's average payment to the United States is 2.87% of its total foreign trade, and the combined payments to the United States and England 6.32% of its total foreign trade. Great Britain's average annuity represents .94% of its national income; Belgium's .80%; Italy to the United States alone .97%, and to the United States and Great Britain 2.17% of its total national income. If we averaged the three indices, the comparative Italian burden of war debts would be represented by 6.72, the British 2.4, and the Belgian by 1.75. If instead of using the average annual annuity we should compare the present value of the settlements with the sum of these three indices—the total budget, the total foreign trade, and total national income for a year of each of the countries—the burden of the British settlement represents 11.7% of this sum, the Belgian settlement 7%, and the Italian war debts to the United

States and England combined 19.8%. Suppose that America had to assume a burden comparable to the burden of war debts upon Italy based upon the above indices, the present value of this burden would be over $15,000,000,000, or ¾ of our present public debt, and if we were to pay this war debt on the same scale as in the Italian agreement, after five years we would be paying an annuity of over $400,000,000, after 30 years of over a billion dollars, and by the end of the period of considerably over two billion a year. Consideration must be given in these comparisons to the income and standard of living in Italy, which are lower than in either England or Belgium and very much lower than in the United States, and which, therefore, would make the same burden relatively higher in Italy than in other countries.

In its negotiations for the funding of the debt, the American Debt Commission has been forced to consider these facts: No nation, except by the pressure of public opinion and the necessities of its own credit, can be compelled to pay a debt to another nation. An insistence on a funding agreement in excess of the capacity of the nation to pay would justify it in refusing to make any settlement. None can do the impossible. If the debtor is to be able to pay and if the creditor is to receive anything, a settlement fair to both countries is essential. It follows that those who insist upon impossible terms are in the final analysis working for an entire repudiation of the debts. The only other alternative which they might urge is that the United States goes to war to collect.

Europe is our largest customer. Unless the finances of Europe can be restored, her currency placed on a sound basis, and her people able to earn and to spend, this country will not be able to dispose of its surplus products of food, materials, and goods. Our exports to Belgium last year were $114,000,000, and imports $66,-000,000. Our exports to Italy were $185,000,000, and imports $75,000,000. Of the total exports to the two countries, 26% were foodstuffs and 36% were cotton. Nearly two-thirds of the exports represent the surplus products of the American farmer.

Germany began a reestablishment of sound currency in the latter part of 1923. In that year it imported $149,000,000 of cotton from us. With the Dawes plan and a proper financial system exports of cotton increased in 1924 to $223,000,000 and in the first ten months of 1925 to $198,000,000 or at the rate of $231,000,000 a year. Here is the real interest of America in the stablization of Europe, in which prompt debt settlements are an integral part.

The countries of Europe must be restored to their place in civilization. In this process of reconstruction certain essentials have to be met: First, the budgets must be balanced. This is a domestic question for each nation to solve. Second, payments coming due in the future must be ascertained. Inter-allied debts constitute the principal item in this essential, and in order that their settlement be effective the terms must be definite in amount and time and within the capacity of the debtors. We have learned the folly of imposing indefinite and impossible terms from the experiment with Germany before the Dawes plan. And, third, America with its excess of capital seeking profitable investment, must aid by making private loans to Europe for productive purposes.

Only from these private loans during the past year have the countries abroad been able to pay for our wheat and cotton. It is these new loans which make our exports possible. The American Commission has not recommended settlements of the debts to profit those who wish to loan money abroad. It is possible since any payment necessarily involves a strain on the debtor country, that the insistence on impossible terms which would justify a, refusal of the debtor to fund, might be more acceptable to the international bankers. But the settlements are made in the real interests of those American producers who must have a foreign market able to pay. The American producer needs these debt settlements. The entire foreign debt is not worth as much to the American people in dollars and cents as a prosperous Europe as a customer.

The capacity of a nation to pay over a long period of time is not subject to mathematical determination. It is and must be largely a matter of opinion, but we have been fortunate in the constitution of the American Debt Commission to have a representation from the Administration, from Congress, and from private life, and from both political parties. We have facilities to acquire information through the State Department, the Treasury, and the Department of Commerce. We bring a varied experience to the consideration of the debt settlements, and our recommendations are unanimous. While some may believe our recommendations too lenient and others too harsh, I know that it is the honest judgment of the Commission that they are just settlements in the real interests of our country. The President has approved each settlement.

B. STATEMENT TO THE WAYS AND MEANS COMMITTEE OF THE HOUSE OF REPRESENTATIVES, MAY 20, 1926.

On January 4, 1926, I appeared before the Committee in connection with the debt settlements with Belgium, Czechoslovakia, Esthonia, Italy, Latvia and Rumania, which were then before you for consideration. I discussed briefly the principles applied by the Commission in negotiating and effecting a settlement.

It is not necessary for me to repeat what I stated at that time. Since then the Commission has concluded two additional settlements: one with France, the other with the Kingdom of the Serbs, Croats and Slovenes, or Yugoslavia. These have been presented to Congress for approval.

Referring to the settlement with France: The amount to be funded has been calculated on the same basis as in the other debt settlements at 4¼ per cent interest to December 15, 1922, and at 3 per cent interest thereafter to June 15, 1925, the date of the agreement. The total to be funded, after a cash payment of $386,686.89 to adjust the amount to round figures, is $4,025,000,000. Of this amount $3,340,000,000 represents principal and $685,-000,000 the accrued interest to the date of the agreement. There is attached to my statement a schedule showing the total annual payments to be made by France.

Under the agreement France pays $30,000,000 a year the first two years; $32,500,000 a year the third and fourth years, and $35,000,000 the fifth year. The annuities increase each year, reaching $125,000,000 in the seventeenth year, thereafter continuing at that figure, except for the sixty-second year when the payment is approximately $118,000,000. Under the agreement the total principal of the funded debt (including $685,000,-000 accrued interest) will be repaid in full with interest on the funded principal as follows: after the first five years and for the next ten years, one per cent per annum; for the succeeding ten years, two per cent per annum; for the succeeding eight years, two and one-half per cent per annum; for the succeeding seven years, three per cent per annum and for the remaining twenty-two years, three and one-half per cent per annum.

The total payments to be received from France on account of the $3,340,000,000 originally loaned is $6,-847,674,104.17. The present value of these payments on a 4¼ per cent basis is $2,008,122,624, or practically 50 per cent of the debt funded, as compared with the Italian settlement of 26 per cent.

Although the United States has outstanding a substantial amount of Liberty Bonds bearing 4¼ per cent interest, a large part of the Government's requirements are now being financed at a much lower rate. The average cost of money to the United States probably will continue to decline. Securities with high interest rates issued during the war will be paid, redeemed or refunded. If we assume that the average cost of money to the United States for the next 62 years will approach a 3 per cent basis and if we determine the present value of the French annuities on that basis, we arrive at a figure which would approximate their actual value to-day. The present value of the French payments on a 3 per cent basis is $2,734,000,000. This is approximately 82 per cent of the principal amount of the $3,340,000,000 French debt.

Until the present negotiations and settlement the best offer received from France was made last October after two weeks of negotiations with a French Commission. Under that offer France was to pay $40,000,000 a year for five years; $60,000,000 a year for the next seven years and $100,000,000 a year for the succeeding fifty-six years. There was included, however, as an essential element of the proposal, a so-called "safeguard clause", the effect of which was to relieve France of making payments to the United States if Germany did not pay reparations. The receipt by the United States of the payments, therefore, would be uncertain. A comparison of the previous offer with the present settlement shows the following:

(1)   The "safeguard clause" has been eliminated.

(2)   Under the settlement the total payments to be received from France are $6,847,000,000, against $6,220,000,000 under the offer, an increase of $627,000,000. The present value of this settlement on a 4¼ per cent basis is $2,008,000,000; the present value of the former offer was $1,755,000,000, an increase of $253,000,000.

(3)   In the first five years France offered last October $200,000,-000. Under this settlement we are to receive $160,000,000. The slightly smaller payments for the first five years were made necessary because the present fiscal condition of France is less strong than it was at the time of the negotiations last fall. Under present exchange rates the payment of the first annuity of $30,000,000 requires that France find approximately 1,060,000,000 francs. Last October to make a payment of $40,000,000 France would have been required to find 846,000,000 francs. The lower annuity in dollars represents today a higher annuity in francs.

(4)   From the sixth to the tenth year under the offer the United States would receive $300,000,00; under this settlement the United States will receive $305,000,000.

(5)   From the eleventh to the fifteenth year France offered $420,000,000; under this settlement France will be required to pay $520,000,000.

(6)   The maximum annuity under the offer was $100,000,000, reached after the twelfth year; the maximum annuity in this settlement is $125,000,000, reached after the sixteenth year.

In conducting negotiations for settling the war debts we meet with criticism from two extremes. One body of opinion would have us forgive entirely the debts because the money was loaned during or immediately after a war against a common enemy. Those who maintain such a position fail to recognize the responsibility of the representatives of a government to its citizens.

Public officials, whether in the legislative or executive branch of the Government, are essentially trustees. They are trustees for the citizens of their own country. They are not free to give away the property of the beneficiaries of the trust. An individual can do what he will with his own property. A public official, however, must keep firmly in view that he is dealing not with his own property but with property entrusted to his care by the citizens of his country.

Moreover, those who urge a complete forgiveness of debts ignore entirely the effect upon the country whose debt is forgiven. All self-respecting people desire to discharge their obligations. This is true of nations as of men. It is true of France.

At the other extreme are those who insist that we should collect the full principal and interest of the debts. In its final analysis the maintenance of this position could but reach the practical result that nothing would be collected since the full payment of the debt is beyond the capacity of the debtor. While a trustee may not give trust money away, while he may not even be generous at the cost of those for whom he is trustee, it is equally true that a trustee must manage the trust with business intelligence. Any trustee would be derelict in the performance of his duty if by demanding the impossible he should lose the possible.

The settlement with France is but another application of the principal of capacity to pay. I appreciate, as all reasonable men must, that it is not possible for any set of men to determine with mathematical accuracy the future capacity of a great nation to tax itself and to transfer the avails of taxation to another nation. We are forced to look at the present, and to estimate the future.

France at present is not able to set apart large sums to be transferred abroad as payments on account of her external debts. Despite great efforts she has not yet fully repaired the losses in man power and property caused by the war. Her domestic debt has reached enormous proportions, her currency is inflated and it is becoming increasingly difficult to raise by taxation sufficient funds to meet the charges on her debt and to pay her ordinary governmental expenditures. Subject to the ill effects of a fluctuating currency, she has been making every effort to balance her budget. France must fix the amount of her obligations abroad so that she may definitely know all her commitments. Having completed a settlement of her obligations to this country, she has started negotiations with her other large creditor. When a settlement has been reached with Great Britain, she will then be in a position to balance her budget, check inflation, stabilize her currency and put her finances on a permanently sound basis. Until these have been accomplished, France cannot be expected to make large payments on account of her war debts to the United States and Great Britain. To insist on too heavy payments in the early years might well jeopardize the accomplishment of these reforms essential to her economic and financial rehabilitation.

Criticism has been made of France for the situation in which she now finds herself. In our criticism we are likely to forget the factors which contributed to that situation. The French people gave so fully of their man power and their industry during the four years of war, fought mainly on their own soil, that French taxation during the period of the war and the period immediately following could not be so heavy as in those countries which were never occupied by the enemy. The richest industrial section of France lay directly in the course of the German armies, and when recovered was in a destroyed condition.

France was faced with the problem of deciding whether it would leave the country in this condition, with its industry permanently crippled, or would recondition the soil and rebuild its plants at whatever cost, and thus increase the wealth producing power of the nation. The former course might have permitted more immediate taxation. The latter course was in substance the re-creation of industries able in the future to bear a proper burden of taxation. France chose the latter course.

In my statement of January 4, 1926, I compared the burden of the various settlements in terms of the total budget, total foreign trade and total national income and an average for the three indices.

The total budget represents what the government collects from the people; the total foreign trade has an
important bearing on the capacity to transfer sums
abroad and the total annual income in is final analysis
the ultimate source of the country's capacity to pay.

The British settlement calls for an annual average
payment equivalent to 4.6 per cent of the total British
budget expenditures; the Belgian settlement 3.5 per cent;
the Italian settlement to America alone 5.17 per cent and
the French settlement 7.33 per cent. The British settlement calls for an average annual charge corresponding to
1.9 per cent of the total British foreign trade, the Belgian
settlement 0.88 per cent, the Italian settlement 2.87 per
cent and the French settlement 2.64 per cent. Great
Britain's average annuity represents 0.94 per cent of
its national income, Belgium's 0.80 per cent, Italy's 0.97
per cent, France's 1.47 per cent. If we average the three
indices, the comparative French burden of her debt
would be 3.81 per cent, the Italian, 3.00 per cent, the
British 2.4 per cent, the Belgian, 1.75 per cent.

If, instead of using the average annual annuity, we
should compare the present value of the settlements with
the sum of these three indices—the total budget, the
total foreign trade and total national income for a year
of each of these countries—the burden of the French
settlement represents 15 per cent, the British settlement
11.7 per cent of this sum, the Belgian settlement 7 per
cent and the Italian settlement 8.58 per cent.

When discussing other debt settlements I have stressed
the importance to America of the economic revival of
Europe. When viewed as a market for the surplus
products of our fields, our mines, and our industry,

Europe must be taken as a whole. While the finances of its nations are closely related, each presents a distinct problem requiring individual treatment, but responsibility rests upon each nation to effect its own stabilization. Our efforts to that end during the past three years are known to all of you. We have concluded debt settlements with 13 nations, among the larger being England, Italy and Belgium.

France is the last of our large debtors. Her future is bright. She has been and is one of the great nations of the world. Her people are able, hard-working and frugal. While the burden of the debt settlement is relatively light in the earlier years, it is heavy in the later years.

To have imposed too heavy a burden at the outset would have rendered doubtful any subsequent payments.

The Commission is confident that the settlement, giving due consideration to the ability of the debtor as well as to the rights of the creditor, is a just settlement, fair both to the American taxpayer and to the French people.

APPENDIX C

BRITISH DEBT SETTLEMENTS

I. THE BALFOUR NOTE*

Note addressed by the British Secretary of State for Foreign Affairs to the French Ambassador in London and to the Diplomatic Representatives in London of Italy, Yugoslavia, Rumania, Portugal, and Greece.

Foreign Office, August 1, 1922.

Your Excellency,

As your Excellency is aware, the general question of the French debt to this country has not as yet been the subject of any formal communication between the two Governments, nor are His Majesty's Government anxious to raise it at the present moment. Recent events, however, leave them little choice in the matter, and they feel compelled to lay before the French Government their views on certain aspects of the situation created by the present condition of international indebtedness.

Speaking in general terms, the war debts, exclusive of interest, due to Great Britain at the present moment amount in the aggregate to about £3,400,000,000, of which Germany owes £1,450,000,000, Russia £650,000,000, and our allies £1,300,000,000. On the other hand, Great Britain owes the United States about a quarter of this sum—say £850,000,000, at par of exchange, together with interest accrued since 1919.

No international discussion has yet taken place on

* Official text.

the unexampled situation partially disclosed by these figures; and, pending a settlement which would go to the root of the problem, His Majesty's Government have silently abstained from making any demands upon their allies, either for the payment of interest or the repayment of capital. But, if action in the matter has hitherto been deemed inopportune, this is not because His Majesty's Government either underrate the evils of the present state of affairs, or because they are reluctant to make large sacrifices to bring it to an end. On the contrary, they are prepared, if such a policy formed part of a satisfactory international settlement, to remit all the debts due to Great Britain by our allies in respect of loans, or by Germany in respect of reparations.

Recent events, however, make such a policy difficult of accomplishment. With the most perfect courtesy, and in the exercise of their undoubted rights, the American Government have required this country to pay the interest accrued since 1919 on the Anglo-American debt, to convert it from an unfunded debt, and to repay it by a sinking fund in twenty-five years. Such a procedure is clearly in accordance with the original contract. His Majesty's Government make no complaint of it; they recognise their obligations and are prepared to fulfil them. But evidently they cannot do so without profoundly modifying the course which, in different circumstances, they would have wished to pursue. They cannot treat the repayment of the Anglo-American loan as if it were an isolated incident in which only the United States of America and Great Britain had any concern. It is but one of a connected series of transactions, in which this country appears sometimes as debtor, some-

times as creditor, and, if our undoubted obligations as
a debtor are to be enforced, our not less undoubted rights
as a creditor cannot be left wholly in abeyance.

His Majesty's Government do not conceal the fact
that they adopt this change of policy with the greatest
reluctance. It is true that Great Britain is owed more
than it owes, and that, if all inter-Allied war debts were
paid, the British Treasury would, on balance, be a large
gainer by the transaction. But can the present world
situation be looked at only from this narrow financial
standpoint? It is true that many of the Allied and
Associated Powers are, as between each other, creditors
or debtors, or both. But they were, and are, much more.
They were partners in the greatest international effort
ever made in the cause of freedom; and they are still
partners in dealing with some, at least, of its results.
Their debts were incurred, their loans were made, not for
the separate advantage of particular States, but for
a great purpose common to them all, and that purpose
has been, in the main, accomplished.

To generous minds it can never be agreeable, although
for reasons of State, it may perhaps be necessary to
regard the monetary aspect of this great event as a
thing apart, to be torn from its historical setting and
treated as no more than an ordinary commercial dealing
between traders who borrow and capitalists who lend.
There are, moreover, reasons of a different order, to
which I have already referred, which increase the dis-
taste with which His Majesty's Government adopt so
fundamental an alteration in method of dealing with
loans to allies. The economic ills from which the world
is suffering are due to many causes, moral and material,

which are quite outside the scope of this despatch. But among them must certainly be reckoned the weight of international indebtedness, with all its unhappy effects upon credit and exchange, upon national production and international trade. The peoples of all countries long for a speedy return to the normal. But how can the normal be reached while conditions so abnormal are permitted to prevail? And how can these conditions be cured by any remedies that seem at present likely to be applied?

For evidently the policy hitherto pursued by this country of refusing to make demands upon its debtors is only tolerable so long as it is generally accepted. It cannot be right that one partner in the common enterprise should recover all that she has lent, and that another, while recovering nothing, should be required to pay all that she has borrowed. Such a procedure is contrary to every principle of natural justice and cannot be expected to commend itself to the people of this country. They are suffering from an unparalleled burden of taxation, from an immense diminution in national wealth, from serious want of employment, and from the severe curtailment of useful expediture. These evils are courageously borne. But were they to be increased by an arrangement which, however legitimate, is obviously one-sided, the British taxpayer would inevitably ask why he should be singled out to bear a burden which others are bound to share.

To such a question there can be but one answer, and I am convinced that Allied opinion will admit its justice. But while His Majesty's Government are thus regretfully constrained to request the French Government to make arrangements for dealing to the best of their ability

with Anglo-French loans, they desire to explain that the
amount of interest and repayment for which they ask depends not so much on what France and other Allies
owes to Great Britain as on what Great Britain has to
pay America. The policy favoured by His Majesty's
Government is, as I have already observed, that of
surrendering their share of German reparation, and writing off, through one great transaction, the whole body of
inter-Allied indebtedness. But, if this be found impossible of accomplishment, we wish it to be understood that we do not in any event desire to make a profit
out of any less satisfactory arrangement. In no circumstances do we propose to ask more from our debtors
than is necessary to pay to our creditors. And, while
we do not ask for more, all will admit that we can hardly
be content with less. For it should not be forgotten,
though it sometimes is, that our liabilities were incurred
for others, not for ourselves. The food, the raw material,
the munitions required by the immense naval and military efforts of Great Britain and half the $2,000,000,000
advanced to allies were provided, not by means of foreign
loans, but by internal borrowing and war taxation. Un-
fortunately, a similar policy was beyond the power of
other European nations. Appeal was therefore made to
the Government of the United States; and under the
arrangement then arrived at the United States insisted,
in substance if not in form, that, though our allies were
to spend the money, it was only on our security that
they were prepared to lend it. This cooperative effort
was of infinite value to the common cause, but it cannot
be said that the rôle assigned in it to this country was
one of special privilege or advantage.

Before concluding I may be permitted to offer one further observation in order to make still clearer the spirit in which His Majesty's Government desire to deal with the thorny problem of international indebtedness.

In an earlier passage of this despatch I pointed out that this, after all, is not a question merely between allies. Ex-enemy countries also are involved; for the greatest of all international debtors is Germany. Now His Majesty's Government do not suggest that, either as a matter of justice or expediency, Germany should be relieved of her obligation to the other allied States. They speak only for Great Britain; and they content themselves with saying once again that, so deeply are they convinced of the economic injury inflicted on the world by the existing state of things that this country would be prepared (subject to the just claims of other parts of the Empire) to abandon all further right to German reparations and all claims to repayment by allies, provided that the renunciation formed part of a general plan by which this great problem could be dealt with as a whole and find a satisfactory solution. A general settlement would, in their view, be of more value to mankind than any gains that could accrue even from the most successful enforcement of legal obligations.

I have, &c.,

(Sgd.)   BALFOUR.

II. ANGLO-RUSSIAN TREATY REGARDING DEBT SETTLEMENT *

Initialed in London, August 8, 1924, but not ratified by the British Parliament.

Great Britain and Northern Ireland, of the one hand, and the Union of Soviet Socialist Republics, of the other hand, being animated with the desire to extend and develop the commercial relations established after the signature of the trade agreement of March 16, 1921, and to remove all causes of friction and disagreement between the two countries and to place their relations on a firm, just, and durable basis, have decided to conclude a treaty with this object, and for the conclusion of which they are represented as follows:

Great Britain and Northern Ireland by the Right Honorable James Ramsay MacDonald, M. P., First Lord of the Treasury and Prime Minister, Principal Secretary of State for Foreign Affairs; Mr. Arthur Augustus William Harry Ponsonby, M. P., Under-Secretary of State for Foreign Affairs; the Union of Soviet Socialist Republics by Christian Georgievich Rakovski, Member of the Presidium of the Central Executive Committee of the Union of Soviet Socialist Republics, Deputy People's Commissary for Foreign Affairs, Chargé d'Affaires in London of the Union of Soviet Socialist

* Articles 2-5 are omitted from the text as not being pertinent to the debt question: Articles 2, 3 and 4 enumerate the treaties between Great Britain and Russia concluded prior to 1918 which are now considered as having lapsed, as well as those which are recognized as being still in force; Article 5 deals with the fisheries question. The text of the treaty is from the *London Times*, August 9, 1924.

Republics; Adolph Abramovich Joffe, Member of the Central Executive Committee of the Union of Soviet Socialist Republics; Andrei Fëdorovich Radchenko, Member of the Central Executive Committee of the Union of Soviet Socialist Republics, President of the Provincial Council of Trade Unions of the Donets Basin; Aron Lvovich Scheinmann, Member of the Collegium of the People's Commissariat of Finance; Mikhail Pavlovich Tomski, Member of the Presidium of the Central Executive Committee of the Union of Soviet Socialist Republics, President of the All-Russian Central Council of Trade Unions.

These plenipotentiaries having communicated their full powers, found in good and due form, have agreed as follows:

ARTICLE 1

The present treaty constitutes the formal general treaty adumbrated in the preamble to the trade agreement between His Britannic Majesty's Government and the Government of the Russian Socialist Federative Soviet Republic signed in London on March 16, 1921, and as between Great Britain, including Northern Ireland, and the Union replaces that agreement.

Commercial relations between the two countries will in future be regulated by the Commercial Treaty signed this day by the representatives of the two parties.

·   ·   ·   ·   ·   ·   ·

ARTICLE 6

In pursuance of the declaration annexed to the trade agreement of the 16th March, 1921, the Government of the Union of Soviet Socialist Republics declares that by way of exception to the decree of the 28th January, 1918 (concerning the annulment of debts of the former Imperial and Provisional Governments), it will satisfy, in the conditions prescribed in the present treaty, the claims of British holders of loans issued or taken over or guaranteed by the former Imperial Russian Government, or by the municipalities or towns in the territory now included in the Union, payable in foreign (non-Russian) currency.

The Government of His Britannic Majesty recognizes that the financial and economic position of the Union renders impracticable the full satisfaction of the claims referred to in the preceding paragraph of this article.

The Government of the Union agrees to meet the claims referred to in the first paragraph of this article in respect of holdings by British subjects or companies other than holdings which were acquired by purchase since the 16th of March, 1921, and were in other than British ownership on that date.

After negotiations between the parties concerned, the terms on which the claims referred to in the first paragraph of this article shall be satisfied will form the subject of an agreement with His Britannic Majesty's Government, which will be included in the treaty referred to in Article 11, provided that His Britannic Majesty's Government is satisfied that such terms have been accepted by the holders of not less than one-half of the capital values of British holdings in the loans referred to in this article.

ARTICLE 7

All questions connected with the claims of the Government of the Union of Soviet Socialist Republics against the Government of His Britannic Majesty, or with the claims of the Government of His Britannic Majesty against the Government of the Union, arising out of events which took place between August 4, 1914, and February 1, 1924, are reserved for discussion at a later date. This provision includes claims in respect of—

(a) War loans advanced by the Government of His Britannic Majesty to the former Russian Imperial or Provisional Governments;

(b) Gold belonging to the former Russian Imperial or Provisional governments, and handed over to the Government of His Britannic Majesty by either of those governments;

(c) Russian gold handed over to Germany under the supplementary agreement to the Treaty of Brest-Litovsk;

(d) Sums owed by the former Russian Imperial or Provisional•governments to British Government Departments, or *vice versa;*

(e) The claims advanced by the Government of the Union on the ground of intervention between November 7, 1917, and March 16, 1921; and also any adjustments made or to be made in the accounts relating to such claims on either side.

There shall similarly be reserved all questions connected with claims by the nationals of either party against the other party, in respect of loss or damage suffered in the territory of the party whose national the claimant is, and resulting from warlike operations or hostile measures during the above-mentioned period.

ARTICLE 8

Claims by nationals (including juridical persons) of the one party against the other party in respect of loss or injury due to events which took place between the 1st of August, 1914, and the coming into force of the present treaty, other than (1) claims covered by other articles of the present treaty, and (2) claims arising out of normal trading relations between the Government of the Russian Socialist Federative Soviet Republic or governments allied to or federated with it, or its agents, and British nationals, or between the Government of His Britannic Majesty and citizens of the Union of Soviet Socialist Republics, shall, in view of the admitted preponderance of the claims of British nationals, be finally settled as between the contracting parties by the payment of a lump sum by the Government of the Union to the Government of His Britannic Majesty.

The distribution of this sum shall be effected by the Government of His Britannic Majesty in such manner as they shall consider just. The Government of the Union undertakes to furnish the Government of His Britannic Majesty with any relevant papers or information in their possession which may facilitate the just distribution of such sum.

ARTICLE 9

Each of the contracting parties shall appoint three properly qualified persons to examine the claims of which the settlement is to be effected by the payment of the lump sum provided for in Article 8. These six persons shall make a joint examination of the claims, and shall report to the two contracting parties the amount at which they consider the lump sum should be fixed. If they are unable to agree as to the amount of the lump sum, they shall present separate reports. They will arrange their own procedure, and shall, in particular, be entitled by agreement between themselves to refer the examination of any particular category of claims to two of their number.

Each of the contracting parties shall defray the remuneration and expenses of the persons appointed by it, together with one-half of the expenses incurred jointly.

ARTICLE 10

Being desirous of re-establishing the economic cooperation between their two countries, the Government of His Britannic Majesty and the Government of the Union of Soviet Socialist Republics agree as follows:

The Government of the Union will, by way of exception to the decrees nationalizing industrial businesses and land, negotiate with British nationals (including juridical persons) in respect of industrial businesses or concessions which have been nationalized or canceled by it, in order to arrange for the grant of just compensation for such claims.

Furthermore, a commission shall be appointed to examine the validity and ascertain the amount of the claims.

Each of the contracting parties agrees to assist the commission so far as possible with regard to supplying or collecting papers or information required for the proper accomplishment of its task.

If the members of the commission are unable to agree

on a joint report in respect of any particular property, they may present separate reports.

In cases where the Government of the Union concludes an agreement with an individual claimant, the commission shall be informed of such agreement in order that the claim in question may be withdrawn from the competence of the commission.

The commission shall consist of six persons possessing the necessary qualifications for their task, three being appointed by the Government of His Britannic Majesty and three by the Government of the Union.

The commission shall settle its own procedure, which shall be approved by the two governments. Each of the contracting parties shall defray the remuneration and pay the expenses of the persons appointed by it, together with one-half of the expenses incurred jointly.

ARTICLE 11

A second treaty will be entered into, which will contain:

(1) The conditions accepted in accordance with Article 6.

(2) The amount and method of payment of compensation for claims under Article 8.

(3) An agreed settlement of property claims other than those directly settled by the Government of the Union of Soviet Socialist Republics.

ARTICLE 12

Upon the signature of the treaty referred to in Article 11 His Britannic Majesty's Government will recommend Parliament to enable them to guarantee the interest and sinking fund of a loan to be issued by the Government of the Union of Soviet Socialist Republics.

The amount, terms, and conditions of the said loan and the purposes to which it shall be applied shall be defined in the treaty provided for in Article 11, which will not come into force until the necessary parliamentary authority for the guarantee of the said loan has been given.

ARTICLE 13

The provisions of this chapter constitute a single and indivisible unit.

ARTICLE 14

On the coming into force of the treaty referred to in Article 11, Article 10 of the trade agreement of March 16, 1921, will be abrogated, until which time it will be maintained in force, Article 1 of the present treaty notwithstanding.

ARTICLE 15

Documents and papers of every kind, which, on November 1, 1917, belonged to individual subjects or citizens of either party, and are now withheld from the owners and are in the possession or under the control of the government or a public institution of the other party, shall be returned to the owners, or to such representative as they may appoint, within two months from the date of a request to that effect.

ARTICLE 16

The contracting parties solemnly affirm their desire and intention to live in peace and amity with each other,

scrupulously to respect the undoubted right of a State
to order its own life within its own jurisdiction in its
own way, to refrain and to restrain all persons and
organizations under their direct or indirect control, including organizations in receipt of any financial assistance from them, from any act, overt or covert, liable in
any way whatsoever to endanger the tranquillity or
prosperity of any part of the territory of the British
Empire or the Union of Soviet Socialist Republics or
intended to embitter the relations of the British Empire
or the Union with their neighbors or any other countries.

ARTICLE 17

The present treaty is drawn up and signed in the
English language. A translation shall be made into the
Russian language as soon as possible and agreed between
the parties. Both texts shall then be considered authentic
for all purposes.

ARTICLE 18

The present treaty shall be ratified, and the ratifica-
tions shall be exchanged in London·as soon as possible.

In witness whereof the respective plenipotentiaries have
signed the present treaty and have affixed thereto their
seals.

III. BRITISH-ITALIAN DEBT AGREEMENT *
(Signed January 27, 1926.)

Whereas Great Britain holds Italian Sterling Treasury
Bills to the value of £610,840,000, representing the war
debt of Italy to Great Britain,

* Text from the *London Times*, January 28, 1926.

And whereas Italy and Great Britain desire to arrive at a friendly settlement of this debt, within the capacity of Italy,

Now, therefore, the Rt. Hon. Winston Leonard Spencer Churchill, Chancellor of the Exchequer of Great Britain, and the Count Giuseppe Volpi di Misurata, Finance Minister of Italy, after having taken into account all relevant considerations, duly authorized thereunto by their respective Governments subject to such ratification as may be required, have agreed as follows:

1. Italy agrees to pay, and Great Britain to accept, in satisfaction of the aforesaid war debt the following Annuities:

In respect of the current financial year	£2,000,000
In respect of the next two financial years......	4,000,000 a year
In respect of the next four financial years.....	4,250,000 a year
In respect of succeeding financial years until 1986-87	4,500,000 a year
In respect of the financial year 1987-88........	2,250,000

The above payments will be made in sterling at the Bank of England, London, on March 15, 1926, and thereafter in equal half-yearly instalments on September 15 and March 15 of each year, so that the last payment will be made on September 15, 1987.

2. Italy will issue and deliver to the British Treasury on or before February 20, 1926, a bond substantially in the form set out in the annex to this agreement in respect of each of the payments provided for in Article 1 of this Agreement.

3. The payments due under all bonds issued in accordance with this Agreement shall be made without deduction for, and shall be exempt from any and all taxes

and other public dues, present or future, imposed by or under authority of Italy or any political or local taxing authority within Italy.

4. Italy, at its option, upon not less than 90 days' notice to Great Britain, may postpone such part of any of the half-yearly instalments falling due on or after September 15, 1928, as exceeds the sum of one million pounds (£1,000,000) to any subsequent March 15 or September 15, not more than two years distant from its due date, but only on condition that in case Italy shall at any time exercise this option as to the payment of any instalment, the instalments falling due in the second succeeding year cannot be postponed at all unless and until the instalments due two years and one year previous thereto shall actually have been paid in full. All such postponed payments shall bear interest at the rate of 5 per cent, per annum, payable half-yearly.

5. The accounts relating to the war debt of Italy to Great Britain, including the accounts in connexion with the Wheat Executive and War Risks Insurance schemes, shall be finally closed, and the British Treasury shall be entitled to retain any sums credited or to be credited to Italy in respect of such accounts. Save as provided in this Agreement, the contracting parties and their agents reciprocally renounce all claims or counter-claims against the other contracting party or their agents in respect of the above-mentioned accounts or the services and supplies to which they relate.

Great Britain likewise renounces all claims outstanding against Italy in respect of the hire of ex-enemy shipping.

6. If at any time it appears that the aggregate pay-

ments effectively received by Great Britain under Allied
War Debt Funding Agreements and on account of Reparations or of Liberation Bonds exceed the aggregate payments effectively made by Great Britain to the Government of the United States of America in respect of war
debts, an account shall be drawn up by the British
Treasury, interest at 5 per cent, being allowed on both
sides of the account; and if that account shows that the
receipts exceed the payments, Great Britain will credit
Italy against the payments next due by Italy under
Article 1 of this Agreement with such proportion of that
excess as the payments effectively made by Italy under
Article 1 of this Agreement bear to the aggregate sums
effectively received by Great Britain under all Allied
War Debt Funding Agreements.   Thereafter, a similar
account will be drawn up by the British Treasury each
year, and any further excess of the receipts over the payments shall each year give rise to a credit to Italy of
a proportion of such excess calculated in the manner indicated above.   On the other hand, any deficit shall be
made good by an increase in the payments next due by
Italy up to a similar proportion of such deficit within
the limit of the total amount of the credits already
allowed to Italy under this Article.

For the purpose of this Article any capital sums which
may hereafter be realized by Great Britain in respect of
Reparations or of Liberation Bonds will be taken at their
annual value, taking account of amortization.

7.   The £22,200,000 of gold, belonging to Italy, which
was deposited under the Agreements of 1915 against the
Italian war debt, will be retained by Great Britain as a
non-interest-bearing deposit and will be released to Italy

as to the sum of £1,000,000, in eight equal instalments on September 15 and March 15 of each of the four years commencing September 15, 1928, and terminating March 15, 1932, and, as to the balance, in equal half-yearly instalments commencing September 15, 1932, and terminating September 15, 1987, provided always that all the annuities due under Article 1 of this Agreement have been integrally paid to date.

8. Upon the execution of this Agreement and the delivery to Great Britain of the bonds of Italy to be issued hereunder, duly executed, the British Treasury will cancel and surrender to Italy the Italian Treasury bills held by Great Britain.

Signed in duplicate at London on the twenty-seventh day of January, 1926.

For the Kingdom of Italy:

GIUSEPPE VOLPI DI MISURATA,
Minister of Finance.

For the United Kingdom of Great Britain and Ireland:

WINSTON S. CHURCHILL,
Chancellor of the Exchequer.

ANNEX

(Form of Bond)

Dated   1926. Maturing

The Government of the Kingdom of Italy for value received promises to pay to the Government of His Britannic Majesty, or order, on March 15/September 15, 19   , the sum of   pounds sterling at the Bank of England, London.

The payment due under this bond shall be exempt from all Italian taxation, present or future.

This bond is issued by the Government of the Kingdom of Italy pursuant to the agreement of January 27, 1926, for the funding of the Italian War Debt to Great Britain.

IV. BRITISH-FRENCH DEBT AGREEMENT *

(Signed July 12, 1926)

The British and French Governments having arrived at a definite settlement of the debts due by France to Great Britain arising out of the great war, the undersigned, duly authorized by their respective Governments, subject to such ratification as may be required, have agreed as follows:

1. France agrees to pay and Great Britain to accept the following annuities in full and final settlement (subject to the provisions of Article 7 of this agreement) of the war debt due by France to Great Britain, in respect of which Great Britain holds sterling Treasury bills to the value of £653,127,900, viz:

During the financial year 1926-27, £4,000,000; 1927-28, £6,000,000; 1928-29, £8,000,000; 1929-30, £10,000,000; 1930-31 to 1956-57 inclusive, £12,500,000; 1957-58 to 1987-88 inclusive, £14,000,000.

The above payments will be made in sterling at the Bank of England in London in equal half yearly instalments on the 15th of September and the 15th of March of each year, so that the first instalment shall be paid on the 15th of September, 1926, and the last instalment on the 15th of March, 1988.

* Text from the *New York Times*, July 14, 1926.

2. France will issue and deliver to the British Treasury on or before the 15th of September, 1926, a bond in respect of each of the instalments provided for in Article 1 of this agreement.

3. The payments due under all bonds issued in accordance with this agreement shall be made without deduction for, and shall be exempt from, any and all taxes and other public dues, present or future, imposed by or under the authority of France or any political or local taxing authority within France.

4. France at her option upon not less than ninety days' notice to Great Britain may postpone the payments of one part, not exceeding one-half of any of the half yearly instalments due under Article 1, to any subsequent 15th of September or 15th of March not more than three years distant from its due date, but only on condition that, in case France shall at any time exercise this option as to payment of any instalments falling due in the third succeeding year, they cannot be postponed at all unless and until the instalments due three years, two years and one year previous thereto shall actually have been paid in full. All such postponed payments shall bear interest at the rate of 5 per cent per annum, payable half-yearly.

5. If at any time it appears that the aggregate payments effectively received by Great Britain under the allied war debt funding agreements and on account of reparations or of liberation bonds exceed the aggregate payments effectively made by Great Britain to the Government of the United States of America in respect of war debts, account shall be drawn up by the British Treasury, interest at 5 per cent being allowed on both sides of the account: and if that account shows that

receipts exceed payments, Great Britain will credit France against the payments next due by France under Article 1 of this agreement with such proportion of that excess as the payments effectively made by France under Article 4 of this agreement bear to the aggregate sums effectively received by Great Britain under all the allied war debt funding agreements. Thereafter a similar account will be drawn up by the British Treasury each year and any further excess of receipts over payments shall each year give rise to the credit to France of a proportion of such excess calculated in the manner indicated above. On the other hand a deficit shall be made good by an increase in the payments next due by France up to a similar proportion of such deficit within the limit of the total amounts of the credits already allowed to France under this article.

For the purpose of this Article, any capital sums, which may hereafter be realized by Great Britain in respect of reparations or liberation bonds, will be taken at their annual value, taking account of amortization.

6. Accounts relating to the war debt of France to Great Britain shall be finally closed and the British Treasury shall be entitled to retain any sums credited or to be credited to France in respect of such accounts. Save as provided in this agreement the contracting parties and their agents reciprocally renounce all claims or counter claims against the other contracting party or their agents in respect of the above mentioned accounts, or the services and supplies to which they relate.

7. The sum of £53,500,000 shall remain as a non-interest bearing debt of France to Great Britain, repayment of which will be settled by a further agreement.

Meanwhile, the British Government will retain (without interest) against this debt the gold remitted to London by the French Government during the war under the Calais agreement.

8. Upon the execution of this agreement and the delivery to Great Britain of the bonds of France, to be issued hereunder, duly executed, the British Treasury will cancel and surrender to France the French Treasury bills at present held by Great Britain.

Done in duplicate, both in English and in French, the original English text being the authentic one in case of difference, this 12th day of July, 1926.

INDEX

437

INDEX

For Product Safety Concerns and Information please contact our EU
representative GPSR@taylorandfrancis.com
Taylor & Francis Verlag GmbH, Kaufingerstraße 24, 80331 München, Germany